GERMANY'S BALANCED DEVELOPMENT

GERMANY'S BALANCED DEVELOPMENT

THE REAL WEALTH OF A NATION

KAEVAN GAZDAR

Q

QUORUM BOOKS
Westport, Connecticut • London

Library of Congress Cataloging-in-Publication Data

Gazdar, Kaevan.
    Germany's balanced development : the real wealth of a nation /
Kaevan Gazdar.
      p. cm.
    Includes bibliographical references and index.
    ISBN 1–56720–173–3 (alk. paper)
    1. Germany—Economic conditions—1990– 2. Germany—Social
conditions—1990– 3. Manpower policy—Germany. 4. Infrastructure
(Economics)—Germany. I. Title.
HC286.8.G37 1998
338.943—DC21   97–30745

British Library Cataloguing in Publication Data is available.

Library of Congress Catalog Card Number: 97–30745
ISBN: 1–56720–173–3

First published in 1998

Quorum Books, 88 Post Road West, Westport, CT 06881
An imprint of Greenwood Publishing Group, Inc.

Printed in the United States of America

The paper used in this book complies with the
Permanent Paper Standard issued by the National
Information Standards Organization (Z39.48–1984).

10 9 8 7 6 5 4 3 2 1

To Sabine

who listened, responded, shook her head, smiled,
a paragon of supportive empathy

and to her late tomcat, Whiskey, who spent whole afternoons perched
on the books I was trying to consult, gazing into the far distance with
a philosophical glint in his eyes

Contents

Figures

Introduction

Wealth is a fundamental concept in economics—indeed, perhaps the conceptual starting point for the discipline. Despite its centrality, however, the concept of wealth has never been a matter of general consensus.

—Robert L. Heilbroner
"Wealth," in Palgrave's *Dictionary of Economics*

Early definitions of wealth equate it with welfare and well-being. Later, wealth was held to comprise the stock of economic goods held by an individual or a state. The wealth of nations was first measured in gold and silver, then to an increasing extent in terms of land and labor.

Adam Smith's pathbreaking *Inquiry into the Nature and Causes of the Wealth of Nations* emphasized the centrality of productive labor. Smith's greatest achievement was his discovery of the division of labor's revolutionary impact on productivity: according to him, the wealth of nations ultimately depended on their productivity.

Most contemporary economists continue to emphasize productivity. Paul Krugman echoes the views of many of his colleagues with the assertion: "Productivity isn't everything, but in the long run, it is almost everything."[1]

Statistics apparently confirm the accuracy of this contention: the United States of America, the world's largest economy, also leads in productivity. Data published by the McKinsey Global Institute and OECD between 1990 and 1995 illustrate this lead:

- On an average, Japan's industrial productivity lies at 83 percent and Germany's at 79 percent of American productivity. In the service sector, the American lead is even larger, estimated at between 20 and 40 percent.
- In terms of Gross Domestic Product (GDP) per person employed, Japan's per capita GDP was 74 percent and Germany's 87 percent of America's.
- In terms of growth, Japan outpaced both Germany and the U.S.A between 1960 and 1990. Its Gross National Product (GNP) increased by 537 percent between 1960 and 1990, as against 149 percent in Germany and 147 percent in the United States However, the United States has widened its productivity and growth lead in the 1990s.[2]

The key question is: what constitutes the real wealth of a nation in the long term? Is it a purely quantitative equation comprizing productivity, gross national product (GNP), per capita income, growth and inflation rates, balance of payments surpluses or deficits, employment statistics, and so on? This book argues that wealth is a subtler and more qualitative issue, involving:

- productive potential as much as sheer productivity,
- the quality of a country's financial establishment, its educational system, its transport and communication infrastructure as much as its present GNP and growth performance,
- foundations of competitiveness, such as economic policies and capital-labor relations, as much as individual entrepreneurial achievements, and
- social welfare and personal well-being as much as average income.

In most of the quantitative assessments, Germany is at best second best: it is generally considered to have lost competitiveness since the early 1970s (see Figure I.1).

The country still leads in terms of per capita exports: indeed, during a short period in the 1980s, Germany was the world's largest exporter in absolute terms. Similarly, its currency reserves have been higher and its public debt lower than in the United States and Japan, reflecting Germany's financial stability. However, Germany seems to excel in the "false disciplines":

- Average wages in Germany are the highest in the world, reflecting the enormous social insurance component in wages.
- Germans work fewer hours per year than the Japanese, the Americans, or for that matter, the British, French, and Italians. Beyond this, German employees enjoy an average of forty two days of paid leave and holidays each year, approximately double the number of days that Japanese and American employees are generally entitled to.
- Taxes and social aid account for around 36 percent of Germany's Gross Domestic Product (GDP), as against 30 percent in the United States and 31 percent in Japan.

None of these assessments however considers Germany's hidden strengths. None of them grasps the specific order of the Social Market Economy, the balance it imposes between economic and social priorities, and the enormous foundation this balance provides to wealth creation and distribution. None of them takes into account the enormous productive potential of Germany's

Figure I.1
Germany: Growth Slows Down, Exports Rise Steadily

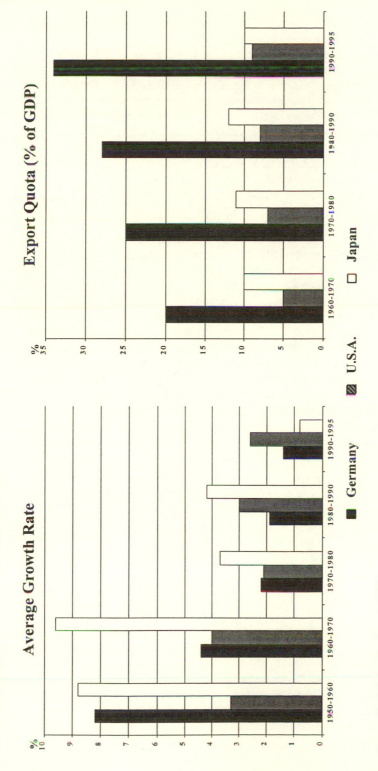

Average Growth Rate

Export Quota (% of GDP)

Germany ■   U.S.A. ▨   Japan ☐

Sources: Statistisches Bundesamt, OECD

infrastructure: an unparalleled system of vocational education, an equally unparalleled degree of financial stability, a superb rail-road-air transport network that provides a strong backbone for industry and trade. In all these areas, Germany is clearly superior to the United States and Japan.

Above all: purely quantitative rankings cannot encompass Germany's consensus-oriented decision-making—which is deeper, more dialectical, and in the final reckoning more coherent than Japan's, while opposed to the more confrontative and divisive U.S. decision-making approach. The Social Market Economy, infrastructure and consensus are this book's leitmotivs. Often overlooked, they explain Germany's uncanny resilience, its ability to recover from two disastrous world wars, rise out of recessions, and continue to provide its citizens with a high degree not only of material wealth but also of social welfare and personal well-being.

Welfare and well-being in the German context are not benefits that the individual acquires if he or she is successful or fortunate. They are concomitants of material wealth and are perceived in communitarian rather than individualistic categories. The German state has traditionally assumed the responsibility to provide the population with a high degree of social welfare. This is the material foundation of personal well-being. Vocational education and professional associations integrate the individual into work-oriented communities. This connectedness is the social foundation of well-being.

Germany's real wealth lies in its ability to balance economic progress with other priorities. This book argues that in the long term, Germany's mastery of balanced development will prevail over the more simplistic U.S. and Japanese growth models.

INVISIBLE OR VISIBLE HAND?

Anglo-Saxon and German perceptions of economic progress differ profoundly. Adam Smith argued—and generations of economists from the classical school have verified, endorsed, reformulated, and extended his arguments —that self-interest, guided by the "invisible hand" of competition, leads to common welfare. Individuals, who only care about their own utility, and enterprises, which only concentrate on their own profits, thus unwittingly contribute to national wealth. "It is not from the benevolence of the butcher, the brewer or the baker, that we expect our dinner, but from their regard to their own interest," is Smith's famous characterization of human affairs.

This Weltanschauung favored the individual rather than the collectivity. According to Smith's logic, a country's government contributes to wealth mainly by ensuring "peace, easy taxes and a tolerable administration of justice."[3]

Influential German thinkers on the other hand have always trusted in the visible hand of the state. They propagated the importance of productive capacity rather than productivity as such, of long-term investments rather than short-term profits.

Friedrich List, a publicist whose fame derives from his promotion of a customs union that preceded the unification of Germany in the nineteenth century, founded a school of thought that concentrated on the national specificity of wealth creation rather than on universal economic laws. List attacked the materialistic orientation of the classical school, criticizing Adam Smith for his cosmopolitan individualism. "Those who breed pigs are, according to this doctrine, more productive than those who teach human beings," he mockingly commented. By contrast, he recognized that stable wealth depended on education, transport, and other elements of infrastructure, influencing German state policies in this direction.[4]

List's emphasis on the foundations rather than the manifestations of wealth was deepened and refined by social scientists like Max Weber in the early twentieth century. Weber perceived the importance of cultural context and relativized the significance of economic laws. In his famous study *The Protestant Ethic and the Spirit of Capitalism*, Weber demonstrated how religious traditions influenced the rise of capitalism in different western countries.[5]

Similarly, Weber's colleague Werner Sombart perceived in his masterpiece, *Modern Capitalism*, that the epoch of high capitalism had ended with the outbreak of the First World War. He recognized the normative nature of what he called "late capitalism": the dislodging of the profit motive as the prime term of reference, the replacement of pure competition through elements of cooperation, and the diminuation of employer-employee antagonism through a complex system of rules and regulations.[6]

Attentive readers of Sombart's works are privy to insights into the true nature of the German economy, insights still relevant to a deeper understanding of the country's wealth. *This book aims at the same depth of understanding, the same emphasis on insights rather than merely on facts and figures.*

The German economy functions—as we shall discover in the course of this book—according to an unwritten constitution. This constitution consists of norms and institutions that integrate economic activity: craftsmanship traditions and vocational education, specialized associations and financial institutions. Just as in Great Britain, the lack of a written constitution led to a high degree of freedom based on common law and a case-law code of justice, so also has the German economy functioned smoothly according to implicit rules rather than explicit regulations.

Ordoliberalism, a contemporary school of economics that propagates a specifically German form of sociocapitalism, bases its recommendations on these unwritten norms and institutions. Its founder Walter Eucken's historically derived concept of order envisaged the state setting the framework for economic activity, while allowing private enterprises a reasonable but not unlimited degree of leeway within this framework. The Social Market Economy established according to ordoliberal principles after the Second World War relies on a high degree of self-regulation on the part of the business community.[7]

Neither before nor after the Second World War was Germany a free-market economy: the state has always ensured both order and free enterprise, thus steering a middle course between laissez faire and dirigiste policies. This book reveals the enormous continuity of the German economy before, during, and after the Nazi period, a continuity that explains Germany's resurgence after two ruinous world wars.

The German emphasis has always been on what a country can make rather than what it can buy. The excellence of "made in Germany" derives from this emphasis on production, just as the chronic U.S. balance of payments deficit reflects the country's orientation toward individualistic consumption. Monetarist Milton Friedman pithily expresses this logic: "Consumption is the sole end and purpose of all production; and the interest of the producer ought to be attended to, only so far as it may be necessary for promoting that of the consumer."[8]

The fundamental chasm between Anglo-Saxon and Germanic perceptions of progress and wealth has never been bridged. Alfred Marshall, the famous economist of the classical school, once cryptically commented: "German economists often lay stress on the non-material elements of national wealth; and it is right to do this in some problems relating to national wealth, but not in all."[9]

PRODUCTIVITY OR CONSENSUS?

Classical economics excels in the precise measurement of productivity, market mechanisms, marginal utility, and many other key factors. It constantly attempts to achieve the exactitude of a natural science. Marshall's contemporary William Stanley Jevons proclaimed in the late nineteenth century: "Economics, if it is to be a science at all, must be a mathematical science." For the classical school, this claim has retained its validity.

The traditional German approach by contrast understands economics as a social science and pays correspondingly less attention to statistics. It fails to pinpoint single issues as precisely as the classical school, but analyzes wealth in a more comprehensive way (see Figure I.2).

Statistics can be misleading indicators of national wealth if they are torn out of a broader context. Great Britain is a case in point. Between 1979 and 1993, for instance, productivity in Britain increased by an average of 4.1 percent, higher than in Japan, the United States and Germany. This implies that Britain's competitiveness and wealth increased commensurately.

Aggregated quantitative and qualitative assessments, however, prove the contrary, showing that Britain lost competitiveness as against Japan, Germany, the United States and France during this period. A deeper view of the British economy shows that short-sighted economic policies, social destabilization, and infrastructure weaknesses were as much responsible for Britain's mediocre performance as quantifiable deficiencies in industrial investment and personal savings ratios.[10]

Figure I.2
Approaches to Wealth

Anglo-Saxon

Free enterprise and free markets lead to wealth

Growth and productivity are prime goals

State ensures law and order, provides basic infrastructure

Short-term gain orientation, favoring consumption

German

A mixture of state control and private sector autonomy leads to wealth

Growth and productivity are balanced by social equity

State creates economic order, ensures social justice, and develops socioeconomic infrastructure

Long-term stability orientation, favoring production

Similarly, the American productivity lead is less impressive than it seems at first sight. The United States in the 1990s exemplifies a country that leads the world in terms of quantitative wealth, but evinces disturbing signs of inner decay within a shell of outer progess:

Infrastructure. In the late nineteenth century, the United States was a world leader in infrastructure investment, in particular in canals and railways, in telephone and telegraph lines. Vocational education was sponsored by large corporations. This contrasts starkly with the present stagnation in investment and corresponding deterioration of roads, urban transportation, and non elitist education.[11]

Banking. America's industrial expansion in the late nineteenth and early twentieth centuries was supported by relationship banking. Bankers belonged to their customers' boards of directors and regularly communicated with top management. The present emphasis on "price banking" has destabilized the American private sector while expanding the range of innovative investment-banking instruments and the scope for profitability.[12]

Society. Social stability in the United States has traditionally relied on the predominantly middle-class identity of most Americans. In this context the radical rise in income disparities and the widely perceived decline of the middle class are probably the most important signals of U.S. inner decay.[13]

Culture. Social disintegration is paralleled by a cultural drift-apart. Militant ethnic groups and the conservative-protestant backlash have weakened U.S. identity. E pluribus unum, the credo that plurality unites, has lost some of its validity.[14]

America's productivity lead in fact masks a profound lack of orientation, a lack of norms and institutions like Germany's Social Market Economy, its consensus-oriented "middle-estate society," its trade unions, and other organizations that create a supportive context for balanced and equitable growth.

Increasingly, America's wealth lacks economic and sociocultural foundations. Germany's wealth on the other hand is more authentic because it is more evenly shared and more aligned toward investing in the country's future.

A similar distinction between surface performance and real potential can be applied to Japan. The country's economic achievements—its manufacturing efficiency and mass marketing skills, the performances of its mighty conglomerates and trading houses, its norms of corporate loyalty and employee participation—remain impressive, though Japan's aura of invincibility has suffered in recent years.

The Japanese deficiencies, however, extend far beyond current issues like the inflexibility of life-long employment and the strong yen. They include:

- substandard infrastructure and inadequate social welfare,
- a comparatively weak small business sector,
- a continuing degree of financial instability in the wake of the "bubble economy" of the late 1980s,
- mechanisms of social control that stunt the individual, and

– an exaggerated sense of national identity and a corresponding lack of inner openness to the outside world.[15]

The significance of Germany's approach to wealth creation and distribution—as against the American and Japanese approachs—is seldom grasped because it is unspectacular, a complex mix rather than a series of easily identifiable achievements. This book shows how German society, culture, and the collective psyche support a form of consensus uniquely capable of balancing socioeconomic and economic-ecological priorities and of achieving stable growth.

Germany already practices sustainable development in the broadest sense of the term: growth balanced by financial stability and ecological and social considerations. This book ends with a forecast: If the world of the future favors sustainable development in the context of regional integration rather than dynamic, unsteady growth in an atomized international environment, the German rather than the U.S. or Japanese approach to economic development will prevail.

FROM MICROCOSM TO MACROCOSM

This book starts with two chapters that analyse small and big business and continues with two further chapters on the socioeconomic environment. Chapters 5 and 6 examine the cultural and psychological roots of the German approach to wealth. The final chapter puts Germany's past, present, and future into a time-frame and reveals the importance of continuity rather than change for Germany's approach to wealth creation.

Chapter 1. Germany's Mittelstand, its small business sector, is a microcosm of the German economy. Its success factors—manufacturing excellence, specialization, and an international orientation—are to a great extent also found in large corporations and its craftsmanship ethos is at the core of Germany's economic identity.

Beyond this, management techniques and leadership styles in small and big business, in companies like Krones and BMW, are remarkably similar. Long-term investment rather than short-term profit-making charcterises business strategies. Similarly, deficiences in cost-effectiveness and time-to-market characterize both Mittelstand enterprises and large corporations.

The Mittelstand's significance is not merely economic: this book will demonstrate that contemporary Germany is a "Mittelstandsgesellschaft," an egalitarian society with norms and attitudes exemplified by the Mittelstand. Lacking clearly identifiable elites, Germany today is remarkably egalitarian, more an estate-oriented community than an atomistic society in the Anglo-Saxon mold. The Mittelstand as the "middle estate" is a point of orientation, just as the U.S. middle class was in the past.

Middle-class norms and attitudes facilitate the politics of consensus-oriented decision-making. Beyond this, estate orientation gives the individual a greater sense of personal identity than in Japan, which is similarly consensus-oriented.

Chapter 2. This chapter on business mentality deepens the insights into success factors and corporate strategies. It also focuses on the fundamental difference between small and big business: organization. The corporate identity of large corporations like Siemens has always been highly orderly with hierarchies, rules, and regulations largely derived from state bureaucracy, though recent attempts at more entrepreneurialism have been made. This atmosphere favors incremental improvements rather than path-breaking innovations.

The quintessence of Germany's business mentality consists of establishing order through control. Stiff quality control in manufacturing and painstaking attention to detail in administrative procedures are characteristic of a management emphasis on organization rather than leadership. Inevitably, German managers tend to be excellent organizers—and mediocre leaders.

Order not only permeates German corporations; mechanisms of cooperation and power integrate the entire business community into a larger order:

- Companies in almost all sectors are members of specialized associations. These associations not only serve as spokesmen for their clientele. They also act as pro-moters of specialized innovations, provide valuable sectorial statistics, and integrate the private sector into the estate-oriented community described in Chapter 1.
- Power in Germany is exercised secretively both through informal cartels and through the financial leverage of relationship banking. A lack of volatile financial markets and the paucity of openly available corporate data contribute to order, secrecy, and stability in the business community rather than the fragmentation, openness, and dynamism characteristic of the Anglo-Saxon countries.

Ecology illustrates the effectiveness of the German "order mentality," just as the electronics sector reveals its weaknesses. Germany is a world leader in eco technology and eco management because technical skills in manufacturing are supported by sophisticated organizational techniques, in particular eco controlling and eco reengineering. Specialized associations have been founded to coordinate the exchange of expertise between companies in different sectors and to provide a forum for new ideas.

At the same time, ecology illustrates the importance of the business environment, to be explored in Chapter 3. Germany's ecological lead can be traced back to strict state legislation regulating waste, emission, and other issues. The business community was forced to rethink its production and distribution techniques and responded with a series of incremental improvements. German society increasingly endorses ecological priorities and public opinion has pressurized the private sector to align towards these priorities.

Germany's "eco consensus" is part of a deeper consensus on sustainable development that extends to financial policies and social issues. Public servants, political representatives, entrepreneurs, trade union leaders and representatives of interest groups increasingly agree on basic priorities and policies to implement these priorities, while disagreeing on details.

For similar reasons, Germany lags behind both the United States and Japan in electronics. On the one hand, it lacks the United States' volatile business environment: quick technology transfer, venture capital financing, and dynamic marketing skills. On the other hand, it also lacks the Japanese combination of quick technology assimilation, standardized production techniques and synchronized corporate strategies. Its business environment is aligned toward the evolutionary nature of ecology as against the revolutionary impact of electronics.

Chapter 3. Wealth creation in Germany, as opposed to the United States, involves the pursuit of collective rather than individual happiness. Economic progress is characterized by a complex balance of power, priorities and responsbility. This balance favors the business environment—defined as comprizing the state, trade unions, and society—rather than the individual entrepreneur.

As mentioned earlier, the German state has traditionally guided economic progress and influenced the corporate identity of major companies. Wealth creation thus relies on a strong state role—and on a power balance between the public and private sectors. Beyond this, state officials have served as role models for private-sector leaders. These officials have set the tone for an unspoken commitment to public welfare, a kind of honor code subscribed to by managers and trade union leaders alike.

The Social Market Economy (SME), Germany's form of sociocapitalism, relies on this basic commitment rather than on explicit policy formulation. SME is an adroit mixture of Ordnungspolitik—policies aligned to establishing order—and elements of Anglo-Saxon liberalism. The public sector ensures a high degree of social justice by means of an elaborate system of social aid, while the private sector is granted a large degree of autonomy within the parameters of "competitive order" (Wettbewerbsordnung). German economic policies have tended toward Keynesian deficit spending between 1966 and 1982 and have shown neoclassical tendencies since 1982, but SME's basic principles retain their validity. They ensure a balance of economic and social policy priorities.

As we have seen, specialized associations coordinate the interests of enterprises in the private sector. Correspondingly, trade unions represent a large percentage of the workforce and integrate them into the Mittelstandsgesellschaft. Associations and trade unions are involved in a constant process of negotiations on wage agreements, social benefits, and job security. This ensures a balance of responsibility between entrepreneurs and workers.

Significantly, major trade unions are organized in the same formalistic, bureaucratic way as large companies. Thus, in spite of the autonomy of the private sector, the German state normatively influences both capital and labor.

Trade unions play a largely constructive role in Germany's business environment. Because of trade union affiliations, their vocational qualifications, and codetermination procedures in German corporations, workers are not part of a largely anonymous labor-force as in the Anglo-Saxon countries. On the contrary, they are active participants in SME. They also enjoy more rights and a greater degree of autonomy than their counterparts in Japan.

German society, the third component of the business environment, is—as we have seen—an estate-oriented community composed of vocationally qualified individuals organized in specialized associations. This Mittelstandsgesellschaft, supported by SME's policies of social justice, ensures a large degree of social cohesion. The individual is committed to fulfilling a vocational role.

Cohesion and commitment to common priorities favor a broad-based medium level of achievement, rather than the pursuit of individual excellence that characterises the Anglo-Saxon ethos. At the same time, German-style consensus allows the individual more scope for individuality than in Japan.

The commitment of the average German citizen to ecological principles and the participation of a sizable percentage of Germans in the Green party, in ecological pressure groups, and in various professional and personal associations have for instance contributed to Germany's success in eco management and eco technology. Just as order pervades the business mentality, so also does commitment penetrate the business environment. Commitment supplements order and ensures participation rather than sheer obedience on the part of individuals and social groups.

Chapter 4. Both the business mentality and the business environment derive their stability from Germany's socioeconomic infrastructure. Germany's monetary system, its educational and technological institutions and its transport and telecommunications networks constitute major elements of infrastructure, which will be examined in this chapter. The German approach to wealth creation involves consistent investment in infrastructure, regardless of economic ups and downs.

Financial stability is a prerequisite for the economic order established by SME. Stability is not only imposed by the rigorously monetarist policies of the Bundesbank. It is also a norm to which Germany's banks, corporations, and private citizens subscribe.

The structure of Germany's banking sector, financing mechanisms in German business and the savings habits of a large cross-section of Germans make the Deutschemark's stability the product of collective commitment. This contrasts with banking practices and consumption trends in the Anglo-Saxon countries. However, this preoccupation with stability has also limited the profitability of Germany's banks, curbed the development of financial markets, and reduced the potential of venture capital. As we shall see, the mechanisms of balanced development preclude dynamic growth.

Vocational education is an equally vital element of infrastructure. Germany's unique dual system of theoretical and practical training effectively integrates young individuals into the working world and provides them with a sense of vocational identity. Beyond this, excellent facilities for life-long education ensure a high general standard of knowledge.

University education is less effective at first sight. None of the German universities can claim the excellence of America's Ivy League or of Oxford and Cambridge; many have lost their former prestige. German higher education is, however, well adapted to a nonelitist society and to a business mentality oriented toward incremental improvement rather than revolutionary innovations.

Similarly, German research and technology have lost their former preeminence, though the country has retained a relatively strong position in the natural sciences. As we have seen, German industry favors specialized innovations rather than path-breaking novelties. Inevitably, Germany trails both the United States and Japan in terms of patent statistics. This is particularly evident in key high-tech sectors like microelectronics and telecommunications.

However, in a number of other advanced technologies like medical equipment, energy production, and ecological installations, Germany excels. This is equally the case in specialized microelectronics applications like electronic process-control in manufacturing and electronic traffic-control equipment.

The comparison between Germany's performance in transport and telecommunications—two important infrastructure elements—also reveals quintessentially German strengths and weaknesses. Germany excels in transport because the coordination of road, rail, and air transport requires sophisticated organizational techniques. Beyond this, traffic management draws on the cooperation between car manufacturers, producers of electronic equipment and local authorities. The transport consensus, which involves the integration of economic, social, and ecological considerations in the planning process, is a further example of the German approach to achieving balanced development.

Conversely, Germany lags behind other countries in introducing modern telecommunications. Formalistic structures in German corporations and conservative user attitudes have limited the introduction of value added networks and services. Similarly, Germany is unlikely ever to become a major player in Internet: the network's uncontrolled flow of information and exchange of messages challenges rather than reinforces order and commitment. Innovative forms of telecommunication thus face major nontechnological obstacles in Germany.

Infrastructure in the German context does not merely represent an investment in the foundations of wealth. The contrast between transport and telecommunications also provides important insights into Germany's economic identity.

Chapter 5. Order and commitment, the central qualities that characterise Germany's business mentality and environment, have both cultural and psychological roots. In particular SME and Germany's mechanisms of consensus are culture-bound. This chapter examines the influence of culture—specifically religion, philosophy, and language—on the German economy, while also highlighting the significance of the Prussian ethos for the business community.

In Germany as elsewhere, the Protestant faiths represented the rejection of empty ritual in favor of a search for spiritual substance. Lutheran Protestantism was however more community-oriented than the Calvinistic forms of Protestantism in the Anglo-Saxon countries. It led Germany to become a moralistic community rather than an urbane society. Here lie the roots of the Mittelstandsgesellschaft described earlier.

German Catholicism, traditionally overshadowed by Lutherism, gained a strong influence on SME. Its principles of solidarity and subsidiarity have both defined and limited the purview of the social state. Beyond this, the Catholic emphasis on compromise through discussion has proved a valuable corrective to Lutheran inflexiblity. It has   encouraged the growth of consensus in contemporary Germany.

Germany's churches, whether Protestant or Catholic, are rich institutions with a social role: they run a large percentage of Germany's kindergartens and hospitals. Like corporations and trade unions, they support the order of the Social Market Economy. Their bureaucratic structures equally reflect the normative influence of the state.

Similarly, Germany's philosophical traditions are at the core of order and commitment. Enlightenment thinkers like Kant and Lessing emphasized the need for both the inner order of the soul and for state-imposed order. This strongly contrasts with the Utilitarian approach to individual welfare adopted by philosophers like Locke and further explains the profound difference between Anglo-Saxon and German perceptions of real wealth.

The complexity of German philosophy is reflected in Germany's mastery of complex industrial sectors. Its remarkable ability to master complexity has for instance helped Germany become a world leader in "Anlagenbau," the construction of entire industrial installations. This ability is also visible in eco management: in the redesigning of entire production and distribution processes according to ecological criteria.

The ecological sector also profits from Germany's romantic tradition, particularly its deep inner commitment to the forest and the soil. Romantic philosophers emphasized wholeness rather than individualism. The movement's leading political thinker, Adam Müller, opposed Adam Smith by emphasizing the individual's integration into the community rather than the importance of self-interest. Here lie the roots of Germany's communitarian commitment.

The structural depth of Germany's philosophical thought is paralleled by the versatility of the German language, in particular by an enormous linguistic potential for word constructions. Linguistic complexity is well attuned to formalistic organizational procedures in German companies. Because of the state influence on the private sector, business terminology and means of communication often echo an unnecessary amount of formalism and functionality.

Business German is the language of organisers—not of innovators, who need the English language's eclectic vocabulary and freedom of expression. However, German companies are well versed in gradually adopting innovations and tend to instrumentalise them more efficiently than their Anglo-Saxon competitors.

Similarly, German rhetoric is a blend of the formalistic and the ritualistic. Speakers tend to constantly express commitment to common goals and values, rather than displaying individual eloquence or advancing original opinions.

Public debates in Germany are often dominated by representatives of vocational groups; they serve the purpose of domesticizing the dialectic of divergent opinions so that a consensus can be reached. In ecology, transport, energy, and other areas where Germany has achieved remarkable success through processes of consensus, this form of rhetoric can be observed.

The Prussian military ethos has more directly influenced the business mentality than the economy in general. The influence is twofold: emphasis on systematic planning in German corporations is derived from the Prussian general staff, in particular from Moltke's careful analysis of long-term trends and his attention to logistics. Secondly, leadership attitudes in German companies still reveal the impact of the "Reserveoffizier," of brusquely authoritarian modes of behavior derived from the officers' corps. These attitudes are slowly changing, but the emphasis on order through control ensures the continuing influence of the Prussian ethos.

Chapter 6. The psychological roots of order and commitment are examined in this chapter. Order through control, the quintessence of Germany's business mentality, relies as much on the compulsive orderliness of those involved in manufacturing and administration as on Prussian modes of leadership described in the last chapter.

The compulsive personality internalises order without reflecting on it, exalts thoroughness, and thus achieves a high standard of operational efficiency. A compulsive commitment to perfection on the part of the average worker, coupled with vocational skills, is responsible for the legendary quality of products "made in Germany." *Compulsiveness, however, also leads to over-engineering and over-administration, two key problems faced by German business.*

Since the students' movement and the rise to power of the Social Democrats in the late 1960s, however, values and attitudes in Germany have shown a slow evolution toward a more balanced sense of priorities, in particular a more relaxed work ethic. A higher degree of personal commitment to social and ecological issues characterises the new "psychology of consensus."

This form of consensus contrasts with the individualistic antagonism that characterises public life in the United States. The difference between Germany and Japan is less apparent at first sight: both countries have authoritarian traditions, take a long-term view of development, and are consensus-oriented. However, Germany's collective psyche is, as we shall see, more balanced and more open than Japan's, its consensus-orientation correspondingly different.

The psychology of consensus involves a constant dialogue between representatives of conflicting interests and a constant search for harmony in the face of diversity. This dialogue is vitally important: *balanced development relies on balanced identity.*

Chapter 7. This book ends with a chapter that puts Germany's past, present, and future into perspective. Using the Mentality-Environment-Foundations-Roots framework developed in Chapters 2 to 6, it examines the "Wirtschaftswunder"—Germany's economic miracle after the Second World War—and reveals how unmiraculous, how inevitable the miracle really was. Germany's postwar business success is closely linked to a process of technical rationalization and organizational improvement visible during the Nazi period and earlier.

Beyond this, major SME principles were developed and discussed during the 1930s and belonged to the policy agenda during the Nazi period. Social modernization during this period facilitated the transition to a Mittelstandsgesellschaft after the war. *In contrast to conventional perceptions of the fundamental difference between the Nazi period and contemporary Germany, this book reveals a greater degree of continuity than of change.*

Deterministic explanations of the causes of national wealth like Mancur Olson's controversial *Rise and Decline of Nations* inevitably ignore the complexity of national economies and the importance of continuity rather than change. Olson contends that stable societies encourage "distributional coalitions," which block decision-making and slow down growth. According to him, countries like Germany, in which a new order was established after World War II, initially lacked the "institutional sclerosis" that slowed growth in stable countries like Britain.[16]

As we shall see in the course of this book, the opposite is the case. Germany succeeded so spectacularly after the Second World War not because it radically changed, but because it adhered to its former precepts of organized development. It prospered because it remained stable and became a more egalitarian society. Its "distributional coalitions"—in particular the industrial associations, trade unions and other pressure groups—continued to function smoothly. *Regulatory complexity in Germany was and still is greater than in the United States, Great Britain, and Japan. It is in fact an integral part of the German approach to wealth.*

Germany's present challenges consist of integrating the former East Germany into its complex policy framework while simultaneously gaining the flexibility needed to deal with unemployment and with institutional inertia.

After reunification, massive progress has been made in improving infrastructure in the east. Drawing on its reasonably high level of vocational education, the East German Mittelstand thrives particularly in craftsmanship and service enterprises. Technology transfer between the West and the East is rapidly upgrading product quality and manufacturing techniques.

However, in the interests of social justice, the East German workforce was given munificent wage hikes between 1990 and 1995. Industrial productivity has not risen to a commensurate extent. Equally munificent social aid has sparked off a wave of unrealistic expectations, both of material wealth and of welfare and well-being. Germany's greatest challenge consists in establishing SME in the East, in a region that lacks experience in the quid pro quo of consensus-oriented negotiations and in the interplay between economic order and social commitment.

To cope with elements of structural inflexibility that have promoted unemployment, united Germany needs to gradually link social benefits to market conditions. Equally, the German state must slowly relinquish its role as a kind of universal insurance company and reorient toward the original Social Market Economy emphasis on solidarity and subsidiarity.

The state's success as the stimulator of ecological reorientation is a heartening signal for the future. This reorientation has been organic: it has not upset the delicate interplay between the state, business, trade unions, interest groups, and society at large. Changes in the role of the social state will need to be equally organic. *Future wealth creation will hinge on Germany's capability to adapt to global change while retaining and extending its unique balance of wealth, welfare, and well-being. Its present mastery of balanced development needs to be practiced more consciously.*

This book ends with an estimate of Germany's future prospects. It predicts that the world of the future will neither fulfill deterministic forecasts, such as those propagated by Marx and Schumpeter, nor conform to radically optimistic or pessimistic visions such as those of Francis Fukuyama's end of history or Samuel Huntington's clash of civilizations. The future will be less apocalyptic, more complex. It will favor steady and sustainable development rather than rapid, uncontrolled growth.

Violent clashes between disparate ethnic groups such as those visible in the former Soviet Union and Yugoslavia and clashes of interest between peace-loving countries will continue to recur. However, this book assumes that alliances of nation states such as the European Union (EU), NAFTA, Mercosur, and APEC will gain in importance and in influence.

Despite a multitude of problems, the EU is and will remain the most cohesive and coherent of all federations of states. It has pioneered a transition from nation-states to member-states. Nation-states belonging to alliances will be increasingly constrained to adhere to group norms rather than impose their own norms on other countries. Complex consensus procedures in the EU favor countries with a proven ability to master complexity and to adapt to collective decision-making, as against countries that favor simple, unilateral solutions and try to assert their national identities on other nations.

Germany's mastery of balanced development, coupled with its consensus approach to solving problems and its constructive role in the EU, are its keys to future wealth. In an epoch of sustainable development, Germany will be better equipped—in geographic and cultural as much as in socioeconomic terms—than the United States and Japan, its major national rivals.

Germany's superiority is normative rather than "dominative." The norms of financial stability propagated by the Bundesbank, for instance, are already the world benchmark for monetary policies. German "Ordnungspolitik"—policies geared towards ensuring economic order—already guide legislation and policies in the EU. *In a world marked by complexity rather than simplicity and by consensus rather than power-play, Germany's economic-social-ecological policy matrix will prevail.*

THE GESTALT APPROACH TO NATIONAL WEALTH

Most analyses of the German economy highlight specific aspects rather than the connectedness of economy, society, culture, and the collective psyche. As Kirsten S. Wever and Christopher S. Allen point out in their *Harvard Business*

Review survey of economic literature on Germany: "Observers are so preoccupied with praising—or blaming—individual components of the German economy that they fail to see the dynamic logic that ties these components together into a coherent system. And yet it is precisely in the system that the real lessons of the German model lie. "[17]

This book sees the national economy not as a model or a system but as a Gestalt, a complex form that needs to be recognized in its entirety. Gestalt is an approach toward grasping wholeness, practiced by social scientists and cultural historians of predominantly German origin in this century. Major Gestalt protagonists like Max Wertheimer emigrated to the United States in the 1930s and strongly influenced academic institutions like the New School in New York.[18]

Gestalt incorporates the recognizable part of a country's identity. It postulates that the whole is more than the sum of its parts, that an entity like a national economy is a coherent organism and that quantitative data and qualitative observations can be meaningfully linked, so that a country's identity—and the potential derived from this identity—can be recognized.

Quantitative-qualitative linkage leads to a deeper understanding of the connection between wealth and welfare. For instance, the gap between highest and lowest incomes in Germany is smaller than in the United States and Japan. Between 1980 and 1995, the gap widened in the United States, remained the same in Japan, and actually narrowed in Germany. However, the social cohesion indicated by these statistics becomes an important wealth factor only when allied to qualitative factors such as vocationally derived identity in Germany as against an ethos of individual achievement in the United States and feudalistic bonds of fealty in Japan.[19]

Gestalt is clearly opposed to the "best practice" paradigm. Best practice relies largely on quantitative indicators and measures the success of nations in terms of competitive advantage. Harvard Business School professor Michael E. Porter's celebrated study *The Competitive Advantage of Nations* is an excellent example of this mind-set.

Porter acknowledges the importance of qualitative attributes: "Differences in national economic structures, values, cultures, institutions, and histories contribute profoundly to competitive success." His analysis, however, exemplies the quantitative approach to determining economic success. It postulates the importance of culture without exploring ist influence on the economy. Porter in fact explains cultural differences as the result of varying economic circumstances, thus placing the cart before the horse.[20]

By contrast, Gestalt reveals the connectedness between national wealth and economic identity. Why for instance does Germany excel in ecology while lagging behind the United States and Japan in electronics? As we shall see in the chapter on business mentality, Germany's quality orientation and its emphasis on specialized product segments has given it competitive advantage with both end-of-pipe and integrated eco products and processes. However, the roots of Germany's ecological excellence are qualitative: state legislation and incentives, social pressure, a deep cultural commitment to nature. These factors will be explored in the chapters on the business environment and the cultural roots of wealth.

Similarly, the reasons why Germany is an electronic laggard are a mix of the quantitative and qualitative. As the McKinsey study *Excellence in Electronics* shows, companies with the highest growth rates and returns on turnover in the electronics industry flourish under Darwinistic competitive conditions. Successful corporations restructure and grow simultaneously, while reducing complexity in their production processes.[21]

This is entirely contrary to Germany's ethos of refined craftsmanship, of steady improvement rather than radical restructuring, of specialized complexity rather than mass-production simplicity. In sum, Germany's economic identity is attuned to ecology, not to electronics.

A country's Gestalt is characterized by continuity rather than change. Important elements remain basically the same, despite the passage of time, and can best be understood in an historic context.

Historic portrayals of Germany have often tended to emphasize its authoritarian-totalitarian heritage. From Luther to Hitler: this reduction of German history to a uniform archetype is now considered outmoded. However, the structuralists, who concentrate on class structures, the evolution of institutions, and other non-mentality abstractions, often tend to overlook the woods by concentrating on the trees.

This book adopts a different approach. It examines the importance of institutions like the state, the trade unions and business assocations and emphasizes the enormous role played by the Mittelstandsgesellschaft, Germany's middle-estate oriented society. Simultaneously, it acknowledges Luther's seminal influence and begins the chapters on cultural and psychological roots with a brief analysis of the great reformer's impact on cultural norms and psychological proclivities. But it also highlights countervailing factors such as Catholicism's impact on social policies. Similarly, it acknowledges but relativises Hitler's role by arguing that business strategies, economic policies, educational norms, and other primary sources of Germany's economic identity survived and outlived the Nazi period.

This book argues that Germany's real wealth is not excellence but balance. Mittelmaß, best translated as a happy medium of policies, priorities, and accomplishments, is a quintessentially German phenomenon, an amalgam of Mittelstandsgesellschaft, a philosophical search for synthesis and rituals of consensus. *Paradoxically, the excesses of the Nazi period stimulated the potential of an economy, a society, and a cultural ambience uniquely attuned to balanced development—and thus uniquely equipped for an age of sustainable development.*

NOTES

1. Paul Krugman, *The Age of Diminished Expectations* (Cambridge, MA: MIT Press, 1994), p. 13.

2. See *OECD Economic Surveys: United States* (Paris: OECD, 1993), p. 53; William Lewis et al., "Service Sector Productivity and International Competitiveness," in *The McKinsey Quarterly*, 4/1992, pp. 69–91; A. Steven Walleck et al., "How Competitive Are U.S. Manufacturers?" in *The McKinsey Quarterly*, 2/1992, pp. 105–112; see also "America's New Productivity," in *Business Week*, October 16, 1995, pp. 38–46.

3. Adam Smith, *An Inquiry into the Nature and Causes of the Wealth of Nations* (Oxford: Clarendon Press, 1976), p. 22.

4. Friedrich List, *Das nationale System der politischen Ökonomie* (Stuttgart: Cotta, 1883), especially pp. 46–49, 136–141; for an Anglo–Saxon assessment of List, see James Fallows, "How the World Works," in *Atlantic Monthly*, December 1993, pp. 61ff.

5. Ludwig M. Lachmann, *Drei Essays über Max Webers geistiges Vermächtnis* (Tübingen: Mohr, 1973), pp. 2–9, 16–21.

6. Werner Sombart, *Das Wirtschaftsleben im Zeitalter des Hochkapitalismus*, Book 1 (Munich: Duncker & Humblot, 1927), pp. XIIff.

7. Walter Eucken, *Die Grundlagen der Nationalökonomie* (Berlin: Springer, 1965), especially pp. 170–171.

8. Milton Friedman, "A Deficit That's Good for Us," in *Washington Post National Weekly Edition*, August 16–22, 1993.

9. Alfred Marshall, *Principles of Economics* (London: Macmillan, 1961), p. 59.

10. For productivity statistics see "Winner und Loser," in *Informationsdienst der deutschen Wirtschaft*, 29, September 1994, p. 1; for aggregated assessments of competitiveness, see *OECD Economic Surveys 1994–1995: United Kingdom* (Paris: OECD, 1994) and Howard Vane, "The Thatcher Years: Macroeconomic Policy and Performance of the UK Economy, 1979–1988," in *National Westminster Bank Quarterly Review*, May 1992, pp. 26–42.

11. See *OECD Economic Survey: United States* (Paris: OECD, 1993), pp. 63–81; for education, see "American Education: Still Separate, Still Unequal," in the special issue of *Daedalus*, Fall 1995.

12. Michael T. Jacobs, *Short-term America* (Boston: Harvard Business School Press, 1991), particularly p. 143; see also M. Colyer Crum and David M. Meerschwam, "From Relationship to Price Banking: The Loss of Regulatory Control," in Thomas K. McCraw (ed.), *America versus Japan* (Boston: Harvard Business School Press, 1986), pp. 261–298; for financial instability, see Thomas Geoghegan, "Why Americans Don't Save," *The New Republic*, July 17 and 24, 1995, pp. 26–33.

13. For statistics, see Theodore Caplow, *Recent Social Trends in the United States, 1960–1990* (Frankfurt: Campus, 1991), pp. 185–188; see also Jack Beatty, "Who Speaks for the Middle Class?" in *Atlantic Monthly*, May 1994, pp. 65–78.

14. Martin E. Marty, "Religion in America," in Luther S. Luedtke (ed.), *Making America: the Society and Culture of the United States* (Chapel Hill: University of North Carolina Press, 1992), especially p. 402; see also Wade Clark Roof, *American Mainline Religion* (Trenton: Rutgers State University, 1988), especially p. 28.

15. For infrastructure and welfare, see Margaret Powell and Masahira Anesaki, *Health Care in Japan* (London: Routledge, 1990), pp. 1–5, 226–234; for small business, see D.H. Whittaker, "SMEs and Entry Barriers," in Masahiko Aoki and Ronald Dore (eds.), *The Japanese Firm* (Oxford: Oxford University Press, 1994), pp. 210–225; see also J.A. Stam: "New Patterns of Cooperation among Enterprises in Japan, " in Sung-Jo Park (ed.), *Managerial Efficiency in Competition and Cooperation* (Frankfurt: Campus, 1992), pp. 231–242; for financial instability, see Kent E. Calder, *Strategic Capitalism* (New Jersey: Princeton University Press, 1993), pp. 136–139 and Michael Hirsh, "Why

Japan Won't Change," in *Institutional Investor*, September 1994, pp. 57–69; for social control, see Ross Mouer and Yoshio Sugimoto, *Images of Japanese Society* (London: Kegan Paul, 1986), pp. 239–243 and Karel van Wolferen, *The Enigma of Japanese Power* (London: Macmillan, 1989), pp. 87–91; for national identity, see Wolferen, *The Enigma of Japanese Power*, and Harumi Befu, "Symbols of Nationalism and Nihonjinron," in Roger Goodman and Kirsten Refsing (eds.), *Ideology and Practice in Modern Japan* (London: Routledge, 1992), pp. 26–46.

16. Mancur Olson, *The Rise and Decline of Nations* (New Haven: Yale University Press, 1982), pp. 74–81.

17. Kirsten S. Wever and Christopher S. Allen, "Is Germany a Model for Managers?" in *Harvard Business Review*, September–October 1992, p. 36. For conventional views on the German economy, see Herbert Giersch et al., *The Fading Miracle* (Cambridge, GB: Cambridge University Press, 1992) and Hans-Werner and Gerlinde Sinn, *Jumpstart* (Cambridge: MIT Press, 1994).

18. For a general discusssion of Gestalt, see Solomon E. Asch, "Gestalt Theory," in David L. Sills (ed.), *International Encyclopedia of the Social Sciences, Volume 6* (New York: Macmillan & Free Press, 1968), pp. 158–175; for a cultural history viewpoint, see Alois Closs, "Integration als Gestaltungsbegriff, " in Robert Mühlher and Johann Fischl (eds.), *Gestalt und Wirklichkeit* (Berlin: Duncker & Humblot, 1967), pp. 277–283.

19. See "Winners and Losers" in a survey of the world economy published by *The Economist*, September 28, 1996, pp. 24–33.

20. Michael E. Porter, *The Competitive Advantage of Nations* (New York: Free Press, 1990), p. 19; see also in this connection European criticism of Porter's "diamond," for instance Frans A.J. van den Bosch and Arnot A. van Prooijen, "The Competitive Advantage of Nations: The Impact of National Culture—a Missing Element in Porter's Analysis?" in *European Management Journal*, June 1992, pp. 173–177; see also Porter's rejoinder on p. 178.

21. McKinsey & Company, *Wachstum durch Verzicht* (Stuttgart: Schäffer-Poeschel, 1994), pp. 4–5, 25–31.

CHAPTER 1

The Mittelstand: Microcosm of the Germany Economy

Heil Sachs! Heil to you, Hans Sachs! Heil to Nuremberg's dear Sachs! Heil! Heil!

—Richard Wagner
Die Meistersinger von Nürnberg

Richard Wagner's "Mastersingers of Nuremberg" is the most significantly German opera ever written. In the scene quoted from above, the people of Nuremberg welcome the shoemaker and "master singer" Hans Sachs with enthusiasm. Some 400 years later, the populace hailed Hitler with similar fervor at the Reichsparteitage—the annual Nazi party meetings held in Nuremberg.

The *Meistersinger* was in fact Hitler's favorite opera, performed every year at the Reichsparteitage. Goebbels called it the "sheer incarnation of our folklore." Nietzsche characterized it as German in the best and worst sense of the term, emphasizing its spirituality—and its formlessness.

However, the opera's significance transcends folklore and aesthetics. The master singers existed in reality. They were members of recognized guilds, who practiced a highly formalized type of singing—"Meistergesang"—in their spare time. Hans Sachs was also no figment of Wagner's imagination: he was a respected craftsman and follower of Luther's Reformation in the sixteenth century, the time frame of the opera.[1]

The Mastersingers contrast with the "Minnesingers" or troubadours from the Middle Ages, with their aristocratic origins and romantic intentions. In the opera, Sachs announces that the goldsmith's daughter will be married to the singer who wins a Meistergesang contest. The contest is won by Walther, a young Minnesinger who has fallen in love with the heroine. His rival, Beckmesser, a pedantic town clerk, tries unsuccessfully to discredit Walther by proving his inability to conform to the prescribed rules of Meistergesang. True talent ultimately triumphs over contrivance and mediocrity, and Walther can marry the woman he loves. Beyond this, the hero is persuaded to join the Meistersingers by Hans Sachs, who appeals to his loyalty toward "holy German art."

The "Meistersingers of Nuremberg" has been interpreted as a victory of true art over pedantry. But observers of economic affairs can dwell on other significant aspects:

- The German craftsmen's guilds have continued to maintain stringent regulations for the admission of new members that parallel the strictures applying to "Meistergesang." These regulations define quality in craftsmanship and reward those with a master's title who have been through the training and have achieved the prescribed quality standards. To be a meister in contemporary Germany is still a highly respected sign of accomplishment. Beyond this, the guilds are prototypes of today's trade associations that, as we shall see in Chapter 2, integrate the business community into society.
- The Meistersingers symbolize the cultural assertiveness of a productive "middle estate," the Mittelstand. The craftsmen formed the nucleus of this estate, which successfully challenged the hegemony of the upper classes from the late Middle Ages onward. The Mittelstand played a vital role in Germany's upsurge as an industrial nation. Its social importance grew even further after the Second World War: contemporary Germany is, as we shall see in Chapter 3, a Mittelstandsgesellschaft, an estate-oriented society.
- In the opera, a talented outsider, helped by a craftsman, triumphs over a bureaucrat. In reality, Beckmesser's cautious, suspicious attitude is as typical of contemporary Germany as Hans Sachs's homely generosity; "beckmesserisch" is a modern German word used to describe pettiness. Today's Beckmesser plays an important role in both large companies and the public sector, just as the Mittelstand features a large percentage of Sachs-type Craftsmen.[2]

Craftsmanship remains the quintessence of Germany's economic identity, which is primarily that of a manufacturer of high-quality products. Germany's unique dual system of vocational education for factory workers is modeled on traditional craftsmanship training. Thus, the guilds in Germany are not quaint relics of the past: they still exercize a powerful influence on the economy and society.

In postwar Germany, craftsmen have retained their distinctive and privileged identity. An all-party consensus led to the reestablishment of the old strictures for the qualification of master craftsmen. This "Handwerksordnung" of 1953 effectively restored the old order of the guilds, though the qualification process has been slightly liberalized.

The exclusive privileges of the guilds have been heavily criticized as an anachronistic anomaly, favoring an entrenched social group. However, they have ensured an invaluable continuity in economic development. As we shall see, *continuity is the key to stable wealth creation in the German context, the prerequisite of balanced development.*

A comparison between Germany and its two major economic rivals, the United States and Japan, reveals the unique role played by the Mittelstand. A number of analyses—among others Michael T. Piore and Charles F. Sabel's *The Second Industrial Divide* and the MIT Commission on Industrial Productivity's "Made in America" study—have commented on the basic difference between the U.S. emphasis on mass production as against the continuance of crafts traditions in countries like Germany.[3]

Small business in the United States consequently lacks the Mittelstand's specific ethos, though it plays an important role in sectors as diverse as software, health care, and retailing. The small business ethic is, as several commentators point out, closely linked with middle-class values and the growing decline of America's middle class endangers the Jeffersonian ideal of the independent entrepreneur. Beyond this, small business's lack of associational representation can be construed as symptomatic of a more general atomization of the U.S. private sector.[4]

In Japan on the other hand, small and medium-sized enterprises have lower status than big corporations. Their dependence on large companies is larger than in Germany, their exporting capabilities far smaller. They too lack the proud craftsmanship identity that distinguishes the Mittelstand.[5]

Germany's reunification opened new frontiers for medium-sized enterprises. In 1988, a year before the Berlin Wall fell, there were only about 3,000 small businesses in East Germany. Now, there are estimated to be half a million. Enterprises founded by craftsmen are in the forefront. Not only do they provide the largest percentage of new jobs in the east: their productivity has already reached 80–90 percent of West German standards, as against the 50 percent reached by industrial enterprises in East Germany.

THE MITTELSTAND APPROACH TO WEALTH CREATION

The Mittelstand contributes to Germany's economy in various ways. It accounts for almost two-thirds of total employment, half of all business turnover in Germany and over 40 percent of all investment. It also plays a vital role in perpetuating Germany's unique system of vocational education: 80 percent of all apprentices learn their professions in Mittelstand enterprises (see Figure 1.1).

Small business is even more important in qualitative terms. Management writer Tom Peters, a great admirer of the Mittelstand, defines it as "a state of mind, an attitude that emphasizes focus and flexibility, long-haul commitment to a demonstrably superior product and its end user."[6] It is indeed a business attitude that stresses Wertschöpfung, value-creation, rather than money-making.

Mittelstand enterprises are oriented toward long-term investment rather than short-term profit-making. In one large-scale survey of Germany's small businessmen, 70 percent indicated that they would reinvest a large percentage of the profits in the business, while 15 percent went as far as to commit themselves to investing the entire profits. Only 3 percent wanted to withdraw all profits for themselves. Investments were planned in capital equipment, rationalization procedures, and the expansion of product ranges.[7]

This business approach clearly has a negative impact on the profit and loss account. A survey of Europe's "hidden champions"—medium-sized companies with turnovers in the 24–240 million dollar range—conducted in 1995 showed German companies trailing their competitors from Italy, Britain and France in terms of profitability. Only eight German companies figured in the list of the top 100, as against thirty-two from Italy, twenty-three from Britain, and fourteen from France.[8]

According to the criteria of classical economics—productivity and profitability—the Mittelstand performance is substandard. In actual fact, however, these enterprises have other priorities. The Mittelstand's productive potential—its specialized expertise, the educational standards of its employees, its range of products and the quality of its technical installations and equipment—far exceeds its actual performance. Moreover, the Mittelstand is not unique in its principles and priorities: *this emphasis on potential rather than performance is the quintessence of the German approach to wealth creation.*

The craftsmanship ethos is, as we shall see in this chapter, aligned to matured quality, not to the time-to-market or design-to-cost strategies that U.S. and Japanese manufacturers excel in. The specialization of the Mittelständler is oriented toward niches rather than to cannibalizing the market. Similarly, international strategies are linked to niches, not to large-scale dominance of world markets.

The big business success factor mix differs from the Mittelstand success formula in detail rather than in substance: while medium-sized companies specialize, large corporations exploit economies of scope deriving from a closely linked range of products. Otherwise, however, they subscribe to the same norms of quality and internationality.

In its priorities and its approach to wealth, the Mittelstand is a microcosm of the German economy. It is also the nucleus of the Mittelstandsgesellschaft. Contemporary Germany is, as we shall discover, an estate-oriented community rather than an atomized society in the Anglo-Saxon mold. Vocational education, craftsmen's guilds, and specialized associations for members of other professions give individuals a sense of vocational identity and provide them with representation. *Since Germany lacks clearly defined elites, the Mittelstand is a vital point of focus. It contributes to social cohesion as much as to gross national product.*

Figure 1.1
Importance of the Mittelstand for the German Economy

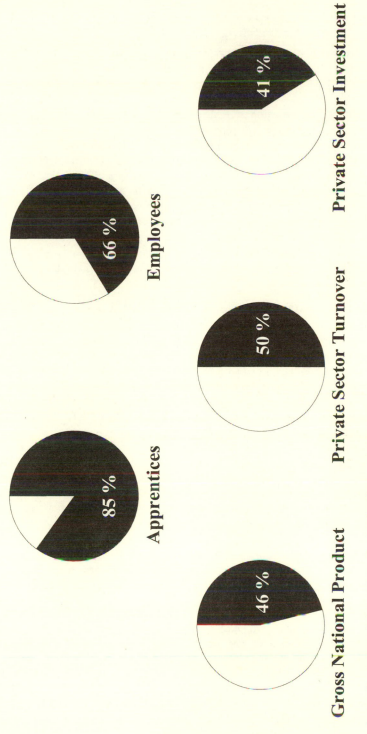

Apprentices   **Employees**

85 %   66 %

46 %   50 %   41 %

Gross National Product   **Private Sector Turnover**   **Private Sector Investment**

Sources: Bundeswirtschaftsministerium, Institut für Mittelstandsforschung

SECTION 1: QUALITY AS TOP PRIORITY

German industry—whether Mittelstand or Big Business—adheres to one important paradigm: the mechanical. It excels in industries with a strong mechanical base and has lost ground in sectors where electronics plays a pivotal role.

Germany's perception of quality is that of the master craftsman: attention to detail in all aspects of the manufacturing process. Given this quality orientation, German manufacturers are virtually unbeatable with specialized mechanical products—and are often helpless in volatile, electronics-driven mass markets. They succeed however in sectors where electronics can be adapted for specialized applications or where electronic components can be combined with traditional mechanical elements. In machine-tools, manufacturing process-control, traffic control equipment, and many other industrial segments, the Germans have mastered the mechanical-electronic symbiosis and remain world technology leaders.

Quality in the German context means: technology, design, and service.

TECHNOLOGICAL QUALITY: THE ART OF BUILDING MACHINES

Machine building is the sector that exemplifies best the German commitment to quality. Germany is the world's leading exporter of machines and machine tools. Statistics show German manufacturers leading in twenty-nine out of forty-two product categories, the United States in eight, Japan in three. In machine-building, which employs more workers than any other sector in Germany, the Mittelstand dominates: only three percent of all machine-building companies are large corporations.

Krones AG is a typical Mittelstand machine-builder. Founded in 1951 by a technician called Hermann Kronseder and located in a small Bavarian town, Krones is a world leader in technology for filling and labeling bottles for breweries and soft-drinks manufacturers.

With an annual turnover that now exceeds a billion marks and with around 7,000 employees, Krones's success formula comprizes:

- Own technology (more than 800 registered patents)
- Highly qualified and specialized workers, mostly trained in-house (more than 500 apprentices trained simultaneously)
- Self-sufficient production rather than outsourcing (Krones has its own factories in the United States, Canada, and Brazil as well as in Germany)
- A high export quota (70 percent)
- Personal technological and organizational involvement of the CEO, Hermann Kronseder, for over four decades[9]

Krones is more than a company: it is a model for the German way to economic success, a model adopted by companies in various sectors. The Fischerwerke in the Black Forest town of Tumlingen, for instance, is more diversified than Krones: its product range includes fixing elements, learning and simulation systems, and audiovisual storage elements. Otherwise, however, similarities are striking: the company's founder, Artur Fischer has some 5000 patents to his credit. His invention, the "Fischerdübel"—a fixing element made of nylon—is used across the world.

The export quota of the Fischer group, which makes a yearly turnover of around 500 million marks and employs 2,300 people in factories in Germany and five other countries, is around 50 percent. Like Krones, Fischer has invested a large amount in training and motivating his employees. Though the Fischerdübel has been copied all over the world, the company has retained its competitive niche in the fixing elements market by constantly improving product quality.[10]

Technological Quality and Big Business: The Automobile Saga

While machine building is predominantly a Mittelstand domain, automobile production is dominated by large corporations. The quality of Germany's cars—of Mercedes Benz and BMW, of VW, Audi, and Porsche—is the most visible worldwide symbol of "Made in Germany." Cars account for four of the ten best-known German brands in the world. State-of-the-art technology, streamlined design, und reliable service characterize the German automobile industry. BMW's advertising slogan—"the ultimate driving machine"—applies to the other brands as well: the country's cars represent machine building at its best.

From the beginning onward, German automobiles were technically advanced and built by skilled workers. The perfection of the finished product was of paramount importance. The Germans emulated but did not excel in the mass production techniques that characterized car-making in the United States—and later Japan. Thus the marketing focus of the German automobile industry—with the exception of VW—has traditionally been to serve high-quality segments within a mass market, not to capture world markets on the basis of cost superiority or marketing skills, as the Japanese have done. The German car manufacturers have always possessed a strong international orientation—Daimler Benz exported 75 percent of its production as far back as 1905—and have continued to concentrate on high-end niche markets (see Figure 1.2).

Germany's automobile industry profits immensely from the following factors:

- The German state imposes high security norms and ecological standards. The roadworthiness of all automobiles on Germany's roads is stringently controlled.
- Trade unions generally support rationalization while exacting high wages and social benefits as the price for a basic consensus.
- German consumers are highly criticial: they voice high expectations in terms of the quality and reliability of the cars they drive.

Beyond this, the auto industry profits from the country's superb road networks; in particular from the Autobahn, its highways without speed limits.

It also benefits from a longstanding "know-how infrastructure": major automobile technology institutes were founded in Aachen, Karlsruhe, Hannover, and Stuttgart as far back as the 1920s. Germany's technical universities provide the car industry with an ample supply of excellently qualified engineers. In sum, the quality of the automobile sector derives to a great extent from Germany's business environment, and its infrastructure, from factors that will be explored later in this book.

In spite of these longstanding strengths, the crisis of Germany's auto industry in the early 1990s was inevitable—Germany's overheads were simply too high, there were too many variations in car models, and the industry lacked adequate financial controlling.

The car makers' deficiencies were commercial rather than technical, typical for an industry that exemplifies the craftsmanship ethos described earlier. Their recovery from 1994 onward illustrates the efficacy of retaining high technical standards, and simultaneously adopting commercial strategies.

BMW is a case in point. It almost quadrupled its turnover between 1982 and 1994, and in 1992, it surpassed the annual production of its arch-rival, Mercedes Benz. Next to Toyota, BMW is the only company in the international automobile industry to have consistently made profits for the last thirty years. In terms of productivity, it rivals the leading Japanese and U.S. manufacturers.

BMW's success formula is a mixture of typically German and universal strategies:

- With its Model 3 cars, BMW occupied the market niche of the sportly compact limousine, a niche that Mercedes discovered far later with its less attractive Model 190.
- BMW is a master of the fine art of varying models and motors, and thus providing sophisticated customers with a broad choice of options, without undertaking significant production-line investments. In other words, it revels in economies of scope.
- Earlier than other German manufacturers, BMW carried out sophisticated cost analysis and explored methods of reducing overhead.
- The Munich-based corporation systematically developed a core group of components suppliers in the 1980s, adopting strategies later called simultaneous engineering.
- BMW adopted lean management long before Mercedes Benz: its personnel costs were 20 percent of turnover in 1993, as against 33 percent at Mercedes Benz.
- By the late 1980s, BMW had flattened its hierarchies and established a matrix organization.[11]

BMW's market niche and economies-of-scope strategies are classically German. The other strategies listed above are followed by excellent companies across the world.

Mercedes, on the other hand, concentrated exclusively on product quality and consistently lacked professional marketing and financial controlling. It has however recovered its leading position by cutting costs, developing attractive new models, and by imaginatively marketing them.

Figure 1.2
Autos: Worldwide Symbol of Made in Germany

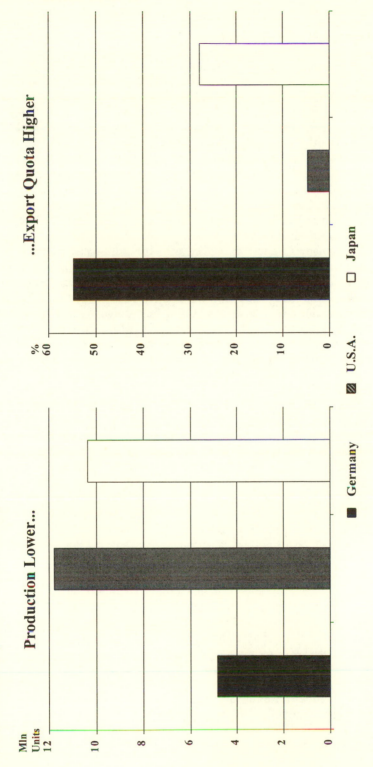

Mln
Units

Production Lower...

...Export Quota Higher

%

■ Germany   ▨ U.S.A.   □ Japan

Source: VdA (Figures for 1996)

DESIGN QUALITY: THE MEISTER TRADITION

The Mittelstand profits from the German tradition in industrial design. Bauhaus in the 1920s and the Ulm school in the 1950s played a pioneering role in sensitizing consumers to the harmony between form and function. Significantly, the Bauhaus school—whose architects and product designers like Gropius, Breuer, Scharoun, and Mies van der Rohe achieved world fame—was oriented toward the German craftsmanship tradition. The Bauhaus professors were in fact designated as "Meister."

Today, German designers tend to be less prominent. Hartmut Esslinger of Frogdesign, who has conceived the Apple Macintosh, Louis Vuitton luggage, and other prominent artifacts, is an exception. However, in sectors as diverse as light installations and office furniture, products designed in Germany have achieved worldwide success.

One company that has triumphed with the minimalist Bauhaus motto of "less is more" is the lighting specialist Erco. Erco products light up the Louvre, the Hong Kong Shanghai Bank, and many other prestige sites across the world. They have even found their way into New York's Museum of Modern Art. One of the major protagonists of the Ulm school, Otl Aicher, was responsible for product design at this Mittelstand enterprise with a thousand employees and a yearly turnover of around 200 million marks.

Erco's corporate philosophy is that of a "Designer for Architects." Like Krones and Fischerwerke, Erco is located in the German province, in a North German town called Lüdenscheid. It relies on local suppliers for all components it does not produce itself. Exports to more than twenty countries account for approximately half the turnover.[12]

Design combined with manufacturing quality is the success formula for sectors like Germany's domestic furniture industry. Interlübke for instance, one of Germany's leading manufacturers with yearly turnover at around 150 Million marks, combines exclusive design with premium quality. The raw materials—wood, leather, and steel—are carefully processed so that they retain a natural flair. The finished products are subjected to rigorous tests through in-house and outside specialists before they leave the factory. They are delivered by Interlübke's own transport department. This ensures that the quality chain does not end at the factory door.

Hülsta, a furniture manufacturer whose yearly turnover is more than twice as high as Interlübkes, has a double-pronged strategy. On the one hand a systems approach ensures that all furniture elements—beds, cupboards, dressing tables and so on—harmonize with each other. On the other hand, Hülsta furniture systems have an in-built potential for variations adjusted to the individual needs of consumers. The company thus assumes the function of an interior decorator. It aims at allowing the buyer to discover his own taste and then purchase a comprehensive furniture system. Modern electromechanic technology in the Hülsta factory enables the furniture makers to cope with the special needs of larger individual customers.[13]

Design in the German context augments technological excellence. It also supports mass customization, as the Hülsta case illustrates.

SERVICE QUALITY: CONTRASTS IN EXCELLENCE

Service is part of the quality chain in successful Mittelstand companies. Krones, for instance, employs around 400 highly trained specialists in customer service and guarantees prompt attention to customers' needs across the world. Interlübke has its own transport department to ensure that the quality chain does not end at the factory gate.

Because of Germany's unique system of vocational education, German technicians are better trained and more versatile than their counterparts in other countries. Technical service is a more invulnerable competitive advantage than product quality, because it stands and falls with the specialized training of service staff.

In his analysis of thirty-nine "hidden champions"—Mittelstand manufacturers that excel in their market segments—Hermann Simon traces the links between service, market research, and Research and Development (R&D). Service provides Mittelstand enterprises with valuable tips on market developments and innovation potentials. Customers are in fact, as surveys have shown, the primary source of information about technological and market trends, followed by industrial fairs, competitive analysis, and professional magazines.[14]

Service in the German context is closely linked with technological excellence—it is seldom a purely commercial strategy. Docter Optik in Wetzlar for instance, a company that manufactures precision lenses and other optical products for leading corporations in the automobile and optoelectronic industries, enjoys a reputation for both meticulous product quality and superb service.

The truck-drivers who deliver Docter components are company-trained: if necessary, they can repair or readjust the products on the spot. The company provides extensive training to all of its own employees and many of its customers' employees. Its major customer, Kodak, testifies: "Docter is the benchmark."[15]

Service Follows Technology

Service rather than technological excellence has helped German companies to success in sectors with declining growth rates. Germany has for instance managed to become the world's leading exporter of harvesting machines, though it was not a technology pioneer. U.S. technology and production methods were superior until the early 1960s.

German manufacturers closed the U.S. lead by pursuing a strategy of incremental innovations. Improvements in product reliability and flexibility, in fuel consumption, and in spare-parts-logistics rather than sheer product quality were responsible for success.

Stagnating home markets forced the German harvesting machine producers to go abroad. Before achieving an export ratio of over 60 percent, the sector rationalized sharply: through fusions and closures the number of enterprises decreased in the course of the 1980s from 450 to 300 and 20,000 jobs were eliminated.

A cost-cutting production strategy is the success formula of Germany's market leader Claas, whose yearly turnover totals approximately a billion marks. Claas has invested heavily in flexible manufacturing systems. But it has also maintained its investments in customer service, carried out by highly trained staff. Its R&D quota of 4.6 percent of total turnover has enabled it to reach the technical forefront in the development of multifunctional machines for farming and forestry. The Westfalian firm has succeeded in living its motto: "We bring quality into the fields."[16]

The Mittelstand excels in technical service. *Service in the German context is indeed an extension of product quality, not an end in itself. It derives from the dedication of the master craftsman or industrial specialist to reaching perfection and is often not part of a calculated strategy to gain customers.* Thus, service deficiencies can be perceived particularly in sectors like gastronomy and retail trade, where flexibility is of paramount importance.

Bad service is probably the most strongly criticized aspect of the German economy. Inflexible opening hours and unfriendly attitudes on the part of service staff are the most common complaints. This criticism is legitimate. However, most critics ignore the high level of functional efficiency that enables the vast majority of Germany's industrial and trade enterprises to deliver punctually and replace spare parts punctiliously.

Basically, it is easier for German companies to adjust toward customer needs than for U.S. companies to obtain the skilled technicians and specialists needed to achieve the functional efficiency that is taken for granted in Germany. The German barriers toward customer service are historic and psychological, concomitant to a craftsmanship ethos. The U.S. weaknesses on the other hand are far more tangible and systemic: vocational education is virtually nonexistent and technicians with specialized skills are therefore in short supply.

At its best, the German approach to service quality is less cosmetic and more sustainable than the "Total Quality" and "Best Practice" strategies followed in the United States and elsewhere. The quintessence of the German approach is the "Konzeptkunde," the conceptual customer:

- Europe's leading special glass manufacturerer Schott developed its best-selling ceran cooking range by organizing workshops and conferences with the cooking equipment manufacturers that integrate Schott components into their product lines. They also invited professional cooks to their workshops and thus supplemented their own research with expertise from their buyers and end-users.
- Heidelberger Druck, the world's leading offset-print manufacturer, not only guarantees customers across the world that a qualified technician will attend to repairs within 24 hours of a complaint being lodged. It also systematically engages in a constant dialogue with selected customers. The Heidelberg Druck teams that visit customers include product developers, marketing experts and service technicians. Thus, service is part of a comprehensive concept that encompasses R&D, manufacturing and marketing.

Quality orientation—in technology, design, and service—can turn out to be an irresistible success factor when combined with cost reduction, a strategic approach to R&D and clever merger & acquisition policies. Manufacturers like BMW and Claas, who synthesize Germanic perfectionism with market orientation and flexibility, have proved that they can survive and prosper under conditions of intense competition.

SECTION 2: STRATEGIES OF SPECIALIZATION AND ECONOMIES OF SCOPE

Specialization is the Mittelstand's key to entrepreneurial success. All the country's "hidden champions" have successfully concentrated on specific product segments. This has helped Mittelstand enterprises to survive in niches, even when the mainstream market is dominated by foreign products. The photographic industry illustrates this point: major manufacturers like Agfa and Zeiss Ikon were unable to resist the mass market penetration of Japanese competitors in the 1970s and 1980s and reduced or discontinued production.

Mittelstand enterprises managed to survive by specializing and simultaneously rationalizing. Linhof for instance, a Munich-based manufacturer of precision-made large-format cameras, has retained its product segment. For professional applications like product photographs in brochures and aerial photography, the Linhof cameras—which can cost upto 100,000 marks per piece—have a great international reputation. By rationalizing production, this company has managed to reduce its staff by 75 percent in the last thirty years while retaining a yearly turnover of approximately 20 million marks.

Similar strategies have been followed by the famous film-camera makers Arnold & Richter in Munich. Arriflex film cameras in 16–65 millimeter formats are renowned all over the world for their mechanical perfection and have won several Academy Awards. However, rising production costs and teething problems with new products reduced profits significantly in the early 1990s. By automatizing production, Arnold & Richter have managed to reduce costs and raise profitability.[17]

Through specialization, Mittelstand companies can achieve a deep knowledge of technology, markets, and customer needs. Their success formula involves concentrating on high-end product segments and rationalizing the manufacturing process.

SCOPE RATHER THAN SCALE: THE BIG BUSINESS APPROACH

In his authoritative study of industrial capitalism in the United States, Great Britain, and Germany in the late nineteenth and early twentieth centuries, business historian Alfred Chandler points out that German corporations exploited the economies of scope rather than of scale, thus differing from their Anglo-Saxon competitors. Scope signifies a range of closely interlocked products requiring minimal changes in raw materials and intermediary manufacturing processes. This contrasted with the Tayloristic preoccupation with size, speed, and standardization.[18]

As we have seen, car makers like BMW and harvesting manufacturers like Claas have achieved competitive advantage by efficiently manufacturing a large range of car models and multifunctional farming machines using basically the same processes. This is also the prime strategy of Germany's powerful chemicals industry. Its three giants, BASF, Bayer, and Hoechst, have achieved impressive synergies in research, production and distribution. Bayer, for instance, manufactured more than 2,000 kinds of dyes by 1913.

Several generations later, scope remains a prime strategic orientation. The percentage of specialized products in Hoechst's product line rose between 1980 and 1990 from 54 to 62 percent, with a corresponding drop in the percentage of basic chemicals. Bayer, BASF, and Hoechst each consist of 100 to 130 business units. Each unit makes a yearly turnover of 300 to 400 million marks—in other words, the turnover of a normal Mittelstand company—and addresses specific market niches.

Successful German corporations follow the same basic specialization strategies as Mittelstand enterprises. They concentrate on filling as many niches as possible by using the same intermediate products, and processes. Big companies can thus economize on fixed costs and accumulate specialized expertise.

At the same time, the scope orientation of major German corporations leads to deficiencies in diversification strategies. Degussa for instance, Germany's largest manufacturer of electrolytically produced cyanides, has traditionally found its market niches by chemically processing precious metals. In the 1970s and 1980s, however, the company dabbled in business areas like fine mechanics and optics, while ignoring the market potential for natrium cyanide, an area in which Degussa was potentially both a technology and a market leader. Faced with a downturn in profits and a loss of reputation, Degussa was forced to restructure its activites. Characteristically, it now plans to expand in areas like ecology and nutrition, where it already enjoys an excellent reputation.[19]

Most German corporations lack clearly formulated diversification and disinvestment policies. The accent is on a risk-minimizing portfolio strategy rather than on proactive exploitation of strengths in key sectors.

As we shall see later in this book, such caution derives from a deeply ingrained Prussian administrative tradition. This tradition influences large corporations, just as the craftsmanship ideal of the Meistersinger pervades the atmosphere in Mittelstand enterprises. In the case of Degussa, its managers have been accused of possessing a "Beamtenmentalität," literally: the mentality of public officials.

The mission of the typical German company is aligned toward stability rather than profitability. Thus, top managers tend to act like judicious trustees rather than adventurous ship captains. They excel in the organizational capabilities needed to exploit the economies of scope, but not in the more imaginative skills that would enable them to make shrewd merger &

acquisitions decisions. They are, as we shall see, talented organizers but mediocre leaders.

SECTION 3: GLOBAL SPECIALIZATION

The export orientation of leading Mittelstand companies is a natural consequence of specialization. In order to find enough outlets for their products, German enterprises seek customers and distributors around the world. In his "hidden champions" study, Simon points out that each of these Mittelstand companies had an average of around ten production sites or distribution outlets abroad.

DGF Stoess has become a global player in the market for photographic, pharmaceutical, and edible gelatine by acquiring companies in the United States, Britain, and Sweden. Stoess's expansion strategy is aligned to the raw materials for gelatine: animal bones and connective tissues, purchased from local slaughter houses. The company's local presence in key markets is oriented toward ensuring an efficient supply of raw materials. Between 1990 and 1994, turnover increased by more than 50 percent to 450 million marks yearly, of which Stoess's foreign subsidiaries contributed the lion's share.[20]

Mast-Jägermeister, based in the Lower Saxon town of Wolfenbüttel, is the rare example of a successful consumer goods manufacturer with aggressive international brand marketing (yearly turnover around 370 million marks). Corporate founder Günter Mast has imaginatively marketed the Jägermeister schnapps in both the West and the East. In the United States, innovative marketing techniques—more than a thousand free tastings a month in bars across the country organized by a group of 800 Jägerette hostesses—made Jägermeister the third largest imported liqueur. Five million bottles were sold in the United States in 1994.

To cater to U.S. tastes, the original Jägermeister schnapps was offered in various blends (JägerMonsters mixed with orange juice, JavaMeisters mixed with coffee). The company had similar success with their free-tasting strategy in East Germany: in early 1990, shortly after the Berlin Wall fell, Jägermeister's marketing organization made contacts in 42,000 bars and shopping outlets. Brand recognition has reached 90 percent in the East, the same level as in West Germany.[21]

Global sales are an important priority for large companies as well. Leading German corporations like BASF, Siemens, and VW earn more than half their turnover abroad. And as a comparative study of CEOs in 100 leading companies in the United States, Japan, France, Great Britain, and Germany shows, Germany's top managers are more proficient in foreign languages and have a greater amount of experience abroad than their colleagues in other countries.[22]

CATERING TO THE JAPANESE

This international orientation is a vital asset in difficult markets. A case in point is Japan. BMW, for instance, was the first foreign automobile corporation to establish a subsidiary in Japan. BMW's German representatives learned Japanese, offered superb after-sales-service through their own, company-trained network of distributors, and provided low-interest purchasing credits. They succeeded in adapting to the Japanese while retaining their German brand image.[23]

BMW can be seen to have profited from its international corporate image and from the high reputation attached to luxury cars made in Germany. Wella, one of Germany's leading manufacturers of cosmetics, also flourished in Japan. Though consumer products are a sector in which German companies rarely excel, Wella has achieved the apparent paradox of becoming an insider in Japan, while still retaining a German business approach.

The Wella success formula is typically German:

- emphasis on long-term presence rather than short-term profitability, with German staff staying six to twelve years in Japan to ensure personnel continuity,
- a top quality/high price approach to product management, with Wella Japan initially concentrating on hair-cutting salons as a professional target group,
- the systematic opening of other distributory channels after a high reputation was established in the hair-cutting salons: cosmetic stores, perfume-selling stores, druggists, and chemists, and also specific department stores,
- an equally systematic approach to training, with special programmes for retailers and hair cutters.

While these are standard German business strategies, practiced as much in the home market as abroad, Wella showed an enormous amount of cultural empathy in gauging the preferences and proclivities of the Japanese. Wella's official policy was that German staff in Japan should empathize with the Japanese, their culture, and their life-styles.

Wella's first top representative in Japan spoke Japanese, read books on Japanese culture, and studied the Japanese mentality. He personally visited the hair-cutting salons, wholesalers, and retailers together with his Japanese subordinates, working side-by-side with Japanese workers on the assembly lines when time was short. He even attended marriages and funerals—this being standard business practice in Japan. Thus, he gave the impression of really caring for his workers, of serving the company, and of belonging to the local business community.[24]

Just as German companies revel in economies of scope rather than diversification, so also do they excel in serving specific market segments abroad rather than in conquering world markets. According to internationalization specialist Manfred Perlitz, even major German corporations making more than 50 percent of their turnover abroad lack clearly planned globalization policies. This accounts for their lack of visibility on world markets. Germany is the world's leading exporter in per capita terms (testimony to its international competitiveness), but its achievements are unspectacular—and hence often overlooked.

Whereas U.S. companies generally concentrate on the profitability of their foreign subsidiaries and Japanese corporations pursue strategies of conquering market shares, German enterprises lack empire-building ambitions. Their quality orientation coupled with their concentration on specialized market segments preclude spectacular visibility, but ensure long-term presence.

SECTION 4: SMALL AND BIG BUSINESS: CARDINAL DIFFERENCES IN CAPITALIZATION—AND ORGANIZATION

Germany's leading corporations are paragons of financial stability. Siemens, for instance, has been ironically termed the "bank with a manufacturing unit," an ironic tribute to its immense liquidity of over 20 billion marks.

The average Mittelstand enterprise on the other hand lacks capital. This is a general problem faced by small business in the whole world. However, since Germany's Mittelstand often competes for market niches in the "top league" both in Germany and abroad, undercapitalization is a strong competitive disadvantage. The working capital ratio in the average Mittelstand company lies between 15 and 20 percent, while 30 to 40 percent is considered adequate. Some Mittelstand companies are however vastly more stable: Mast-Jägermeister for instance has a ratio of 80 percent.

Since most Mittelständlers are fiercely opposed to allowing outsiders to participate in ownership, they remain dependent on their own resources. Various lobbies have urged the Mittelstand to look for sleeping partners or for professional capital participation, but with little success so far. Thus, the entrepreneurs remain dependent on bank loans to finance expansion and obviously suffer more than big business under the high interest rates prevalent in Germany. Over 90 percent of all insolvencies in Germany derive from weak capitalization.

One prime example of an excellent Mittelstand company that verged on bankruptcy and was finally taken over by a large foreign corporation is Heckler & Koch, producer of the famous Mauser guns, which were used in both world wars by the German army. Heckler & Koch decided not to go public, in spite of a heavy capital deficiency deriving from its diversifications in machine building, robotics, and electronics. Instead, the company borrowed from different banks.

In 1990, a 60 million mark contract for the production of a new G11 infantry rifle, the most advanced weapon of its kind in the world, was canceled by the German armed forces. Though the Heckler & Koch group's annual turnover was over 300 million marks at the time, this family-owned company was practically bankrupt. Corporate debt rose to 200 million marks and the burden of interest payments became unbearable. Heckler & Koch Maschinenbau was finally taken over by Britain's Royal Ordnance, while the electronics subsidiary was the subject of a management buyout.

As the Finance Director of Royal Ordnance pointed out: "They fell down on basic financial planning. There was insufficient discipline on investment and stock holding."[25]

Lack of capital also plagues the Mittelstand in East Germany. Between 1990 and 1995, more than half a million companies have been founded in East Germany, no small achievement considering the fact that when the Berlin Wall fell, only some 3,000 companies existed. However, besides lacking management experience, in particular professional marketing skills, East Germany's entrepreneurs are still dependent to a great extent on official subsidies and capital from the western part of the country.

INFORMALITY VERSUS OVER-FORMALIZATION

The fundamental difference between small and big business can be summed up in one word: organization. Mittelstand companies are characterized by a comparative lack of hierarchic organization. Personnel policies tend to revolve round the top leader. While typical Mittelstand entrepreneurs have a strong social conscience and also invest heavily in training apprentices, they lack human resources strategies for developing "high potentials."

Lack of formalization can be an advantage or disadvantage, depending on the situation. Innovation is a case in point. Mittelstand companies are strong where they can quickly identify a "techno niche" and develop custom-built technology to match the market need. They are weak when exploratory R&D work needs to be done in the initial stage and are obviously disadvantaged when new products or processes require a prolonged gestation period.

One survey shows that 44 percent of the Mittelstand enterprises "stumbled on" innovations, as against 9 percent of the large companies. Innovative activity in big corporations is to a major extent the result of a planning process: 62 percent of all large companies have formalized procedures for developing innovations, as against 33 percent of the smaller firms. In complex innovation processes, large companies tend to outpace the Mittelständler, using professional techniques of managing projects, building task forces, and carrying out feasibility studies.[26]

Large companies in Germany are excellently organized, as we shall see in the next chapter. Their problem is an over formalization of organization. Corporate bureaucracies in big business rival those in the public sector. Meticulous attention to detail characterizes both managers and clerks. This is the "Beamtenmentalität" described in connection with Degussa. Formalization cramps creativity in the initial innovative phase while ensuring that innovations, when adopted, are efficiently implemented. As mentioned at the beginning of this chapter, there are many Beckmessers in big business— meticulous bookkeepers with a passion for detail.

In the Mittelstand, on the other hand, delegation of authority is the central management problem. Many entrepreneurs complain about the load of routine tasks they are forced to accomplish, but few have learned to delegate.

Those entrepreneurs who fail to delegate authority during their lifetimes are often faced with the existential problem of finding a successor. Experts estimate that at the end of the 1990s, around 700,000 small- and medium-sized companies will face problems of succession. However, only a tiny percentage of these companies has actively tackled the issue.

According to one survey that covered the nonfamily managers of 200 Mittelstand companies, 93 percent saw the question of succession as the major problem. More than one-third of the entrepreneurs for whom they worked were over fifty years old and the question of succession was apparently not being directly tackled. The same survey pointed out that few managers were informed about the possibilities of management buyins or buyouts (MBI/MBO) and that most of them were skeptical about the entrepreneur's readiness to consider such a solution.[27]

Lack of formal organization limits the growth of Mittelstand companies. Companies like Siemens, Bosch, and Krupp originally started as small craftsmanship enterprises. Beyond manufacturing excellent products, these companies mastered organizational change. Siemens in particular was highly proficient in financial planning and controlling. This mastery has enabled Siemens to become one of Germany's largest—and stablest—corporations, though not one of it's most profitable ones.

MICROCOSM RATHER THAN MODEL

In recent years, the Mittelstand has attracted a growing amount of attention in Germany and abroad. The wealth and stability of the German economy has been attributed in large part to the contribution made by small business. Mittelstand entrepreneurs have found recognition as "hidden champions"—an expression used by management writer Hermann Simon—while Tom Peters contends that the Mittelstand could well be a model for the world economy.[28]

Peters and others attribute a large percentage of the Mittelstand's success to the leadership skills of entrepreneurs and to the strategies followed by enterprises. They thus individualize—and inevitably glorify—the Mittelstand.

In actual fact, as we have seen, small and big business derive their success from the same factors. The Mittelstand has no magic recipe and its entrepreneurs are not necessarily more talented than managers in large corporations. Its particular success can mostly be traced back to flexiblity.

Since the Meistersingers, the Mittelstand has always been a symbol of social ties as well. Because of their strong vocational identity, deriving from the craftsmanship traditions described in this chapter, Germans are very conscious of belonging to various estates. To understand how Germany could develop into an estate-oriented community rather than an urbane, Anglo-Saxon kind of society and why the Mittelstand is a microcosm of this community, we need to briefly review its role in German history.

As we have seen, the term Mittelstand designates a "middle estate." Its origin harks back to the Middle Ages, when the craftsmen in the cities began to assert their independence from feudal ties. The craftsmen in cities like

Nuremberg constituted a kind of middle class, poised between the nobility and the serfs.

By the nineteenth Century, the term Mittelstand encompassed a cultural bourgeoisie, traders, and financially well-situated burghers. However, the heart of the Mittelstand remained the craftsmen. United Germany's Chancellor Otto von Bismarck recognized their political importance as a counterbalance to the rising class of industrialists and bankers. As early as 1849, he hailed the craftsmen as constituting the backbone of the German state.

In spite of Bismarck's moral support, rapid industrialization threatened the independence and the very existence of traditional craftsmen. The Mittelstand's representatives expressed bitter criticism of official policies during the Republic of Weimar, accusations that echo in contemporary Germany, albeit in more moderate form. This criticism peaked in the years after the stock exchange crash of 1929 and culminated in the accusation that the mostly Social and Liberal Democrat government coalitions favored big business and the trade unions at the expense of small business.

The National Socialists were easily able to mobilize the Mittelstand in their favor, since they pretended to support traditional artisanship. Ironically, when the Nazis came to power, they favored big business far more than small business, while paying lip service to the crucial importance of the craftsmen and small traders.

Despite this neglect, the Mittelstand fitted well into the National Socialist vision of a "Ständestaat"—a state ordered according to estates. Heinrich August Winkler contends in his authoritative analysis of the Mittelstand's historic role that the Nazis and the craftsmen shared the same norms of "brutal introspection," allowing them to justify the exploitation of the workforce in the pseudo-idealistic terms of a working community. As Winkler states: "The artisans incorporated in almost ideal purity the values of authoritarian family structure, employer status, and a subservient mentality toward the state."[29]

Authoritarianism and subservience were traditional German values that the Mittelstand personified. Equally, in contemporary Germany, the Mittelstand forms the nucleus of what the sociologist Helmut Schelsky called the "nivellierte Mittelstandsgesellschaft"—a community that has remained estate-oriented and that has simultaneously progressed toward egalitarian, middle-of-the-road values.

Several factors have contributed to the Mittelstand's preeminence in contemporary Germany:

- The economic recovery after the Second World War led to a boom in individual enterprises. In the 1950s, there were 8.2 million Mittelstand companies in Germany, as against approximately 3.5 million in Germany today. This has led to fears of an "Unternehmerlücke," an entrepreneurial gap. However, the immediate postwar period offered exceptional opportunities for startups. Today's dynamism results from MBOs in existing firms.
- Leading policymakers like Ludwig Erhard promoted the Mittelstand: until 1956 for instance, profits invested in enterprises remained taxfree. Erhard himself founded the Institute for Mittelstand Research in 1958 as a means of improving knowledge of the "middle estate's" problems and priorities.

- To a greater extent than in the past, the Mittelstand became partners rather than opponents of big business. The ideological conflicts of the past receded into the background. Instead, the Mittelstand played an important role as suppliers of components for sectors like the automobile industry.
- After the war, the old elites—in particular the military and the aristocrats—were discredited. German society became more egalitarian, and the Mittelstand became the focus of a reconciliation between the former "haves" and "have-nots."

In terms of social values, Germany's small business community personifies socioeconomic norms shared by all sections of the "Mittelstandsgesellschaft." These specifically German norms have been systematically investigated since the 1950s by the Institute for Demoscopy in Allensbach, supplemented by a large-scale study of the Bertelsmann foundation carried out at the end of the 1980s.

Respondents of the Bertelsmann study were asked to identify typical qualities discernible in the characters of the people in their regions. The findings reveal qualities like efficiency and diligence, honesty and decency. As we have seen, these are the human qualities that particularly characterize the craftsmen, the prevalent Mittelstand archetype.[30]

A CULTURE OF FUNCTIONAL PESSIMISM

Any conversation with a representative of a Mittelstand association or with a Mittelstand entrepreneur inevitably develops into a litany of woes—the Mittelstand evidently suffers under the excessive demands of the trade unions, excessive taxation, economic policies that favor large corporations, and so on. The list of inequities is long, and at some stage one asks oneself how the Mittelstand has at all managed to survive, let alone prosper.

It is certainly true that the established political parties have their own priorities: the Social Democrats still rely strongly on support from the trade unions, while the Christian Democrats, Christian Socialists, and Free Democrats are more on the lookout for big business contributions to reduce the chronic financial deficits faced by all major parties in Germany—and thus more attuned to their needs. All parties pay lip service to the virtues of the Mittelstand, but none are truly committed to them.

Beyond this, bureaucracy burdens the Mittelstand. The application procedures for subsidies are often so complex that Mittelstand companies, which cannot afford to employ separate staff for the processing of applications in the way that large companies do, are often incapable of profiting from available funds. According to one survey of Mittelstand entrepreneurs, 60 percent criticized the administrative work necessary to tap public funds, while 55 percent felt that big companies were favored by the existing government regulations.[31]

However, the Mittelstand also indulges in a peculiarly German psychological phenomenon that an eloquent parliamentarian during the Wilhelmine period, Eugen Richter, aptly called the "capacity to complain without suffering!" Large corporations also constantly complain about high wages and social charges, tariff restrictions, bureaucratic obstacles and so on. Beyond this, all social groups in Germany—representatives of specialized associations, state officials, trade union representatives and others—indulge in lavish bouts of dissatisfaction about the state of the world and their own lots in life, mixed with self pity—and sometimes with self criticism.

This peculiarly Lutheran form of long-winded severity, sometimes tempered with a more Catholic touch of "mea culpa, mea maxima culpa," has been raised to a fine art in Germany. In simple terms, it can be said that many Germans are talented hypochondriacs. Molière's malade imaginaire would probably feel very much at his ease in today's Germany! For this reason, economic success in Germany is seldom perceived with the clarity that it deserves. As we shall see in the chapter on cultural roots, religious, and philosophical traditions have led to a culture of functional pessimism—as opposed to the optimism typical of the United States.

Constant dissatisfaction and self-criticism simultaneously signal a steady search for improvement. As we shall see in the next chapter, strategies of incremental innovation are a part of the business mentality. Thus, *the pessimism expressed by the Mittelstand also serves the function of verbalizing a specifically German approach to innovation, one that constantly stresses present deficiencies and the need for improvement.*

Functional pessimism is not only a culturally induced mindset in the German business environment: it is a kind of lingua franca for the constant dialogue between representatives of capital, labor, government, and interest groups that characterizes German society. Pessimistic statements and viewpoints serve the purpose of curbing the demands made by the other party in tariff negotiations, tax debates, and many other issues.

The Mittelstand embodies typically German norms. It has contributed to social cohesion as much as to economic wealth. The Mittelstand is thus a microcosm, an integral part of a larger whole.

NOTES

1. Richard Wagner, *Die Meistersinger von Nürnberg* (Stuttgart: Reclam, 1993).

2. For information on the real Hans Sachs, see Kurt Pahlen (ed.), *Die Meistersinger von Nürnberg* (München: Goldmann, 1981), pp. 394–398; for a deeper analysis of the operas, see John Hamilton Warrack, *Richard Wagner, Die Meistersinger von Nürnberg* (Cambridge, GB: Cambridge University Press, 1994), pp. 49–59; for a stimulating commentary on the opera, see Marcel Reich-Ranicki, "Die Meistersinger von Nürnberg," in *Frankfurter Allgemeinen Zeitung*, June 19, 1993.

3. Michael T. Piore and Charles F. Sabel, *Das Ende der Massenproduktion* (Berlin: Wagenbach, 1985), pp. 162–163; Michael L. Dertouzos et al. (eds.), *Made in America* (Cambridge, MA: MIT Press), 1989, pp. 46–47.

4. Rowland Berthoff, "Independence and Enterprise: Small Business in the American Dream," in Stuart W. Bruchey (ed.), *Small Business in American Life* (New York: Columbia University Press, 1980), pp. 33ff; for recent reports, see "Hot Growth Companies," in *Business Week*, May 25, 1992, pp. 49–60 and Andrew E. Serwer "Lessons from America's fastest-growing companies," in *Fortune*, August 8, 1994, pp. 16–27.

5. D.H. Wittaker,"SMEs and Entry Barriers," in Masahiko Aoki and Ronald Dore (eds.), *The Japanese Firm* (Oxford: Oxford Unviersity Press, 1994), pp. 210–225; see also J.A. Stam, "New Patterns of Cooperation among Enterprises in Japan," in Sung-Jo Park (ed.), *Managerial Efficiency in Competition and Cooperation* (Frankfurt: Campus, 1992), pp. 231–242.

6. Tom Peters, "Mittelstand—The Mighty Minnows," in *German Brief*, August 9, 1991, p. 10.

7. Droege and Comp., *Zukunftssicherung durch strategische Unternehmensführung* (Düsseldorf: Wirtschaftswoche, 1991), pp. 21–22, 27–28.

8. Faisal Rahmatallah, "The Hidden Champions," in *World Link*, March-April 1995, pp. 34–39.

9. For a very journalistic description of Krones, see Horst Biallo, *Die geheimen deutschen Weltmeister* (Vienna: Ueberreuter, 1993), pp. 87–108; see also Rainer Nahrendorf, "Spitzentechnik und hohe Spezialisierung können Standortnachteile kompensieren," in *Handelsblatt*, August 20, 1993.

10. Biallo, *Die geheimen deutschen Weltmeister*, pp. 33–46; see also "Fischer hat nicht nur mit Dübeln durchschlagenden Erfolg," in *Süddeutsche Zeitung*, December 31, 1994.

11. Stephan Schlote and Frank A. Linden, "Münchner Himmel," in *Manager Magazin* 2/1995, pp. 31–43; Rolf Antrecht and Thomas Luber, "Nur BMW so gut wie Japan," in *Capital*, 9/1993, pp. 8–12.

12. See "Unsere Produkte gewinnen viele Preise und verkaufen sich glänzend," in *Impulse*, 1/1992, pp. 44–45, 48–49.

13. For Interlübke, see "Der Cor-Geist," in *Manager Magazin*, June 1994, pp. 144–156; for hülsta see "Markenpflege zahlt sich für Hülsta aus," in *Frankfurter Allgemeine Zeitung*, January 20, 1995; "An der Herstellermarke scheiden sich die Geister," in *Süddeutsche Zeitung*, January 17, 1995.

14. See "Know-how von außen," in *Absatzwirtschaft*, April 1992; see also "Erfolg mit Nischen-Produkten" in *IWD*, September 5, 1996.

15. Hayo Koch, "Doktor Optik," in *Manager Magazin*, 6/1991, pp. 73–79; see also "Stark im Markt durch Eigenentwicklungen," in *Handelsblatt*, December 29, 1994.

16. See "Die Bauern kaufen wieder mehr Landmaschinen," in *Frankfurter Allgemeine Zeitung*, February 25, 1995 and "Claas zwischen Saat und Ernte," in *WirtschaftsWoche*, October 10, 1986, pp. 143ff.

17. For Linhof and Arri, see "Für Lichtbildner mit gutem Leumund," in *Manager Magazin*, 3/1991, p. 90; sse also "Arnold & Richter setzt sich in Szene," in *Süddeutsche Zeitung*, August 16, 1994.

18. Alfred D. Chandler, jr., *Scale and Scope* (Cambridge, MA.: Harvard University Press, 1990), p. 24.

19. See the mismanagement report "Der Glanz ist dahin," in *Manager Magazin*, 8/1990, pp. 30– 33; see also "Ohne Kostenabbau hätte die Degussa keinen Gewinn erzielt," in *Frankfurter Allgemeine Zeitung*, February 2, 1995.

20. Biallo, *Die geheimen deutschen Weltmeister*, pp. 17–30; see also "In fünf Jahren ein internationales Netzwerk geknüpft," in *Frankfurter Allgemeine Zeitung*, March 29, 1995.

21. "Recipes for wide success, " in *World Link*, March-April 1995, pp. 43–44; scc also "Internationalität stärkt die Mast-Jägermeister AG," in *Lebensmittelzeitung*, February 17, 1995.

22. See a report on the study, "Wege zum Club der Weltelite," in *Top Business*, August 1993.

23. Walter Sawallisch, "Die Strategien eines deutschen Autombilunternehmens auf dem japanischen Markt: Das Erfolgsbeispiel BMW," in Dieter Schneidewind and Armin Töpfer (ed.), *Der asiatisch-pazifischer Raum: Strategien und Gegenstrategien von Unternehmen* (Landsberg: Verlag Moderne Industrie 1991), pp. 353–376.

24. Makato Tobari, "Zum Hintergrund des Erfolges von Wella Japan," in Schneidewind and Töpfer, *Der asiatisch-pazifischer Raum*, pp. 381–396.

25. "Germany: Heckler und Koch Benefits from New Financial Muscle," in *Accountancy*, 9/1991, pp. 78–79; see also "Heckler & Koch Elektronik," in *Handelsblatt*, November 22, 1990.

26. Jürgen Bethel (ed.), *Mittelständische Unternehmen: Herausforderungen und Chancen für die 90er Jahre* (Berlin: Springer 1988), pp. 27 ff.

27. The results of the survey are reported in *Handelsblatt*, August 3, 1992; for other surveys on delegation of authority, see Thomas Baumgärtner, "Verprellt und zerstritten," in *Die Zeit*, April 28, 1995.

28. See the interview with Tom Peters, "Der Mittelstand ist ein Modell für die Weltwirtschaft," in *Impulse*, 12/1992, pp. 92–94; see also Hermann Simon, "Lessons from Germany's Midsize Giants," in *Harvard Business Review*, March-April 1992, pp. 115–123.

29. Heinrich August Winkler, *Mittelstand, Demokratie und Nationalsozialismus* (Cologne: Kiepenheuer & Witsch, 1972), pp. 21ff.; for the term Mittelstand, see Eberhard Hamer, *Das mittelständische Unternehmen* (Stuttgart: Poller, 1987), pp. 11–18.

30. Meinhard Miegel, *Wirtschafts- und arbeitskulturelle Unterschiede in Deutschland* (Gütersloh: Bertelsmann Stiftung, 1991), pp. 48ff.

31. Eberhard Hamer, *Das mittelständische Unternehmen* (Stuttgart: Poller, 1987), pp. 170–184; see also from the same author, *Bürokratieüberwälzung auf die Wirtschaft* (Hannover: Schlüter, 1979), pp. 1–13, 109–152.

CHAPTER 2

Order and the Business Mentality

We can best reach our targets if we can prove that the autonomous status of our organization is capable of guaranteeing technical security—and of achieving all the tasks that the state is obliged to, but cannot achieve on its own. In technical control and security, we always have to be a step ahead of the state. We have worked this way for the last 60 to 70 years.

—Former TÜV President Siegfried Balke
quoted in Werner Hoffmann
Unabhängig und neutral—die TÜV und ihr Verband

The TÜV (Technischer Überwachungsverein, literally "Technical Control Association") is one of Germany's best-known institutions. It undertakes various technical control tasks on behalf of the German state. In particular, the TÜV certifies the roadworthiness of all motor vehicles registered in Germany.

TÜV's former president, Siegfried Balke, quoted above, drew attention to its traditional raison d'etre. Derived from an association founded by factory owners to check the safety of steam boilers in 1866, TÜV has successfully defended its independence against state interventions on the one hand and critics of its monopoly status on the other hand. The technical expertise of its highly trained specialists and the TÜV's organizational efficiency have commanded respect and justified its privileged position.

TÜV's significance far exceeds its function. It is the symbol of a specifically German business mentality—the mentality of order through control. Though it acts autonomously, TÜV's authority is unquestioned. *Its combination of technical proficiency and organizational efficiency is the key to Germany's business success.*

The association is now exporting its enormous expertise by establishing subsidiaries and working on projects in countries as diverse as Italy, Russia, and China. Quality certification according to the ISO 9,000 norms is a major priority at present. TÜV is rapidly acquiring know-how in subjects like eco auditing and telecommunications security, which will gain importance in the future. Its activities rarely hit the headlines but are quietly influential. In effect, TÜV implants a specific mindset—that of order through control—in the countries where it operates.[1]

TÜV also illustrates the efficacy of private-sector cooperation in Germany. As early as 1873, the first affiliation of technical associations was founded; in 1888 the first foreign organizations joined. Since then, technical specialists from the regional TÜV associations cooperate closely with their colleagues in other regions and, more recently, with specialists from the central ministries. This accumulation of collective know-how through cooperation is a typically German economic achievement. *The TÜV success story unites vital elements of wealth creation in Germany: technical expertise, organizational efficiency, and cooperative acumen.*

MENTALITY AND WEALTH CREATION

A German-U.S. executive at IBM Germany was once quoted as saying that he could not stand the country's "TÜV mentality." This order-control emphasis is culturally rooted in philosophical concepts of order and in the Prussian ethos. It is psychologically traceable to a streak of compulsiveness in the collective psyche. The roots of order will be analyzed later in this book. In this chapter, the impact of Germany's TÜV mentality on wealth creation will be explored.

The term mentality is often used but seldom defined. Historians are in fact the only group of scholars who seriously analyzes mentality: the French "Annales" school has defined it as an ensemble of ways and types of thinking and feeling that manifests itself in actions. More specifically, mentality is, as Peter Burke points out, opposed to the idea of "timeless rationality." It stands between the individual and the collective, between ideas and behavior, as the cultural expression of particular social groups.[2]

In the English-speaking world, the term "business culture" is often used as a synonym for mentality and generally characterizes styles of entrepreneurship and management. For instance, a detailed comparison of national competitiveness in the United States and Europe refers to U.S. business's "short-term business mentality." Similarly, a biomedical newsletter refers to the "new lean and mean U.S. business mentality."[3]

America's business mentality can be characterized as an individualistic search for best results in terms of profitability, productivity, customer service and so on. The individual enjoys a high degree of freedom—and insecurity—in business and in social life. Japan, on the other hand, with its collectivist orientation toward business success, forcibly integrates the individual. Perceptive observers have discerned mechanisms of repression behind the harmonious facades in Japanese companies, and more visible signs of repressiveness in Japanese society.[4]

German business on the other hand offers the individual a degree of autonomy within parameters of tasks defined carefully on the basis of vocational qualifications. Order through control applies to job descriptions and performance checks. It integrates employees and gives them guidelines, but it does not suppress individuality.

Similarly German society, the Mittelstandsgesellschaft described in the last chapter, is organized in occupationally defined estates that imbue the individual with a vocational sense of identity. Industrial, trade, and professional associations integrate both business leaders and normal employees into a larger whole.

The traditional clichés used to explain Germany's economic success, such as hard work and discipline, can easily be empirically refuted. Germany's short working hours, its record number of public holidays, and the high level of absenteeism in German industry all point in a different direction.

This chapter examines the German emphasis on organization rather than leadership. Because of this bias, German corporations are adept at organizing an internal consensus—and in contributing to a more broad-based consensus in sectors such as trade fairs and ecology, where Germany excels.

The U.S. and Japanese economies excel in short-term competitiveness because they quickly adapt to technological and structural changes without paying particular attention to financial stability or to the social costs of change. Germany on the contrary assimilates changes more gradually. The country's ecological success story—Germany is a world leader both in ecological technology and in eco management procedures—illustrates the effectiveness of its gradualist approach.

Germany's "eco consensus" presages its future success in the world economy. Because of this consensus, Germany already practices sustainable development—economic growth balanced by ecological considerations, the need for social justice, and the exigencies of financial stability—to a greater extent than any other country in the world. The German approach to wealth creation is thus more complex (and less impressive at first sight) than the U.S. and Japanese strategies aimed at maximizing gross national product and productivity.

SECTION 1: AN EMPHASIS ON ORGANIZATION RATHER THAN LEADERSHIP

Organization, not leadership, is the key to business management in Germany. The TÜV mentality of order through control is reflected in the formality of organizational procedures and in the functionality of consensus-oriented decision-making.

In his classic study, *Organizational Culture and Leadership*, Edgar H. Schein concentrates on two corporate case studies, that he calls A and B. A, the action company, is obviously quintessentially U.S.: open office atmosphere, dynamism, interpersonal confrontration.

Company B is so quintessentially German that it deserves to be described in Schein's words: "At the level of what is visible, it is more formal—the formality symbolized by large buildings and offices with closed doors; obvious deference rituals among people who meet each other in the hall; many status symbols, such as private dining rooms for senior managers (in contrast to A's open cafeteria); the frequent use of academic and other titles, such as Dr. so-and-so; a slower, more deliberate pace; and much more emphasis on planning, schedules, punctuality, and formal preparation of documents for meetings."[5]

This illustrates the "Beamtenmentalität"—managers with the aura of government officials—already described in connection with Degussa. The punctiliousness and the reverential attitude toward academic degrees and ranks of office commented on by Schein are symptomatic of an attitude transfer from the public to the private sector. The Prussian tradition of public-sector administration has strongly influenced management styles and procedures in large corporations.

While Mittelstand enterprises are to a large extent informally organized, big companies are complexly structured. Great attention is paid to formalized procedures, to organigrammes, job descriptions, and other instruments that regulate power and responsibility.

Business economics ("Betriebswirtschaftslehre"), the German equivalent of business management studies, emphasizes organizational theory and accounting rather than leadership or strategies. Basically, business economics instrumentalizes the primary importance of order for the business world, just as state science ("Staatswissenschaft") formerly provided the public service with a frame of reference. One of Germany's leading business theorists, Erich Gutenberg, once pointed out: "Organization is the execution of order."

Business economics has never achieved the status that business management—as a science or an art—enjoys in the Anglo-Saxon countries. German corporations, like Mittelstand enterprises, have traditionally been dominated by craftsmen rather than commercially qualified managers— engineers, chemists, mining specialists, and so on rather than MBAs or accountants. Since the entrepreneurial emphasis has always been on technical rather than commercial priorities, professional management has remained in the background.

BORROWED CONCEPTS, STANDARDIZED METHODS

Management theory in contemporary Germany is mostly epigonic: it copies U.S. and Japanese models and has virtually no impact on the world outside Germany. As business historian Dieter Schneider points out, it has become a "provincial market that lives from imports."[6]

Management consultants in Germany are similarly epigonic: basically they adopt and adapt standard McKinsey and Boston Consulting Group methods such as value analysis, portfolio management, and time-based management. In recent years, they have increasingly taken over Japanese recipes like just-in-time, Kaizen, and lean management. Roland Berger & Partner, Germany's largest consultancy, has come out with a "time-cost-quality leadership" concept that unites the mostly imported time-and-cost orientation with the quality dimension that almost all German companies, whether large or small, explicitly orient toward.

Even in the area of quality, where Germany can be seen to have remarkable competence, there is a curious lack of imaginative concepts or of international management personalities from Germany. The quality gurus have traditionally come from the United States and, more recently, from Japan: Deming, Juran, Crosby, Shingo, Ishikawa, Taguchi. But though German management is good at the mundane tasks of the quality process—top-level commitment, planning, teamwork, education, cost measurement, awareness, corrective action—it lacks a proclivity for the spectacular proclamation of visions and "philosophies."[7]

The Germans are in fact quiet practitioners, not "defenders of the faith." They concentrate on administering efficiently by optimizing organizational structures and procedures.

Both the Mittelstand and large corporations rely on standardized management methods:

- Value analysis for instance has been used by small business to improve operating efficiency: in one case it involved reducing the time span for processing contracts by 50 percent.
- For the craftsman-type leader, efficiency can involve—as it did in the case of one bakery—devoting more time for marketing and lobbying for large contracts.
- Controlling is an important common priority. A rising number of Mittelstand companies are actively installing procedures to measure financial performance and profitability. One brewery for instance introduced sales controlling, so that sales personnel can judge how far they can offer price reductions without completely sacrificing profits.[8]

Large companies use similar management techniques. The mail-order giant Otto Versand for instance relies on cost management to increase the efficiency of its mail-order activities. Other large companies rely on time-based management, simultaneous engineering, computer-based logistics, and outsourcing.

Until the early 1980s, most management techniques, in particular portfolio planning and strategic marketing, were imported from the United States and adapted to German conditions. In recent years, Japanese procedures like just-in-time, quality circles, and lean management have made the rounds. The functional utility of these strategies is unquestionable. However, they do not always harmonize with "soft factors" in German business like obsession with perfection and social priorities.

Lean management for instance was widely implemented in the context of the 1993–94 recession. However, while cutting overheads is a concrete strategy that many small and large companies can identify with, the normal German enterprise is not really attuned to being "lean and mean." German companies are used to making excellent products regardless of the price.

In the same way, benchmarking is anathema to the German mindset: in a perfection-oriented context, one concentrates on doing the best oneself rather than examining the cost structures and the returns on investment of competitors. For this reason, standardized methods often do not function in Germany with the same efficiency as in the United States or Japan.

ORGANIZATIONAL CONSTRAINTS AND THE SEARCH FOR CONSENSUS

An unimpassioned look at the quality of German management reveals that managers have the same positive qualities as the mass of Germany's white-collar workers: specialized education, solid work experience, and, above all, organizational skills. In contrast to other countries, in particular to the United States and Great Britain, the German business scene is short on mavericks and tough guys.

The Swiss consultancy Prognos surveyed 465 high-level managers from seven European countries including Germany, all of whom were asked to judge the quality of German management. To a major degree, the French, Italian, British, and Benelux managers came to the same value judgments on their German colleagues. Positive qualities like reliability, fairness, and a high educational standard contrasted with criticism: German managers were considered boring, unflexible, and bureaucratic. Significantly, the German practitioners interrogated expressed the same opinions of their compatriots.[9]

In recent years, German managers have come in for more stringent criticism: according to business theorist Fredmund Malik, they are "fair-weather pilots," lacking the tough qualities needed to cope with crises. Similar criticism has been expressed by practitioners.

Such criticism ignores the reality of organizational culture in German corporations. Structural restraints curb the power of German top managers in public-limited corporations. In contrast to the Anglo-Saxon board of directors model, executive power is vested in an executive board (Vorstand), while the supervisory board (Aufsichtsrat) has a mandate to control the functioning of the executive board.

In both boards, the principle of collegial decision-making has been codified by law (the Aktiengesetz). Thus, the executive board decides issues on a majority basis and CEOs have no particular powers. The same applies to the chairman of the supervisory board. However, both chiefs serve as "integrative links" between the two boards and thus wield a certain amount of coordinating influence.

Since the Aktiengesetz gives the supervisory board the authority to renew the contracts of executive board members and given the fact that employees' representatives are allotted several seats on the Supervisory Board, top managers are well advised to be on good terms with the employees' representatives. Moreover, the legal situation—in particular stringent, employee-friendly laws applying to dismissal—militates against German managers playing at being "high and mighty."[10]

Beyond this, managers are well aware of their social responsibilities. Their social orientation helps German managers cooperate in associations and automatically sensitizes them to issues like ecology.

The difference in managerial emphasis between corporations in Germany and elsewhere can be traced back to the Prussian legacy. According to psychologist Manfred Koch, the recruitment system practiced in contemporary Germany resembles that of the Prussian state in the nineteenth century. Appointment is on the basis of formal qualification. Criteria used to measure managerial performance are: steady progress in a specialized department and mastery of administrative procedures. Most managers rise steadily through the hierarchies and tend to be solid practitioners. The cautious "Beamtenmentalität" described earlier is a concomitant of recruiting and promotion procedures.[11]

Beckmesser, the niggling bureaucrat we encountered in connection with the Meistersinger of Nuremberg, is as much a role model for large companies as the craftsman Hans Sachs. Beckmessers tend to rise from the ranks of the book keepers to become financial controllers. However, Sachs-type specialists rather than Beckmessers tend to occupy top managerial positions.

Business management in Germany can best be described as being of impeccable mediocrity. In terms of their qualifications, their personalities, and horizons, German managers do not constitute a true elite. In their skills and aspirations, they are typical representatives of the Mittelstandsgesellschaft described earlier. Germany lacks institutions with the aura of the Harvard Business School, the University of Tokyo, Oxford, and Cambridge, or the grands écoles.

Individual corporate leaders are easily replaceable, an infinite advantage for the continuity of wealth creation. *The true explanation of Germany's business success is not individual excellence: it is expressed in more oblique words like organizational cohesion and consensus.*

ORGANIZATIONAL COHESION AND CONSENSUS—IN TRADE FAIRS

Germany is a world leader in the trade fairs sector: of the 450 international fairs recognized by the Union des Foires Internationales, approximately 100 are held in Germany. Fairs constitute a three billion mark service sector.

Service quality, specialization, and an international approach, the success factors analyzed in the previous chapter, contribute to Germany's proficiency in trade fairs:

- Of the 130,000 exhibitors at Germany's trade fairs each year, almost half are from abroad.
- 95 percent of all fairs are specialized "Fachmessen."
- The service quality of trade fairs "made in Germany" is rooted in the organizational skills of the operational staff.

Germany's business community participates in the decision-making process on issues such as the founding of new fairs and the restructuring of existing fairs. Specialized industrial associations canalize the viewpoints and interests of the companies they represent. Organizational cohesion ensures that trade fairs are attuned to the priorities of the business community.

Though the German state owns the fair authorities, it respects their autonomy and allows them to function in cooperation with the representatives of the private sector. Similarly, the business community accepts the non partisan role of the fair organizers, who are larger than their competitors in the rest of the world and who own the premises on which the fairs are held. This ensures that improvements in the quality of exhibition facilities, exhibitor support services, and visitor information services are made on a continuous basis.

Beyond this, the fair organizers cooperate with the regional authorities to ensure the quality of ancillary infrastructure in terms of transport and accommodation for exhibitors and visitors. Germany's six leading fair authorities—in Hannover and Cologne, Frankfurt and Munich, Düsseldorf, and Berlin—vie with each other in attracting the most prestigious fairs and the local authorities in these towns compete in providing infrastructure. Specialized service-providers monitor the general service quality of the fairs and provide statistical analyzes of the performance of individual fairs.[12]

A viable consensus between the representatives of business, fair authorities, and local administration is achieved through a formalized process of codetermination. Decisions are taken by various committees. The industrial fairs' central association, AUMA, integrates all interest groups involved in the sector and coordinates committee activities.

Neither the fair authorities nor the various exhibitors' associations are under any official pressure to participate in the various committees. Both sides have, however, a vested interest in achieving a consensus. One expert puts it: "In a socially corrected market economy, the state and the private sector are strongly linked to each other, starting with structures and continuing into processes. This is certainly true for fairs, which are particularly subject to public opinion and social judgment."[13]

Trade fairs demonstrate the German consensus approach to business success. Because of their complex organizational structures and the codetermination they internally practice, German corporations are well outfitted to play their role in the trade-fair consensus process. *Organizational cohesion is thus a prerequisite for consensus.*

Through consensus mechanisms, all participants contribute to and profit from wealth creation. The value of cohesion and consensus is easily discernible but difficult to quantify. However, cohesion and consensus are largely invulnerable competitive advantages. Unlike manufacturing processes and marketing strategies, they cannot be easily imitated. As we shall see in the course of this book, *Germany's mastery of consensus is a vital part of its invisible wealth.*

SECTION 2: ASSOCIATIONS AND ESTATE ORDER

Trade fairs illustrate the supportive role played by associations in the consensus process. Beyond this, Germany's "Verbände," its industrial and trade associations, play an even more vital role in integrating the business community into the Mittelstandsgesellschaft, the estate-oriented community described in the last chapter. The country's central and specialized Verbände have achieved this integration by establishing an "estate order," supported by companies from all sectors. The roots of this order lie in the past.

In the nineteenth Century, industrialists like Alfred Krupp considered themselves a part of the "Kaufmannsstand," the commercial estate. Similarly, the Mittelstand has always constituted a specific section of the business community: the middle estate.

The traditional estate-orientation dating back to the guilds has segmented society into a set of vocationally defined groups and has called for mechanisms of formalized cooperation both within these groups and between the various estates. Vocational cooperation and representation characterize public life in Germany, just as the principles of a liberal, loosely organized society are clearly visible in Britain and the United States.

The first modern associations of significance in Germany were the chambers of commerce. Economic modernization, which was decreed by the state, needed support in the private sector. Founded shortly after the Napoleonic wars, the chambers of commerce were quick to seize the chance to propagate their own interests and to influence sections of the Prussian bureaucracy in their favor.

The chambers of commerce are required by their statutes to "bring together and conciliate the interests of their constituents in the context of long-term macroeconomic optimization."[14] This is quintessentially the common-interest component that guides all associations in Germany and that gives them a semi-official status. However, the chambers also profit from their legal status: since membership is compulsory for all enterprises engaging in industry or trade, over two million businesses are members.

Unlike the craftsmen's guilds, however, that are also compulsorily organized in a central chamber, there is no formal qualification test for membership. The chambers of commerce thus represent the collective interests of mostly small businesses. They have recently been subject to severe criticism. Their clientele considers the membership contributions, levied according to a complex method of calculation, to be too high. A sizeable percentage of members seldom use their services. The chambers' officials have also been criticized for being bureaucratic.[15]

Most of this criticism is legitimate. *The value of the chambers of commerce for wealth creation lies however in their role, not in their functional efficiency.* The omnipresent chambers, dotted all over Germany, are forums for "business politics" on the grass roots level. An enormous amount of work is done in committees and working groups. The chambers serve as catalyzers and opinion leaders for technical innovations and issues like environmental protection, they provide advice on exports and offer educational facilities that enable entrepreneurial newcomers to grasp the basics of business administration. They integrate businesses of all types into the mainstream of economic endeavor—and are thus the architects of cohesion.

The chambers of commerce are general-interest associations. Their work is supplemented by an enormous number of specialized Verbände. The roles of these associations are particularly valuable in sectors with potentially cutthroat competition. One excellent example is advertising: Germany is the only country in the world with a "Dachverband," a holding association that unites thirty-nine associations in the ad business. The holding association ZAW serves as a round table for formulating common standpoints and reconciles conflicting viewpoints.[16]

The specialized associations also undertake semiofficial tasks, rather like the TÜV: they provide sectorial statistics and "Betriebsvergleiche," comparisons between enterprises within a sector. The coordination of these activities and the mediation of diverse views is a major organizational achievement. In fact, *associations incorporate the same emphasis on organizational rather than leadership skills that characterize German corporations.*

Their dual role as coordinators and initiators gives the German associations an aura of authority both in business circles and in the business environment. Comparable organizations in the United States, like the National Association of Manufacturers, lack this organizational focus. U.S. business activity is characterized to a greater extent by atomistic antagonism rather than by organic cohesion.

Representation in the U.S. context has more to do with lobbyism than with harmonizing within the business environment. Recently, a number of successful corporations like Microsoft and Walmart have sought "cooperative advantage" by deepening their relationships with suppliers and customers. However, the business climate in the United States is still predominantly atomistic.[17]

The Japanese business associations, the zaikai, are extremely influential. In particular the Keidanren is reputed to hold veto rights on economic legislation. However, Japan's associations lack Germany's specialized orientation, its broad coverage of industrial, trade and service sectors, of small enterprizes and large corporations.

The German associations' role in wealth creation is unique. As Hans Jaeger points out in his history of economic order in Germany, no other country in the world has such a highly developed and influential system of associations.[18]

SUBTLETIES OF COOPERATION AND COMPETITION

Generally, associations in the German context harmoniously coexist: each has its own responsibilities and does not poach on the sectorial specializations of the others. Sometimes, however, two associations serve the same clientele. The quid pro quo that these potentially competitive associations achieve symbolizes the remarkable coexistence of competition and cooperation in Germany.

The machine-tools sector, for instance, is served by two Verbände: the Association of German Machine Tools Manufacturers (VDW), founded in 1891, and the Association of Machines and Equipment Manufacturers (VDMA), founded a year later.

VDMA includes a "specialized community" (Fachgemeinschaft) of machine-tools manufacturers. VDW, on the other hand, is exclusively committed to the specific interests of the machine-tools makers, who sell 30–40 percent of their output to other machine-building companies. Thus a percentage of the customers of VDW members belongs to VDMA.

Beyond this, the two associations differ in their attitudes to industrial policy. VDW has discerned that the inroads made into world machine-tools markets by Japanese competitors are due to innovative strategies initiated by the Japanese state—and is advocating the same strategy for Germany, while also calling for protectionist trade policies. VDMA on the other hand expects the state to restrict its role to supporting private-sector strategies indirectly through specific R&D programs.[19]

In spite of this, VDW and VDMA closely cooperate. In public statements, both emphasize their common interests. Their governing boards are largely identical. Thus, while cooperating closely on certain issues, the associations agree to disagree on others.

While remaining competitors, the German companies manage through their industrial associations to constitute a harmonious community, organized in specific estates. The personal relationships derived from participation in associational activities create unseen bonds between apparent competitors. *Estate order is not imposed by associations: it is voluntarily supported by the business community.*

MERGING BUSINESS INTO A LARGER ORDER

Discussion of the ideology and influence of associations has always been avid in Germany, reflecting their major role in public life. Since the nineteenth century, associations have excelled in playing a dual role. As against their members, they emphasize the need to unite and achieve mutual benefits. In public, they propagate economic viewpoints that go well beyond their missions as representatives of specific estates.

Associations have thus exercized a formative influence on German political discourse, comparable to the Oxford and Cambridge debating clubs in England. From Gustav Stresemann, the outstanding leader of the Republic of Weimar, to Chancellor Helmut Kohl, prominent politicians in Germany have often served in associations before rising to political power. They have learned to mediate the process of consensus in associations and to think organically rather than antagonistically. As Stresemann once pointed out: "I too as an individual am a part of a larger whole, of a great concept."[20]

Stresemann had an intuitive grasp of Gestalt, this book's approach to analysing wealth. As we saw in the introductory chapter, Gestalt postulates that the whole is more than the sum of the parts. The estate order, that Germany's associations coordinate, merges into the larger order of the Social Market Economy (SME). Equally, the business community's representatives integrate their constituents into the Mittelstandsgesellschaft, SME's social foundation.

The influence exercized by associations was widely publicized in the 1950s and 1960s. Contemporary Germany has been described as a "Verbändestaat," this implying that the associations dominate the state. Significantly, criticism often had a strong conservative flavor: it reflects the fear that the sacrosanct powers of the state could be undermined or usurped by business representatives.

These fears are unfounded. As we have seen, the state still serves as an organizational model for large corporations and associations alike. In normative terms, the public sector influences the private sector far more than vice versa. While relativizing the apprehensions refered to above, political scientist Kurt Sontheimer points out that German associations are partially responsible for their own demonization, because they constantly pretend that their activities are in the common interest. Sontheimer sees this as a sign of hypocricy and points out that associations often use a vocabulary more suited to the Last Judgment rather than to the expression of partisan views by an interest group![21].

This exaggerated vocabulary has deeper roots. Estate orientation leads to a stress on mission rather than a clear statement of interest and to constant complaints of injustice and discrimination. This however is not specific to associations: Mittelstand entrepreneurs, trade union officials, political leaders, and other spokesmen similarly equate their own interests with the public good. They too indulge in Zweckpessimisus, the culture of functional pessimism described in the Mittelstand chapter.

SECTION 3: MAINTAINING ORDER—THE ROLE OF POWER

In German business, cartels and banks pull the strings from behind the scenes. Those in power aim at establishing and maintaining the existing order, just as the associations coordinate order. Fittingly, power is quietly exercised, not openly proclaimed.

Analysing the German economy of the late nineteenth century, the famous economist Werner Sombart complained that no information was available on cartels: "Our entrepreneurs and those who work for them have for unfathomable reasons cast a veil on everything to do with cartels. They apparently consider it dangerous to speak with outsiders—and studies of the business practices of the syndicates are despised and feared."[22]

Sombart's observation holds true today. A veritable cult of secrecy surrounds power in Germany. One author of a series of portraits of top managers in German corporations pointed out that entire departments seemed to be occupied with the job of screening off top management from the media.[23]

Both the substance and the spirit of power in German business remain eva-
sive. The desire for secrecy is however not unfathomable, as Sombart felt—the
business world has a vested interest in discouraging curiosity as to its power
mechanisms and financing structures. This was as true of the cartels in the late
nineteenth century as it is for the more informal corporate alliances at the end
of the twentieth century.

After the Second World War, cartels were discredited, mostly because of
the collaborative role played by groups like IG Farben during the Nazi period.
The new doctrine of the SME favored competition and consumer orientation
rather than the consolidation of industrial power. Ludwig Erhard, West
Germany's first minister of the economy, emphasized that market success
should be determined by the quality and price of commodities, not regulated by
the state or by cartels.

However, Erhard was unable to push through stringent legislation. The powerful president of the entrepreneurs' association BDI, Fritz Berg, countered
that quality-based competition was often only possible through "cooperation"
and "communitarian work." Berg prophetically pointed out: "In the modern
industrial economy, competition and cooperation belong together."[24]

The law against "competitive restraints" of 1957 was thus less rigorous
than originally planned. If a cartel unites more than 10,000 employees, if its turnover exceeds 500 million marks or if it holds more than 20 percent market
share, it must be reported to the Cartel Authority, which can forbid its
foundation. However, important sectors of the economy are exempted from the
legislation: financial services, transport, utilities. Cartel-like arrangements can
also be allowed in cases of structural crisis or when rationalization requires a
degree of cartelization. Thus, there has been a recent call for a structural-crisis
cartel in the steel industry.

The cartel law has been sharpened several times to control fusions and
unofficial price agreements. However, the Ministry of the Economy can
overrule the Cartel Authority in the national interest. The entry of the
aerospace giant MBB into Germany's largest corporation, Daimler Benz, is one
prominent example where formal provisions of cartel law were overruled.

The key question is: when is a mode of cooperation in actual fact a cartel?
In cases where information is exchanged, basic research is carried out, or
technical standards are developed, cooperation is permitted. Strategic alliances
or "horizontal cooperation" that overstep the parameters of fair competition, on
the other hand, are not allowed. Thus, the leeway for companies to build virtual
or partial cartels is unlimited—and probably unlimitable.

German companies in the postwar period have proved to be masters in
maintaining interlocking ties and reaching unofficial cartel-style agreements.
For example, the trade corporation Metro was known to be controlling the
departmental store chain Horten at a time when it only held 8 percent of share
capital. Similarly, pharmaceutical companies, mineral oil distributors, and
banks have been accused of having made illicit price agreements.

Cartels thrive in Germany, because they create longstanding bonds. As the
former president of the Cartel Authority, Wolfgang Kartte once pointed out:

"The German mentality plays a major role. The Germans are simply more connected with their companies."[25]

Cartelization is a specifically German method of concentrating power in the hands of those with a vested interest in investment rather than quick profits. Cartels cannot be reconciled with the principles of free markets and fair competition. However, in the German context, they ensure stability and a long-term approach to business, while minimizing risks for all concerned. Thus, they contribute constructively to order in the German context—and to steady wealth creation.

THE FINANCIERS OF ORDER

The financing mechanisms in German business are equally illustrative of the German business mentality. There are around 1,500 public limited companies (Aktiengesellschaften) in Germany, of which only around 700 are traded on the stock exchanges. Banks thus serve as the main source of corporate funds for big companies. For almost three million small- and medium-sized enterprises in Germany, they are virtually the sole source of external capital. The power exercised by the banks has both structural and historic roots.

Structural. The financial power of Germany's banks derives from the country's universal bank system. There is no enforced separation of investment and commercial banking as in the United States and Japan, no Glass-Steagall act or comparable legislation. Consequently, the financial institutes can judiciously allocate their resources and concentrate on long-term priorities.

As a result, Germany's banks offer a wide range of services: conventional loans, real estate financing, brokerage services, trade finance, mergers & acquisitions consulting, and so on This makes the banks virtually invulnerable to crises. It also gives them the status of "house banks" in their dealings with corporate clients. Traditionally, they practice relational rather than transactional banking.

Historic. The strong role of German banks began in the 1860s, during the German industrial revolution. The chronic lack of capital for the newly founded corporations prompted the foundation of financial institutes with share capital such as Deutsche Bank and Commerzbank, who almost immediately surpassed the existing private banks in terms of financial clout and influence. The new banks soon became the "permanent accompaniers" of companies like Siemens and BASF, as one historian points out.[26]

Georg Siemens, the first director of the Deutsche Bank, was the Siemens corporation founder's nephew. One of the bank's founders was Adalbert Delbrück, whose uncle Rudolph von Delbrück belonged to Bismarck's inner circle.

Thus, the Deutsche Bank, the first to be allowed to establish itself in united Germany's new capital city Berlin, started with the support of both the state and the business world of the time. Since then, it has remained at the pinnacle of the German financial world. Its chief executive officer has traditionally been a close adviser to the country's chancellors till the present day.

The Deutsche Bank is respected and feared more than any other private sector institution in Germany, though its reputation has suffered in the early 1990s because of a series of scandals. Its awesome power has survived two world wars. Unlike most German companies, it has been led by a series of charismatic CEOs, including Hermann Josef Abs, Wilfried Guth, F. Wilhelm Christians, and in particular Alfred Herrhausen.

In one book dealing with the power of the Deutsche Bank and fittingly entitled *God in Frankfurt*, the role played by Herrhausen as kingmaker at Daimler Benz is depicted. Benz CEO Werner Breitschwerdt was appointed by Herrhausen's predecessor in the Daimler Benz Supervisory Board, which is traditionally chaired by a Deutsche Bank representative. Breitschwerdt had been R&D director before becoming CEO and was a typically German craftsman, interested in technical rather than commercial priorities.

Herrhausen recognized that in the context of the rapid expansion of Daimler Benz through the acquisition of large corporations like MTU, Dornier, and AEG, a more strategically oriented manager was needed. Breitschwerdt's dislodgment by Edzard Reuter in 1987 was widely seen as a signal of the power of the Deutsche Bank—and for the entrepreneurial ambitions of Alfred Herrhausen. Ironically, Reuter's expansion proved to be a disastrous strategy and he was forced to resign in 1995.

In contrast to almost all his colleagues in leading positions in German business, Herrhausen, who was assassinated by terrorists in 1989, expressed himself in forthright terms. He publicly acknowledged that the Deutsche Bank was powerful, while pointing out that Germany's SME ensured a plurality of power centers. He also admitted in public that he personally liked having power, thus upsetting an unspoken rule in German business.

The power exerciced by German banks has traditionally been founded on the loans given to corporate clients, share capital holdings, voting rights exerciced on behalf of other share-holders, and seats on supervisory boards. The links between Deutsche Bank and the chemical giant BASF illustrate typically German power constellations.

The two corporations have remained linked since the nineteenth Century: the Ladenburg bank, which later became a part of the Deutsche Bank, provided initial capital for BASF. Together with the voting rights it exercices on behalf of other shareholders, the Deutsche Bank has rarely held less than 25 percent of all votes. This gives them an effective veto on important issues that require 75 percent majority voting.

Deutsche Bank together with two other major banks, Dresdner Bank and Commerzbank, have over a long period of time held the majority of all shares in BASF. Thus, the annual general meeting of BASF—as Hermannus Pfeiffer points out in his critical study of the power of Germany's major banks—is for all ends and purposes a formality. Two or three days before the meeting, a "bank meeting" is held and all important decisions are made. These decisions are codified by a notary, who is entrusted with the representation—and the imposition—of the collective views of the banks at the annual general meeting.[27]

THE CULT OF SECRECY AND STABILITY

Under circumstances of quiet power sharing, legally prescribed instruments of communication and control such as the annual general meeting and the supervisory board tend to be farcical. Supervisory boards were instituted as controlling organs in German companies as early as 1904. However, an analysis of interlocking directorships carried out in 1903 discovered that high officials of the Deutsche Bank and Dresdner Bank were personally connected with 221 and 122 corporations, respectively. Thus, an existing system of financial control was merely formalised by the mandatory installation of the supervisory Board.

Germany's share law requires the supervisory board to control the board of directors and gives it far-reaching powers: to appoint and dismiss members of the board of directors, to examine the auditors' report, and to demand further information. A series of scandals involving mismanagement and financial mani-pulation—Daimler Benz and the trading company Metallgesellschaft are two examples—show that the supervisory board rarely intervenes. Its members generally have neither the time nor the desire to really investigate the efficiency or the integrity of corporate management.

As we have seen earlier, the supervisory board is more an instrument of consensus than of control. Employee representation on the board is mandatory and top managers are thus in a constant dialogue with their staff.

Foreign investors, in particular those from the United States, have often felt frustrated and disadvantaged by the existing setup. Foreigners are effectively excluded from the "German Fortress," since company shares are tightly held. The complexity and anonymity of share possession favor the status quo. So also do legal provisions: foreign shareholders for instance would need to possess 75 percent of share capital in order to replace the supervisory board. Considering the fact that German institutional investors hold an average of 60 percent of the total share volume in most important companies, foreigners have no real chance of gradually gaining control.

Beyond this, the stocks and shares markets in Germany are quiet backwaters compared with the volatile markets in the United States and Great Britain. Despite recent liberalization, the market atmosphere is aligned toward channeling investments, rather than toward speculating for quick profits.

Cartels and banks exemplify a peculiarly German cult of stability under conditions of secrecy. Germany's business world has managed to surround itself with an aura of silence, following restrictive information policies with remarkable success.

Perhaps the best example of these policies is the extreme paucity of information available on companies: the German equivalents of Dun & Bradstreet and Disclosure provide only a fraction of the corporate and credit data offered in the Anglo-Saxon countries, while charging exorbitant prices. Many German companies have persistently resisted submitting to ratings of their capital and credit positions by agencies like Standard & Poor's and Moody's and have also sabotaged plans to establish a national rating agency.[28]

Similarly, German bookkeeping procedures make it difficult for outsiders to assess profitability. Many privately owned Mittelstand compnies refuse to publish their turnover or profits. Public-limited corporation, the so-called AGs, are legally required to publish financial accounts. However, most corporations have large stocks of hidden reserves. Lavish risk provisioning results in declared profits being lower than actual profits.

Some internationally oriented corporations like Daimler Benz and Deutsche Bank have now adopted International Accounting Standards (IAS) or Generally Accepted Accounting Practices (GAAP). However, in the vast majority of companies, "opaque Teutonic bookkeeping makes a mockery of shareholder value," as the financial journal *Institutional Investor* points out.[29]

Germany's stringent data protection laws, originally devised to protect citizens from an all-knowing big brother state, actually help companies of all sizes to evade publicity. This is as true of the Mittelstand as it is of the large corporations. The German state has gone out of its way to support medium-sized German companies that are alarmed by new EU provisions requiring them to disclose more information.

The early 1990s have witnessed a new dynamism in Germany. The cozy banking scene for instance has heated up: discount broking and direct banking have made inroads into the traditionally large margins derived from credit transactions. Private customers have become more cost-conscious, while corporate clients are breaking with former loyalty and opting for foreign banks that offer more sophisticated corporate finance services. Trading in swaps, options, and other investment banking instruments has expanded.

However, their universal bank status and their correspondingly wide range of activities shields the country's banks from the harsh realities of cutthroat competition in international financial markets. Leading German banks all enjoy top ratings from Moody's and Standard & Poor's, in stark contrast to most of their competitors in the United States and Japan. No major German bank has faced bankruptcy in the last fifty years. Through steady investments, German banks have contributed to the stability of the business community.

In their internationalization strategies, German banks exercize the same caution and search for stability that characterizes their general business practices. Deutsche Bank, which bought the English merchant bank Morgan Grenfell in 1989, only merged activities in 1994. The *Financial Times* has commented on this gradualist approach in the following terms: "Deutsche Bank, like many German companies, values consensus more than Anglo-Saxon counterparts."[30]

Similarly, Dresdner Bank took over the English investment bank Kleinwort Benson in 1995, planning to slowly absorb it into its own structure. Dresdner Bank CEO Jürgen Sarrazin emphasized his company's gradualist approach, saying (in English): "We don't walk into Kleinwort Benson with our boots on."[31]

U.S. and Japanese banks are on average more productive than their German competitors, but they lack financial stability. U.S. banks have experienced a series of spectacular ups and downs in the 1980s and 1990s. Because of the increasing role of investment banking and the risks involved in dealing with swaps, options, and other innovative investment-banking instruments, the U.S. banking system has a destabilizing impact on the private sector. The change in strategic emphasis from relationship banking to price banking has increased short-term profits while weakening the long-term stability of U.S. banks.

Japan's banks on the other hand are intimately linked with the country's keiretsus and subject to guidelines from the Ministry of Finance. Saddled with enormous debts mostly caused by their real estate speculation during the "bubble economy" in the late 1980s, Japan's banks now detract from rather than contributing to the country's wealth.

The banks symbolize Germany's long-term approach to wealth creation, its accent on stability rather than dynamism. They also incorporate the TÜV mentality—order through (financial) control.

SECTION 4: MENTALITY RATHER THAN MANAGEMENT— GERMANY'S ECO-CONSENSUS

Germany's long-term approach to business success, its orientation toward productive potential rather than productivity at all costs, its emphasis on consensus rather than antagonism and the organizational cohesion in large companies all predestine it to ecological excellence.

Germany is a world leader both in ecological technology and in eco management:

– German exporters hold 21 percent of the world market for ecological technology, ahead of the United States (16 percent) and Japan (13 percent).
– The domestic market for ecological products and services is also booming in Germany: in the 1980s, it increased by 38 percent, as against 17 percent in Japan and 15 percent in the United States.
– Germany is a leader in ecological innovations, accounting for approximately 30 percent of all patents filed worldwide.
– Germany's ecological commitment is visible in terms of the sums spent on environmental protection: 1.74 percent of GNP, in contrast to 1.36 percent in the United States and 1.05 percent in Japan. The private sector contributes 63 percent of the budget. By contrast, in Japan, the state is responsible for 88 percent. This illustrates the business community's financial commitment to ecological reform.[32]

Germany's business world has invested heavily in ecological installations and equipment. For example, of the five billion marks spent on exhaust fume disposal in Europe, Germany's energy suppliers alone spent 1.6 billion and the country's chemical industry contributed a further 600 million marks.

The private sector is equally committed to eco management. German industry is rapidly moving from additive fixtures—so-called end-of-pipe technology—to the integration of ecological components into the entire production and distribution process. This is a revolutionary change in the entire business process, a fundamental restructuring with far-reaching implications for Germany's future competitiveness.

Roger Gale, a former senior official at the U.S. Environmental Protection Agency, comments on Germany's eco strategy in the following terms: "Gains in efficiency from investment in new technologies and services will provide a huge long-term competitive advantage."[33]

Germany's ecological success derives from a mix of the factors described in the last two chapters:

Quality. The integrated approach to ecology restructures the entire manufacturing cycle and results in a new definition of manufacturing quality. Germany's automobile industry, for instance, is ahead of Japan and the United States in terms of recycling, energy saving, and ecologically adjusted production processes. This augments the high quality of German cars and constitutes a huge potential advantage in terms of efficient utilization of increasingly scarce resources.

Specialization. The traditional specialization of German industry is well aligned to customer-determined ecological products and services. Ecological expert Helmut Kaiser points out that the country's traditional emphasis on niche rather than mass markets predestined its excellence in various ecological subsectors.[34]

The market for car varnishes is one example of a subsector. Reacting to stiff legislation, German car markers have already adopted ecologically innovative varnishing assembly lines.

Herberts, a subsidiary of the chemical corporation Hoechst, is a major manufacturer of car varnishes. It develops custom-designed solutions for the assembly lines of various European car manufacturers. Durability, acid resistance, optical quality, and ecological excellence: the exacting standards of the German automobile industry guide the Herberts production strategy. Despite the fact that Herberts and other German varnish producers are world leaders in water-based varnishes, the industry's researchers are already working on a new generation of powder-based varnishes—yet another specialized subsector in which Germany will excel in the future.[35]

Organizational skills. Ecology in the German context has a strong organizational dimension. It involves the restructuring of processes and the imposition of new control mechanisms.

Eco controlling is one management priority that a growing number of German enterprises in different sectors are adopting. Eco audits and eco balance sheets quantify and systematize the process of ecological accounting in leading manufacturing corporations, trading firms, banks, and insurance companies.

Another priority is the central coordination of all ecologically oriented activities. Trade corporations are particularly active in eco organization:

– Otto Versand, the world's largest mail-order company, has adopted an integrated eco concept, which involves removing specific products such as fur coats, products made of tropical wood, and sprays from the Otto catalogue, using recycling paper for all correspondence, and many other activities. This company has developed ecological criteria for purchasing textiles and requires its suppliers to conform to these criteria.[36]

–   Neckermann, also a large mail-order corporation, has founded an "eco circle" to stimulate the flow of ideas from its employees. Beyond this, it has completely reorganized its transport logistics to reduce pollution, transporting its products via railways and shipping instead of trucks; the company has also carried out eco audits in specific product groups such as textiles.[37]

Cooperation. In the early 1970s, Germany's industrial associations realized that public pressure for ecological improvement was increasing. BDI, the central association of German industry, founded an ecological committee to counsel its members. It joined national and international commissions and participated in the drafting of ecological legislation. Beyond this, the business community founded a number of specialised eco associations to coordinate their ecological activities.[38]

Through their associations, Germany's business community grasped the fact that ecology was a common priority that could best be tackled through negotiations with the state and with interest groups. Though conflicts and controversies with ecological pressure groups such as Greenpeace continue to recur, a *constructive dialogue* on specific issues such as air and ground water pollution has now been achieved. This is the *nucleus of the German eco consensus*.

STATE PRESSURE AND THE CRAFTSMANSHIP ETHOS

Germany's ecological lead, both in technology and in management, is not only traceable to its business mentality. It is also the result of severe laws, that have been rigorously imposed.

In the 1960s, the ecological question was ignored in Germany in an attitude symbolized by the phrase: "The solution of pollution is distribution." The Germans were by no means pioneers. However, in the 1970s, several path-breaking laws—regulating waste, emissions, and chemicals—were passed. Today, Germany's ecological regulations are the strictest in the world. The planned ecological tax reform will sharpen the link between taxation and responsibility for pollution, forcing "eco sinners" to contribute commensurately.

At the same time, a large number of national and regional subsidies have been given to promote ecological investments and management procedures like eco audits. Beyond this, state-subsidised technology centers have specialized in supporting new eco tech enterprises.

Germany's reunification stimulated an enormous boom in ecological techology. East Germany's roads, rivers, and parks were in an appalling state:

–   Only 3 percent of the water supply was ecologically intact.

- Air pollution was intense: sulphure-dioxide emissions per square kilometer were 11.5 times as high as in West Germany, while dust emissions were 8 times as high.
- Food pollution was equally intense. East German agriculture used twice the amount of herbicides as in the West and 2.5 times the amount of lime fertilizers.[39]

After reunification, West German laws and regulations were rapidly introduced. New automobile factories, such as those of VW in Zwickau and of Opel in Eisenach, for instance, are outfitted with the latest generation of water-based varnishes. The ecological transformation of East Germany is as profound as the change from a planned economy to a market economy.

The German state's stick-and-carrot tactics of forcing and stimulating ecological investments have been generally accepted by the business world. As many as 40 percent of the eco entrepreneurs covered by a survey in 1989 reported that German regulations compelled them to devise products and processes far beyond the exigencies of the world market. The businesspeople however were confident that the superior quality of their products and services would ultimately give them international competitive advantage. They even praised the government for having initiated stiff regulations.[40]

Germany's stern eco laws have in effect forced entrepreneurs in various industries to rethink production and distribution strategies. After an initial period of protest, they have generally reacted pragmatically, investing in new process technology and distributional mechanisms (see Figure 2.1).

Eco technology—machines, installations, apparatuses—suits the craftsman type of leader described in the Mittelstand chapter. Germany's eco entrepreneurs and managers have excelled in developing custom-made products for various sectors.

Typical of the craftsman mentality is the lack of formal strategies to exploit competitive advantage. One study of eco marketing showed that only half the companies practicing eco management were at all aware of its potential market leverage—and only a tiny fraction of those aware had developed concrete marketing strategies. As seen in connection with quality, the Germans are quiet practitioners, not dynamic marketing experts. Here too, *their market potential exceeds their performance*.[41]

CONSUMER PRESSURE AND CONSENSUS

Public opinion and consumer pressure also pressurize business into adopting ecological strategies. As many as 75 percent of all consumers in Germany now prefer glass or paper as packing materials, because they can be easily recycled; 80 percent would refrain from buying a commodity whose packing could endanger the environment, as two surveys have shown. One further sign of ecological commitment is waste disposal: during the 1980s, the amount of garbage that accumulated in Germany actually decreased by 9 percent, in contrast to increases of 16 percent in Japan and 30 percent in the United States.[42]

Both the United States and Japan have made impressive progress in smog reduction, improvement of water quality, and so on. In both countries however, the approach to ecology is basically technocratic. Companies in the United States are increasingly oriented toward "resource productivity," according to the criteria described by Michael E. Porter and Claas von der Linde in their *Harvard Business Review* article "Green and Competitive: Ending the Stalemate."[43]

The stalemate described by Porter and von der Linde and the many setbacks faced by environmental policies are characteristic of a country with vast natural resources and a frontier tradition of exploiting these resources. Attempts to preserve the environment are quickly denounced as being unrealistic and antibusiness. Beyond this, in the adversarial U.S. context, environmental disputes quickly end in litigation.

As Susan Rose-Ackermann points out in her comparative study of ecological legislation and politics in the two countries, the U.S. Congress rarely passes coherent legislation. Thus, the executive and the judiciary serve as arbiters of legislation. In Germany, on the other hand, the ministerial bureaucracy directly drafts legislation. Quiet negotiations between state and private sector representatives generally result in a constructive consensus, which, however, lacks the democratic legitimacy of the U.S. system.[44]

Water policies are a case in point. In the United States, the Environmental Protection Agency (EPA) relied on legal standards and permits rather than on tax adjustments as in Germany. The EPA developed strict standards for "best practicable control technology" as a technology-forcing policy, largely confronting U.S. industry with the standards rather than coopting them into the decision-making process. Because of the EPA's lack of technical insider knowledge, corporations could successfully topple the standards by going to court.[45]

In Germany, government and business experts are constantly in a process of consultation. The standards imposed are automatically accepted by the business community, because their experts were involved in the policy formulation process. Court cases are virtually unknown.

Significantly, ecology has lost relevance in Japan since the mid-1970s, though Japanese legislation on clean air and on the control of toxic substances is extremely severe. Japanese industry has developed an impressive range of eco products and processes like catalytic converters and flue-gas desulfurization. In contrast to Germany, however, Japan lacks a coherent approach to ecology. It concentrates on specific issues but fails to comprehensively integrate ecology into the entire production and distribution process. Beyond this, Japanese society lacks the acute perception of ecology's importance that distinguishes Germany.[46]

Ecology has in fact given German society a new sense of priorities. From the cradle to the grave, the ecological issue is omnipresent. German children play with the "green spot" on bottles and cans and are made aware at an early age to rules of container disposal. And German cemeteries feature signs that

Figure 2.1
The Eco Innovation Chain

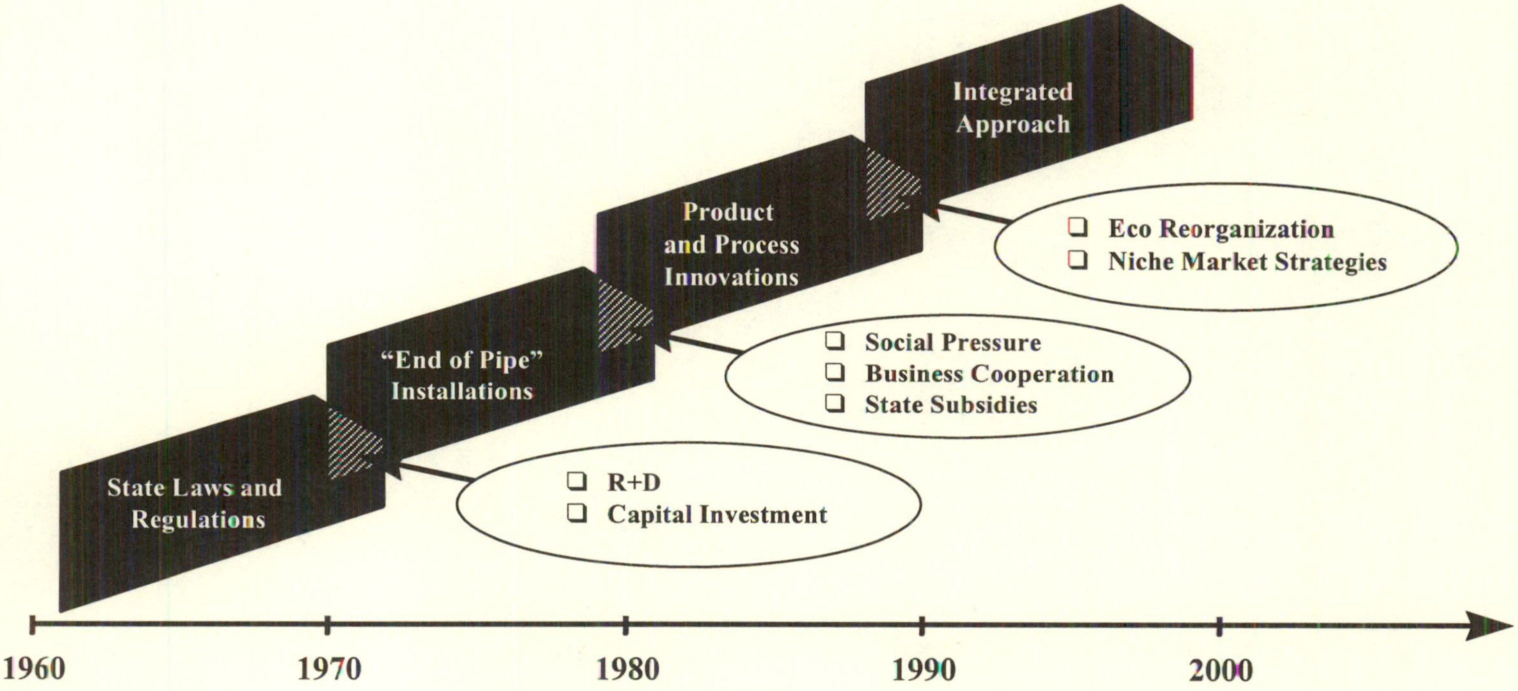

urge visitors: "Act ecologically! Throw organic refuse into the green can!" The symbolism of thinking green pervades public life.

Germany's priorities are by no means shared by its neighbors in the EU. Specific criticism from Britain, France, and other countries has focused on the German packaging rules, which are stricter than those imposed in other EU countries. These rules are considered to be expensive, difficult to implement— and above all a covert form of protectionism.

Enraged producers from other European countries have gone so far as to describe the Germans as "eco Nazis." While such insults are manifestly absurd, resentment on the part of Germany's fellow EU members is understandable, since European ecological norms and regulations are mostly derived from German law. German legislation is already the benchmark in the EU.

A CULTURAL COMMITMENT TO THE ENVIRONMENT

Foreigners are often mystified by the deep German commitment to nature. This commitment is part of Germany's cultural tradition, dating back to the romantic period in the nineteenth century, and will be explored further in the chapter on cultural roots.

Waldsterben for instance, the death of forests, has been a major public issue since the early 1980s. Alarmist reports on the imminent decline of the German forest have been countered by data that proves the opposite. However, public opinion has continued to dramatize the issue and the German state has responded by developing ambitious reforestry plans.

Ecology caters to the German longing for order and wholeness. Order derives from the Age of Enlightenment, wholeness from nineteenth century romanticism Enlightenment and romanticism are however not the only roots of ecological success. There is also an obvious element of opportunism in the endorsement of ecological goals by all German political parties and by a broad cross-section of businessmen: one critical sociologist speaks in this connection of "green Machiavellism."[47]

The endless discussion of ecological issues—Waldsterben, garbage accumulation, water pollution and so on—provides ideal material for pessimistic statements and value judgements. As we saw in connection with the Mittelstand and business associations, Zweckpessimismus—functional pessimism—characterizes the business mentality, just as Kulturpessimismus— cultural pessimism—is a cultural leitmotif.

Functional pessimism has led to many incremental improvements in ecological technology and management. Commitment to ecology in the business community and in society is however not only on a rhetorical level. The concrete changes in industrial processes, management procedures, state policies, and social attitudes can be compared in their magnitude to the genesis of the modern social state in the context of Bismarck's epoch-making social legislation.

Germany's eco consensus is an evolutionary process with revolutionary implications: for product design and component integration, for raw-material procurement and waste disposal, for corporate planning and rationalization. *In sum, the German economy is quietly developing an enormous expertise in practicing a new balance—between the needs of economy and ecology. This balance will give Germany enormous competitive advantage in the context of sustainable development.*

ORDER AND BALANCE

Order through control, estate order, power in the service of order: the centrality of order for German business has been examined in this chapter.

As we have seen, organizational cohesion rather than strategies of leadership characterizes the corporate identity of large companies. This ensures high standards of efficiency in the German corporate world. In one perceptive comparison of the workforces in Germany and the United States, a German manager based in America praised the enthusiasm, spontaneity, and motivation of U.S. employees and then pointed out: " 'Orderliness' in performing daily tasks is miles behind the German standard, thoroughness in solving problems similarly so, and the critical input of knowledge and skills, that Germans are equipped with by virtue of their educational backgrounds, is lacking in the United States."[48]

The average German employee adapts well to order in the business context because he is surrounded by it in his everyday life. The complex system of personal registration and the administration of social insurance ensure that the individual develops organizational aptitude at an early age. *Order is thus not merely an objective principle in the business world. It constitutes the "condition humaine" of all those who live in Germany.*

An internalized sense of order is the most valuable contribution of the average German to the wealth of the nation. The business world in particular profits immensely from the average employee's capability to adhere to routines, to structure tasks, and to keep to schedules. The psychological roots and implications of internalized order will be explored later in this book.

The second element of order analyzed in this chapter is the organization of the business community. Industrial associations, chambers of commerce, and craftsmen's guilds give the individual a sense of identity as a member of a specific vocational group. Explicitly or implicitly, the individual has the feeling of belonging to a larger whole, rather than competing with others for success. *Germans at work are more connected with each other than Americans—and more autonomous, because of their vocational identities, than the more collectivized Japanese.*

The extent of this autonomy in Germany has often been questioned. Writing as far back as 1906, the national-liberal publicist Friedrich Naumann argued that the direction of the economy was being taken out of the hands of the producers by the state and the associations. Naumann pointed out: "A spirit of belonging to a dark totality encompasses us all. It is not as if particularly talented persons could not extricate themselves from these bonds, but the existential conditions of the average person have been fixed. He can try to improve these conditions as a part of his group but not as an individual. That is why he pays fees for those representing his group."[49]

Seen retrospectively, Naumann was unduly pessimistic. Membership in the chambers of commerce and in the craftsmen's guilds has always been compulsory. This was the case long before the twentieth century. Thus the individual was and is automatically bound into larger structures and forced into a vocational mold. Within this mold however, he can develop his own personality and follow his own interests. Contemporary associations continue to play a highly constructive role in fostering group identity, but they do not reduce the individual's autonomy.

Fittingly, individuals who exercize power are rarely charismatic. They adhere more to the Beckmesser archetype that we encountered in connection with the Meistersinger of Nuremberg: they are bookkeepers rather than impressive leaders. Thus, the English employees of Morgan Grenfell, the investment bank taken over by Deutsche Bank, have criticized the parent company's "cumbersome audit and approval procedures" and called their Frankfurt bosses "control freaks."[50]

ORDER IN ORGANIZED CAPITALISM

Order through control—in this case financial control—is indeed the key to Germany's business mentality. The supposed pettiness of Germany's banks, their "TÜV mentality," has however kept them vastly more stable than their competitors in the Anglo-Saxon countries and Japan, while limiting profitability.

In this context, Rudolf Hilferding's famous term "organized capitalism" is an illuminating comment on the German approach to wealth creation. Rudolf Hilferding was a neo-Marxist member of the Social Democrat party, who served twice as minister of finance in the Weimar Republic. He criticized the dependence of German industry on the banks as far back as 1910 and formulated a theory of "organized capitalism" that encompassed many of the elements described in this chapter. Like Karl Marx and Joseph Schumpeter, but for different reasons, Hilferding believed that capitalism would ultimately give way to socialism.

Hilferding, in company with many left-wing observers of the time, underestimated the stabilizing effects of Bismarck's social reforms. These reforms—as we shall see in the next chapter—provided both the material basis and the moral legitimation for the contemporary German social state. They gave economic activity a strong social foundation. Bismarck can thus be seen to have introduced a parallel model of "organized socialism" into predominantly capitalist structures. This capitalist-socialist mixture still characterizes the German approach to wealth creation.

The real strength of the German economy lies in an *imposed equilibrium between capitalism and socialism*. The fundamental balancing act, involving a quid pro quo between the potentially antagonistic representatives of capital and labor, is a process constantly supervised by a state with enormous organizational skills and supported by a largely homogenous society. *The order of Germany's business world is thus a part of a greater whole, a wheel within wheels, organically integrated in its environment.*

NOTES

1. For general information see Günter Wiesenack, *Wesen und Geschichte der technischen Überwachungs-Vereine* (Cologne: Heymanns, 1971), pp. 120–123, 143–150; for a critical review, see Peter Oberender (ed.), *Marktstruktur und Wettbewerb in der Bundesrepublik Deutschland* (Munich: Vahlen, 1984), pp. 661–679, for foreign activities see "Zertifizierungsnachfrage in Italien wächst," in *Nachrichten für den Außenhandel*, August 22, 1994; and "ISO 9000 in Rußland nicht unbekannt," in *Nachrichten für den Außenhandel*, September 5, 1994.

2. Peter Dinzelbacher (ed.), *Europäische Mentalitätsgeschichte* (Stuttgart: Kröner 1993), p. XXI; several French authors contribute to the book *Mentalitäten-Geschichte* edited by Ulrich Raulff (Berlin: Wagenbach 1987), see also Peter Burke, "Stärken und Schwächen der Mentalitätsgeschichte," in Dinzelbacher, *Mentalitätengeschichte*, p. 129.

3. R.S. Collins and W.A.Fischer, "American Manufacturing Competitiveness: the View from Europe," in *Business Horizons*, July-August 1992, pp. 15–23; see also "Are Employment & Executive Search Twisting in the Wind?" in *Biomedical Market Newsletter*, August 1993.

4. See in this connection Mikio Sumiya, *The Japanese Industrial Relations Reconsidered* (Tokyo: The Japan Institute of Labor, 1990), pp. 17–33; Hirosuke Kawanishi, *Enterprise Unionism in Japan* (London: Kegan Paul, 1992), pp. 1–7, 93–99.

5. Edgar H. Schein, *Organizational Culture and Leadership* (San Francisco: Jossey-Bass, 1986), p. 11; see also a differentiation according to personalities (USA) and tasks (Germany) in Knut Bleicher, *Organisation—Formen und Modelle* (Wiesbaden: Gabler, 1981), p. 271.

6. Dieter Schneider, *Geschichte betriebswirtschaftlicher Theorie* (Munich: Oldenbourg, 1981), p. 164.

7. The quality gurus are dealt with in Lesley and Malcolm Munro-Faure, *Implementing Total Quality Management* (London: Pitman 1992), pp. 287–298.

8. For a brief overview of value analysis activities initiated by the Industrie- und Handelskammern, Landesgewerbeämter, Rationalisierungskuratorium der deutschen Wirtschaft and the Fraunhofer Gesellschaft, including the cases mentioned here, see *Impulse* 10/1990, pp. 163–168 and 8/1992, pp. 64–67 and *Top Business* 7/1992, pp. 30–31.

9. Survey results summarized in "Europas Topmanager stellen ihren deutschen Kollegen kein schmeichelhaftes Zeugnis aus," in *Handelsblatt*, February 28–29, 1992; see also Günter Ogger, *Nieten in Nadenstreifen* (München: Droemer Knaur, 1992).

10. For an analysis of the board system, see Knut Bleicher and Herbert Paul, "Das amerikanische Board-Modell im Vergleich zur deutschen Vorstand-/Aufsichtsrats-verfassung—Stand und Entwicklungstendenzen," in *DBW* 46/1986, pp. 263–288.

11. For Koch's ideas, see "Wahlsieg" in *Capital*, 10/1989, pp. 275–278; for more information on bureaucratic practice, see Wilhelm Eberwein and Jochen Tholen, *Euro-Manager or Splendid Isolation*? (Berlin: de Gruyter, 1993), pp. 83–85.

12. Statistics from "Werbung in Deutschland," published by Zentralverband der deutschen Werbewirtschaft (Bonn: ZAW 1993); see also Hans-Gerd Neglein, "Das

Messewesen in Deutschland," in Karl-Heinz Strothmann and Manfred Busche (eds.), *Handbuch Messemarketing* (Wiesbaden: Gabler 1992), pp. 18–21.

13. Quoted from Manfred Busche, "Staat und Wirtschaft als Träger und Gestalter des Messewesens," in *Handbuch Messemarketing*, p. 71; see also AUMA (ed.), *Die Entwicklung des europäischen Messewesen*. (Bergisch Gladbach: Heider 1991), pp. 33–45.

14. Cited in Wolfgang Niopek, "Aufgaben, Organisation und Finanzierung von Industrie- und Handelskammern," in *Zeitschrift für öffentliche und gemeinwirtschaftliche Untenehmen*, 4/1990, p. 445.

15. Michael Roth, "Nicht getraut," in *WirtschaftsWoche* July 9, 1993, pp. 30–32; see also Gerd Kühlhorn, "Unternehmer protestieren gegen das Kartell der Blockierer," in *Impulse*, 11/1994, pp. 8–16.

16. Zentralverband der deutschen Werbewirtschaft (ed.), *Werbung in Deutschland* (Bonn: ZAW, 1993), pp. 315–317.

17. A comparison of associations is touched on in Ulrich von Aleman (ed.), *Neokorporatismus* (Frankfurt: Campus Verlag 1981), pp. 65ff; see also Jürgen Hartmann, *Verbände in der westlichen Industriegesellschaft* (Frankfurt: Campus, 1975); for cooperative advantage see James Moore, "The Death of Competition," in *Fortune*, April 15, 1996, pp. 78–80.

18. Hans Jaeger, *Geschichte der Wirtschaftsordnung in Deutschland* (Frankfurt: Suhrkamp, 1988), p. 221.

19. Hajo Weber, *Unternehmerverbände zwischen Markt, Staat und Gewerkschaften* (Frankfurt: Campus 1987), pp. 89–92.

20. Hans-Peter Ullmann, *Der Bund der Industriellen* (Göttingen: Vandenhoeck und Ruprecht, 1975), pp. 84 ff.

21. Kurt Sontheimer, *Grundzüge des politischen Systems in der Bundesrepublik Deutschland* (München: Piper, 1979), pp. 186–187; see also Elga Lehari, "Zweckpessimismus," in *Handelsblatt*, November 5, 1993.

22. Werner Sombart, *Die deutsche Volkswirtschaft im 19. Jahrhundert und im Anfang des 20. Jahrhunderts* (Darmstadt: Wissenschaftliche Buchgemeinschaft, 1954), p. 316.

23. Sibylle Krause-Burger, *Die andere Elite: Deutsche Topmanager im Portrait* (Düsseldorf: Econ, 1989), p. 9; the author can confirm these observations on the basis of personal experiences, in particular in the course of a book on headhunting in Germany, see Kaevan Gazdar (ed.), *Köpfe jagen* (Wiesbaden: Gabler, 1992).

24. Quoted in Karl Heinrich Herchenröder, "Quellen des Wohlstands," in Herchenröder (ed.), *Soziale Marktwirtschaft—Leistung und Herausforderung* (Düsseldorf: Handelsblatt, 1974), p. 93.

25. See "Wir sind doch nicht blind," in *Der Spiegel*, 15/1992, p. 147.

26. Helmut Dohme, *Deutschlands Weg zur Großmacht* (Köln: Kiepenheuer & Witsch, 1966).

27. Hermannus Pfeiffer, *Die Macht der Banken* (Frankfurt: Campus, 1993), p. 137.

28 See "Viele deutsche Firmen scheuen das Rating," in *Süddeutsche Zeitung*, January 18, 1994; German credit data is provided by Creditreform and Dun & Bradstreet Germany, corporate data is provided by the Hoppenstedt publishing company.

29. Wendy Cooper, "Germany Discovers the Foreign Investor," in *Institutional Investor*, July 1993, pp. 34–40.

30. Nicholas Denton, "Morgan Grenfell's Board Takes a Gradualist Approach to Merger," in *Financial Times*, March 31, 1995.

31. Sarrazin quoted in "Spätzünder," in *Manager Magazin*, September 1995, p. 64.

32. Marianne Halstrick-Schwenk, *Die umwelttechnische Industrie in der Bundesrepublik Deutschland* (Essen: RWI, 1994); see also "Auf hohem Niveau," in *IWD*, April 30, 1992.

33. Quoted in Curtis Moore and Alan Miller, *Green Gold: Japan, Germany, the United States and the Race for Environmental Technology* (Boston: Beacon Press, 1994), p. 25.

34. Kaiser quoted in "Fetter Braten für Vorreiter," in *High Tech*, 7/1990, p. 32.

35. Claus-Dieter Canenbley, "Technologievorsprung bietet europäischen Herstellern Chancen," in *Handelsblatt*, September 4, 1992; see also "Trockene Lösung," in *WirtschaftWoche*, May 14, 1993, pp. 69ff.

36. See "Otto-Motor," in *Impulse*, 11/1991, pp. 217–218.

37. See "Die Natur ist Chefsache," in *Forbes* (Germany), 4/1994, pp. 124–126.

38 For BDI, see Dietrich Herzog and Bernhard Wessels (eds.), *Konfliktpotentiale und Konsensstrategien Opladen* (Westdeutscher Verlag, 1989), pp. 269–286; for the specialized association BAUM, see Andreas Nölting, "Auf grün geschaltet," in *Manager Magazin*, 11/1988, pp. 249–255, for entrepreneurial contacts with pressure groups see "Forsche Schrittmacher," in *Der Spiegel*, 26/1994, pp. 82–84.

39. Klaus Zimmermann, "Ecological Transformation in Eastern Germany," in A. Ghanie Ghaussy and Wolf Schäfer (eds.), *The Economics of German Unification* (London: Routledge, 1993), pp. 206–230.

40. See "Qualität sichert Märkte für die Zukunft," in *VDI-Nachrichten*, April 7, 1989; see also "Keine Stop-and-go-Politik," in *Impulse* 4/1989, pp. 82 ff.

41. See a report on the Wieselhuber & Partner study in "Schlummernde Chancen," in *WirtschaftsWoche*, July 17, 1992, pp. 42–47.

42 See "Verpackungen geraten ins Aus," in *Horizont*, July 14, 1992; for general information on ecological orientation, see Gesellschaft für Konsumforschung, *Die Umwelt- und Abfallproblematik im Spiegel des Konsumentenbewußtseins*, (GfK: Nuremberg, 1993, especially pp. 2–4.

43. See Michael E. Porter and Claas von der Linde, "Green and Competitive: Ending the Stalemate," in *Harvard Business Review*, September-October 1995, pp. 120–134.

44. Susan Rose-Ackerman, Umweltrecht und -politik in den Vereinigten Staaten und der Bundesrepublik Deutschland, Baden-Baden: Nomos, 1995, pp. 13–17, 26–32.

45. Rolf Giebeler, "Zur Setzung von Umwelt- und Gesundheitsstandards," in Cord Jakobeit et al. (eds.), *Die USA am Beginn der neunziger Jahre* (Opladen: Leske + Buderich, 1993), pp. 241–257, see also Ann Reilly Dowd, "Environmentalists Are on the Run," in *Fortune*, September 19, 1994, pp. 59–63.

46. Brendan F. D. Barrett and Riki Therivel, *Environmental Policy and Impact Assessment in Japan* (London: Routledge, 1991), pp. 17–24, 42–45; see also Gerhard Hackner (ed.), *Die anderen Japaner: vom Protest zur Alternative* (Munich: Iudicium-Verlag, 1989), pp. 16–23, 138–147.

47. Ulrich Beck, "Grüner Machiavellismus," in *Süddeutsche Zeitung*, October 30–November 1, 1993; see also for cultural roots Bernd Guggenberger, "Umweltpolitik und Ökologiebewegung," in Wolfgang Benz (ed.), *Die Geschichte der Bundesrepublik Deutschland*, Book 2, (Frankfurt: Fischer, 1989), pp. 394–397.

48. Hans J. Spiller, "Nicht sehr gründlich, aber hochmotiviert und schnell begeistert," in *Blick durch die Wirtschaft*, May 14, 1991.

49. Friedrich Naumann, "Neudeutsche Wirtschaftspolitik," in Gerhard A. Ritter (ed.), *Deutsche Sozialgeschichte 1870–1914* (Munich: Beck 1974), pp. 32–33.

50. John Templeman, "A Cozy World Comes to an End," in *Business Week*, July 24, 1995, p. 48.

CHAPTER 3

Commitment and the Business Environment

The state cannot exist without a certain amount of socialism.
—Otto von Bismarck
quoted in Ernst Engelberg's biography
Bismarck—das Reich der Mitte

Otto von Bismarck, the "Blood and Iron" statesman, united Germany and established its preeminence in continental Europe through a series of wars and through skillful diplomacy. In international politics, Bismarck is famous for having established a power balance between the individual European states that lasted until the outbreak of the First World War.

Bismarck is less known for his socioeconomic policies. Yet, the chancellor's most profound achievement was that he laid the foundations for Germany's long-term economic prosperity, taking a highly unorthodox view of the state's role in society, as is evident in the above quotation.[1]

Bismarck established a balance of socioeconomic priorities that has continued to guide wealth creation and distribution in Germany until the present day. Seen in retrospect, *he was a pioneer of balanced development.*

Bismarck's pioneering public insurance schemes laid the foundation for the modern social state. At the same time, the chancellor's policies reveal a deep understanding of the limits to state power. Bismarck disdained patent recipes, pointing out that the "social question" would never be completely solved. He warned against "total solutions," considering the state to be a slowly evolving organism rather than a construction. Beyond this, Bismarck firmly believed in the importance of vocational estates as a counterbalance to political parties. He planned to administer social insurance through vocationally represented cooperatives and also envisioned a Wirtschaftsrat, an economic council that would have united all major vocational groups into the policymaking process.

Bismarck's insights into the need to link economic progress with social reform still guide policies in Germany. Without him, the Mittelstandsgesell-schaft, a society founded on vocational estates and egalitarian norms, would not have evolved into its present form.

Because of his skilled power brokerage, Bismarck gained a consensus for a modern social market-type economy. This consensus has ensured an amazing continuity for the welfare state despite the different regimes that Germany has experienced in the hundred years after Bismarck: empire, fascism, socialism, and democracy. *A commitment to social welfare has become a part of modern Germany's national identity,* a commitment concretely implemented by the state and supported by all sections of society—by the business community as much as by the trade unions, by the cultural elite as by normal employees.

During Bismarck's chancellorship, national identity was similarly linked with economic expansion. As the historian Harold James points out: "Instead of being a cultural community, or a political unit based on a shared culture, the nation became the framework for an economic process that would in turn create political and cultural consciousness." Thus, modern Germany became a complex Gestalt—a form comprizing an efficient social state, a cohesive private sector with capital and labor organized through associations and trade unions, and a society with many elements of an estate-oriented community.[2]

Wealth creation in Germany has always involved the pursuit of collective rather than individual happiness, in vivid contrast to the Anglo-Saxon ethos. In Germany, the business environment—the subject of this chapter—has always been more important than the individual entrepreneur. At the same time, vocational education and the autonomy of the private sector have allowed the individual to assert his identity within collective parameters. Here, Germany differs from the more feudalistic and collectivistic Japanese model.

WEALTH AND BUSINESS'S ENVIRONMENT

The term "business environment" has been used in different contexts to signify the larger setting within which business functions. In his study of industrial capitalism, Alfred Chandler describes the "historical environment" of three nations, while an article entitled the "U.S./Japanese HR Culture Clash" points out that Japanese companies operating in America "are finding that they must make changes to adjust to the U.S. business environment."[3]

Environment can thus encompass macroeconomic factors like geographical size, population, transport, and communication—as with Chandler—or norms such as individualism or loyalty, as in the second case.

Yet another interpretation of the environment defines it in terms of market players: competitors, suppliers, distributors. Thus, in an analysis of keiretsu-like ties between U.S. enterprises and the establishment of long-term relations with customers, the spirit of cooperation is seen as transforming the business environment. This is a more microeconomic approach that concentrates on changes in entrepreneurial attitudes to competition.[4]

The success and failure of economic sectors depends largely on environment. As seen in the last chapter, Germany is a world leader in ecology because of a subtle interaction between the business community and its environment. Government regulations, official subsidies, pressure from interest groups, and greater environmental consciousness in German society merged with the business community's organizational skills, its long-term approach to profitability, and its incremental approach to the perfectionization of production techniques. This complex factor mix—not entrepreneurial inventiveness or managerial brilliance—accounts for Germany's worldwide lead both in ecological technology and in eco management.

Similarly, Germany has always been a laggard in the electronics industry because it lacks the volatile business environment of the United States, in particular venture capital and the quick marketing of innovations. It also lacks the Japanese combination of synchronized business strategies and standardized production techniques. In short, Germany has lacked both Silicon Valley and the MITI, both the capital markets and the production lines. Its environment supports neither the U.S. archetype of the flamboyant entrepreneur nor the Japanese strategy of efficient mass production and militant market conquest.

Germany's predominantly evolutionary economy was ill adapted to the revolutionary character of electronics. After a gestation period, however, German industry has excelled in a plethora of specialized electronic products and applications. By contrast, the business environment was ideally attuned to balancing economic and ecological priorities.

The environmental focus in this chapter is on institutions with a formative influence on wealth creation: the state and its socioeconomic policies, trade unions in their role as "social partners" of the business community, and society at large.

SECTION 1: BALANCE OF POWER—THE STATE AND THE PRIVATE SECTOR

"The economy is not our destiny, the state is, and the state is also the destiny of the economy." The economist Alexander Rüstow made this point in 1932, during the economic crisis that would soon be followed by a National Socialist regime. Rüstow turned the German businessman-statesman Walter Rathenau's famous phrase "The economy is our destiny," upside down and drew attention to the real center of power. Forced to emigrate during the Nazi period, he was one of the Social Market Economy's (SME) founding fathers after World War II.

"Schicksal"—the German word for destiny used by Rüstow—resonates far more dramatically than its English translation. Traditionally, the state in Germany is not just an institution: it is an almost divine entity, awakening ethical expectations and feelings of attachment. Philosophers like Hegel glorified the Prussian state. The conservative thinker Friedrich Julius Stahl wrote rhapsodically of the state in the nineteenth century as the "sentinel of holy order." Stahl's ideas, which were highly influential in nineteenth century Prussia, reflect a very Germanic idealization for the state and a corresponding disregard for parliament. In one pithy turn of phrase, Stahl sums up the Prussian ethos: "Not majority. Authority!"

Parallel to its ethical mission, the state was responsible for economic progress. It promoted the improvement of technology and the education of workers. Beyond this, it has served as a role model for the business world from the beginning onward. The emphasis placed by German corporations on formalistic organization is clearly derived from the public sector. In the way they reward achievements and promote staff, German companies resemble industrial bureaucracies, as seen in the last chapter.

Bureaucrats in Germany have always been trusted executors of the state's will, enjoying absolute job security in exchange for equally absolute loyalty to the state. This system of Beamtentum—a form of tenured officialdom—is the backbone of the German approach to public service.

The traditional power and prestige of the state contrast with the comparative weakness of Germany's parliament. Contempt of parliament was a leitmotif of the Bismarck period. His famous statement that great issues were not decided by "speeches or majority decisions" but by "iron and blood" is characteristic of a German distaste for parliamentary discourse. Today's parliamentarians are less despised, though the "political class" has lost prestige in the context of corruption scandals. More pertinently, however, politicians lack the specialized knowledge they would need to understand and control the public sector.

Germany's leading public servants, in particular the "state secretaries" in the central and regional ministries, are responsible to a far greater extent than politicians for socioeconomic policies. The 20,000 ministerial bureaucrats in "higher service" at the federal level and their 50,000 colleagues at the regional level are the backbone of concrete policies.

This is particularly true for the Bundeswirtschaftsministerium, the Ministry of the Economy. Ludwig Erhard, Karl Schiller, and Helmut Schmidt were ministers with an acute grasp of economic policies. Since the mid-1970s, however, no politician has mastered the complexity of the ministry's priorities. Top bureaucrats have in effect guided economic policies.

However, the collegial principle of decision-making based on consultation within and between ministries ensures power sharing. Informal networks of specialists—fittingly called "Fachbrüderschaften," specialized brotherhoods—ensure the pooling of expertise between ministries.

Beyond this, bureaucracy is organized on the "bottom-up" principle: the Referat is the basic administrative unit. The specialized knowledge of Referenten and Referatsleiter—the clerks and administrative supervisors—

makes it virtually impossible for higher-level bureaucrats to make dictatorial decisions.

One analysis of administrative efficiency comes to the following conclusion: "Because of their manifold functions, the ministerial bureaucracies have a key role in the consensus-building and conflict-regulation system of the Federal Republic of Germany. In comparison to parliaments and the parties, they have the most competent and subtle resources to gather complex information and watch social reality."[5] Germany's ecological consensus for instance strongly relies on the guidance and control of the public sector.

Entrepreneurial associations are in constant dialogue with bureaucracy. They not only provide specialized information and put forward the standpoints of their clientele, but also participate in the "Fachbrüderschaften." One commentator discerns "symbiotic relations" between the ministries and the large associations. The symbiosis derives from similar organizational structures: associations like BDI also have Referate with highly qualified specialists.[6]

Germany's administrative heritage differs profoundly from those in the Anglo-Saxon countries and Japan. In the United States and Great Britain, codification of administrative law and the formative role of bureaucracy are less pronounced. Britain's House of Commons and the U.S. Congress are far more influential than Germany's Bundestag. As a consequence, Germany's ecological legislation for instance is far more codified and thus easier to enforce than the laws and regulations passed in Britain and the United States. Since the consultation process involves input from various ministries, from private-sector associations and other interest groups, ecological laws and regulations enjoy a general consensus.

CURRENT CRITICISM—AND ITS LEGITIMACY

The public service in contemporary Germany has retained a high degree of functional efficiency—but at a price that its critics consider to be excessive:

– The number of public officials has increased from 2.26 million in 1950 to 4.67 million in 1990.
– In 1950 there were fourteen central ministries with 4,000 officials, forty years later there are nineteen ministries with 18,000 officials.
– The percentage of personnel costs in the public-sector's budget has risen from 30 percent of total costs in 1970 to 50 percent by 1990 (see Figure 3.1).

One former state minister, who now works for a leading management consultancy, contends that 20 percent of all public officials are superfluous. A number of studies have proved that state-owned corporations are less productive than those in the private sector. The present lack of motivation particularly at lower bureaucratic levels is visible from indicators like a high degree of sick leave—higher than in private companies.[7]

Management consultancies have investigated utilities and municipalities, uncovering a large amount of rationalization potential. While in a number of cases, unnecessary public sector expenditure can be curbed by standard managerial practices, the dangers of short-sighted and simplistic reasoning need to be emphasized. The criteria of management consultants are rarely aligned to the social considerations that played a role in the establishment of public services in the first place. Nor do management consultants grasp the long-term foundations and preconditions of Germany's wealth—such perceptions are not a part of their briefs.

Public enterprises are for instance often expected to play a pilot role in initiating ecological policies, to provide liberal apprenticeship training, maternity benefits and so on. Thus, *the public sector is subject to considerations and restrictions that often preempt profitability.*

State officials are often made the scapegoats for the frustration that results from restrictive legislation. Leading chemical companies like Bayer have invested in genetic technology facilities in the United States because they were granted permission within ten months and German procedures could have lasted as many years. Similarly, the auto producer BMW waited five years for a construction permit in Germany, whereas in Japan it was able to get permission to erect a multistoried building in an earthquake-threatened area within six weeks.

The real background to these delays is the massive ethical debate in Germany on the pros and cons of genetic technology in the first case and uniquely severe construction legislation in the second. National Socialism's inhumanity has sensitized German public opinion to the dangers of genetic experiments. And the complexity of construction legislation reflects a German propensity to perfectionize security precautions. In neither case can the delays be ascribed to an obtuse bureaucracy.

Obviously however, the state reflects the "TÜV mentality" of order through control seen in the last chapter. The complexity of laws and regulations reflects this emphasis on control rather than laissez-faire.

Germany's reunification was the "hour of the executive," as one commentator has observed. West Germany's Beamten displayed remarkable administrative skills in quickly integrating a political system that was radically different in terms of organizational mechanisms and ethos. [8]

The East German state's "historic mission" was the dictatorship of the working class. This ideological approach led to absurd value judgments: environmental problems for instance were seen as a "legacy of imperialism." In reality, the East German regime neglected the most elementary rules of environmental protection. The bureaucratic legacy of East Germany's "structural Stalinism"—as it has been called—was that of empty declarations and inefficient administration.

Territorial reform, decentralization of administrative authority, ecological purification and modernization of infrastructure were simultaneously implemented by West Germany's bureaucracy. Within five years, East Germany was successfully molded into the structures and procedures of the West.

A greater degree of achievement-orientation and of flexibility will enable the country's administrators to optimize their contribution to wealth creation.

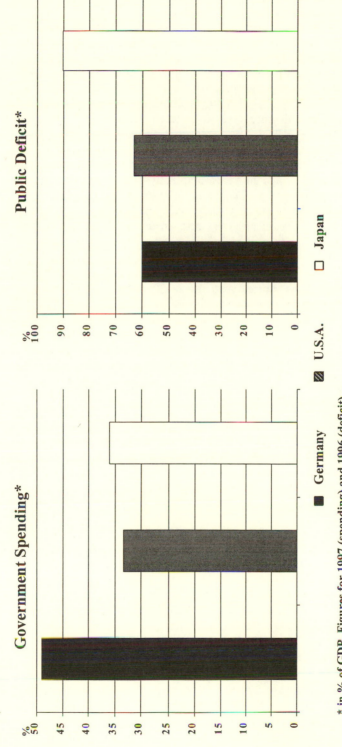

Figure 3.1
High Spending, but Low Public Deficit

Government Spending*

Public Deficit*

■ Germany   ▨ U.S.A.   □ Japan

* in % of GDP, Figures for 1997 (spending) and 1996 (deficit)

Source: OECD

A steady increase in public-private partnerships and in project financing is improving the quality and reducing the cost of municipal facilities. The influential Kronberger Kreis, a policy group manned by independent economic experts, has rightly recommended greater financial incentives for public officials and decentralized decision-taking. [9]

The German state remains the fundament of wealth creation. Its hierarchies and organizational procedures are reflected in Germany's business mentality. Federalism, the collegial principle, and the constant dialogue with private-sector associations ensure that policymaking is a broad-based process.

Beyond this, social self-organization restricts governmental power. Associations and trade unions consequently play important roles. This balance of power between the public and private sectors ensures that Germany's economic development has followed a more humane pace than Anglo-Saxon capitalism. Self-organization has also ensured that business is less subject to state tutelage than in countries with strong central bureaucracies like France or Japan.

The state is thus as much a part of a greater whole as the business world. It reflects the same norms and codes of behavior and has never been a mechanistic monster or monolithic block, clichés that have often served as archetypes in the past. Its dialogue with business associations reflects a balance of power. Its functional efficiency on the other hand ensures a balance of the priorities of economic development and social justice.

SECTION 2: BALANCE OF PRIORITIES—THE SOCIAL MARKET ECONOMY

In his analysis of postwar Germany's Social Market Economy (SME), the economist Viktor Vanberg bravely tries to translate—or rather transliterate— its key terms for the English-speaking reader. "Leistungswettbewerb" is, according to him, a kind of "fair" competition. He describes "Ordnungs-politik" as "a policy providing and enforcing an appropriate framework of rules and institutions."[10]

The virtual untranslatability of SME's basic tenets is symptomatic of its Teutonic depth. On a superficial level, SME represents postwar economic policies implemented by the "father of the Wirtschaftswunder," Ludwig Erhard, and largely followed ever since. Based on "ordoliberal" economic precepts developed mostly at the University of Freiburg by Walter Eucken and others in the 1930s and 1940s, SME postulates that economic policies need a strong institutional framework, that they are in fact based on Ordnungspolitik. The state imposes the institutional framework, plays a major role in enforcing principles of fair competition (the "Leistungswettbewerb") and in ensuring social welfare.

In actual fact, Leistungswettbewerb relies on a prime element in Germany's business mentality: quality-based manufacturing of specialized products. Because of the many product niches that German corporations and enterprises penetrate, competition is rarely fierce as in a mass-market environment. Equally, competition is based on quality rather than on price-cutting or market share. Enterprises compete parallel to each other rather than directly against one another. The state's role in regulating competition is therefore marginal: the business community is responsible for the atmosphere of achievement-oriented competition in Germany.

Official policies in postwar Germany have encouraged Leistungswett-bewerb by providing the Mittelstand with tax benefits, subsidies, and other incentives and thus compensating for the advantages enjoyed by large corporations. Competition in the marketplace has correspondingly increased, though, as we have seen, cartels of various kinds continue to flourish.

Theoretically, SME has always emphasized liberal rather than regulatory policymaking. It thus appeared to provide postwar Germany with economic norms comparable to those in the Anglo-Saxon countries. The administrative reality of ordoliberalism was however a new "Wirtschaftsordnung," an economic order that coopted entrepreneurs and workers alike into adhering to accepting socioeconomic priorities imposed by the state. In particular, the social administration of the economy was intensified. While remaining autonomous, the private sector and the trade unions contribute to order by negotiating tariff agreements for entire sectors and cooperating on issues such as vocational education.

SME does not believe in an abstract market equilibrium. It expects the state to establish and supervize the market economy through Ordnungspolitik while respecting the autonomy of the private sector. *SME is thus classic German state-imposed order, embellished by a judicious amount of free-market leeway derived from Anglo-Saxon traditions.*

Alfred Müller-Armack, the "neoliberal" state secretary at the Federal Economics Ministry during the Erhard era, coined the term Social Market Economy ("soziale Marktwirtschaft"). According to his perception, free-market economics lacks a comprehensive ethos. Müller-Armack called for social stabilizers that would give the anonymous modern citizen a feeling of belonging. These stabilizers—vocational education, representation through associations, and so on—ensure a deeper degree of participation in the economic process.[11]

The importance of these stabilizers is often overlooked by those who perceive SME as a kind of free-market economy with a social state added on. Without them, the consensus that has enabled Germany to excel in sectors as diverse as ecological technology and trade fairs could not exist.

Because of the checks and balances imposed by Ordnungspolitik and by stabilizers, *SME is aligned toward balanced development, not growth at any cost.* Economic stability—rather than dynamism—is ensured by social justice. Thus, growth rates are often lower than in the United States or Japan, but economic stability and social consensus are stronger. *Wealth creation and distribution are a steady, orderly process.*

THE GERMAN APPROACH TO ECONOMICS—AND ITS CRITICS

SME is a symbol of a specifically German economic school of thought. This book's introduction has outlined Friedrich List's seminal contribution. Often characterized as an "economic Luther," List was the first prominent publicist who questioned the rationality and efficacy of the classical school of economics. According to him, the principles propagated by Adam Smith, David Ricardo, and others functioned not because of their accuracy but because of England's industrial superiority and political clout in the early nineteenth century.

Free trade suited England's interests as the world's leading industrial and mercantile power, just as protectionism was suitable for the German states, which were in a fragile process of economic development. List's Zollverein, the customs union propagated by him, helped the German states establish a common market prior to Germany's reunification in 1871. The development of a European customs union in the 1950s and its expansion to a common market and later to a political and economic union can be construed as a confirmation of List's precepts of judicious protectionism as a prelude to economic integration and political unification.

List was in fact the first propagandist of "national economy." In contrast to universal explanations of national wealth such as the "simple cases" used by Ricardo, List penetrated the national core of wealth creation. He emphasized the influence of political power and national character. Because wealth was a national phenomenon, its creation was more important than its distribution. Production prevailed over consumption in List's Weltanschauung.

List's ideas were further extended by Germany's "historic school of national economy." This school was inductive rather than deductive in its approach: it reached conclusions by analysing the development of guilds, trade unions, and economic decentralization, rather than by postulating natural laws. Though ultimately eclipsed by theoretical economics, its criticism of the superficiality of the classical school's "homo oeconomicus" remains valid.

If Carlisle had lived in Germany, it seems likely that he would not have referred to economics as a "dismal science" but would rather have been fascinated by the interconnections made between history, culture, and the economy. These interconnections are the key to the ordoliberal ideas developed by Walther Eucken and others of the Freiburg school.

Eucken attempted to reconcile the theoretical precision of classical economics with the more reality-oriented approach of the historical school. The term "ordoliberalism," which he coined, reflects this duality: ordo harks back to the order of the Middle Ages, liberalism to the ideas of Adam Smith and other classical theorists. Eucken thus integrates the order of the guilds, the craftsmanship ethos, and other vital elements of the Mittelstand seen in this book's first chapter, into the logic of free markets, fair competition, and other elements of classical liberalism.[12]

The economic precepts of ordoliberalism can in fact only be understood in the context of a traditionally powerful state, of associations and chambers of commerce, of apprenticeships and Meisters, of specialized markets and the quality ethos. It lacks both the classical emphasis on natural laws and the schematic character of Keynesianism. Consequently, its significance has often been overlooked or disparaged.

MIT economist Rudiger Dornbusch, for instance, writes off ordoliberalism as "a tame version of laissez-faire which sprouts in Southern Germany." Well-known surveys of the history of economics like John Kenneth Galbraith's *Economics in Perspective* ignore it altogether.

Both for classical economists and for Keynesians, ordoliberalism was highly unorthodox. While the first-mentioned rejected its social orientation—Friedrich von Hayek for instance called the term "social" a weasel word—the Keynesians have reacted allergically to the ordoliberal refusal to adopt interventionist policies such as employment programs. In retrospect, the criticism of Keynesian economist Thomas Balogh is a revealing commentary on the dangers of orthodoxy.

Writing in the early 1950s, Balogh attacked Erhard's monetary reform and contended that it was based on a "wicked formula." He accused Erhard of trying to discredit "enlightened Keynesian economic policy," predicting that because of high interest rates and low relative wage levels, in the long run "this income pattern will become intolerable and this productive pattern unsafe. Both will have to be readjusted. When the attempt is made to recreate mass demand and to wrench the productive system into another shape, a serious crisis and terrible social costs will be inevitable."[13] Needless to say, nothing of the sort has happened in Germany. However, since the 1960s, Keynesian policies have been adopted to a certain extent.

KEYNESIAN DEFICIT SPENDING AND NEOCLASSICAL RECIPES

By the mid-1960s, the postwar boom had slowed down. The 1966–68 and 1973–75 periods were recessionary. Keynesianism entered German policymaking by the back door, in terms of policies aligned to increasing demand. These policies were fiercely opposed by orthodox ordoliberals, who accused Keynes of having provided Nazi Germany with dirigiste strategies such as the employment program of the 1930s and who were generally skeptical of the efficacy of public-sector demand-stimulation.

Keynesianism's leading exponent in Germany was Karl Schiller, minister of economics in the late 1960s. Schiller was a conservative Social Democrat: he propagated employment policies as a necessary means of reaching an optimal level of "social productivity." Beyond this, he was an advocate of deficit spending.

Social Democrats in Germany generally favor policies aligned toward reducing income disparities to a greater extent than their colleagues in the two other leading parties in contemporary Germany, the Christian Democrats (CDU) and the Liberal Democrats (FDP). However, Schiller's dictum, "As much competition as possible, as much planning as necessary," represents a kind of wisdom subscribed to by all political groups. There is a similar consensus on the need for social welfare.

The 1980s and 1990s in Germany have witnessed greater receptiveness for neoclassical approaches. Liberal-Conservative governments, in power since 1982, have tried to adopt policies closer to those in the Anglo-Saxon countries, involving privatization, deregulation, and the reduction of government spending.

The reunification of Germany revealed the serious deficiences of public policies oriented toward market mechanisms. The West German policy elite's initial plans and prognoses for East Germany were wildly off the mark and government spending increased dramatically to cope with unforeseen industrial disasters, social unrest, and widespread unemployment.

Committed as they were to macroeconomic models and microeconomic systems, the West German policymakers and government advisers failed to recognize the enormous social and psychological differences between West and East. As one critic cogently points out: "Because of their frames of perception, the neoclassicists disregarded the complex interconnections between the economy and public administration, as also questions of infrastructure, the mentality of the population and the time required for change."[14]

The German state now finds itself in a schizophrenic situation: in principle, it is committed to demand-oriented Keynesian policies in East Germany. In practice however, it has invested in supply-side politics, as Karl Schiller once pointed out. Characteristically, both Schiller and Helmut Schmidt, who served as minister of finance before his term of office as prime minister from 1974 to 1982, have strongly criticized government policies in East Germany. According to Schmidt, the main mistake was a naive belief in the all-healing power of the market.[15]

The crucial problem however is the need for a new, complex consensus in East Germany, a region that has not organically adopted SME, but been forced to adhere to it after reunification. The psychological ramifications of adjusting to the subtlety of West German checks and balances are enormous—and tend to elude the technocratic preconceptions of contemporary policy planners.

It is of course particularly ironic that in a country where the visible hand of the state has traditionally been the major motor of economic progress, the invisible hand of the market is suddenly considered to be paramount. Behind these attitudes lies an untold story of intellectual subservience on the part of German academics to the supposed wisdom of Anglo-Saxon scholarship after the Second World War.

Economists in contemporary Germany reveal the same medium level of achievement that, as we have seen, characterizes managers and management consultants. Apart from very few exceptions, German economists lack international reputations. To a great extent, they merely restate Anglo-Saxon economic concepts. Inevitably, they lack the broad-based intellectual backgrounds and the knowledge of German history that distinguished SME scholars and practitioners like Eucken, Böhm, Müller-Armack and Erhard. They are thus unable to perceive Germany's economic Gestalt.

Not that the SME protagonists were infallible. The Freiburg ordoliberal Walter Eucken for instance was vehemently against the "estate order," considering it to be an unnecessary relict of the past. Similarly, Erhard condemned what he called Germany's tendency to become an "estate-state with guild-like order." As we have seen however, estate-oriented business associations have greatly contributed to the stability and connectedness of the business world. Germany's unique consensus is founded on this connectedness.

SME is best described as a "gestaltete Marktwirtschaft," a market economy formatively molded by the state to ensure a constant balance of economic and social priorities. As seen in the chapter on Business Mentality, SME is now moving toward a new balance of priorities: the economic-ecological. Technical standards and economic norms imposed by the state provide a framework for quality-oriented competition in the ecological sector. The private sector acts autonomously within this framework, consulting regularly with government. Thus, the existing socioeconomic balance is now being augmented by an economic-ecological balance. *The depth of balanced development has grown accordingly in Germany.*

SECTION 3: BALANCE OF RESPONSIBILITY—TRADE UNIONS AND THE PRIVATE SECTOR

"Arbeit adelt," work enobles. This saying, much misused during the Nazi period, sums up a collective attitude in Germany which dates back to the guilds and to Lutheran Protestantism. It emphasizes the worth of a vocation rather than the profitability of an occupation. Fittingly, this vocational mindset stresses group solidarity rather than individual excellence, as opposed to the Calvinistic ethos. It supports the impeccable mediocrity that, as we saw, characterizes business management in Germany.

The guilds limited solidarity to their members. Those employed by the craftsmen were subjected to a rigid code of rules. However, the master craftsman also offered his employees a certain measure of security. Guilds regulations brought elements of order into the working lives of apprentices and journeymen. Journeymen's associations protected the interests of their members.

Those who became workmen rather than craftsmen during the early phase of Germany's industrialization between 1820 and 1850 enjoyed a greater amount of freedom—and insecurity. They united to face this insecurity in organizations that were modeled on the journeymen's associations. Thus, Germany's trade unions adopted guild norms in their formative phase. This distinguishes them from trade unions in the United States, Japan, and other industrialized countries.

The legacy of the guilds has steered Germany's trade unions toward integration in the Mittelstandsgesellschaft, the estate-oriented community described in the first chapter. Trade unions organize the country's workforce into vocationally defined groups, just as associations coordinate the estate order in the business community. They thus reduce the potential for ideological conflicts and curb fragmentation and particularism.

RITUALS OF CONFLICT

Trade union helplessness in the face of Nazi oppression led to the creation of a central organization, the Deutscher Gewerkschaftsbund (DGB), after World War II. DGB unites sixteen highly autonomous unions with around eight million members. It exercices the same coordinating functions as the employers' association BDI. Similarly, powerful central unions represent white-collar workers and state officials.

Fifty-three percent of all workers and 75 percent of all public officials, but only 24 percent of all white-collar employees are organized in unions. A high degree of formalization characterizes the unions' internal organization and decision-making process. In effect, the trade unions are modern bureaucracies with well-paid functionaries, who generally behave with the decorum of public-sector officials. Like managers in private-sector companies, they too are susceptible to the Beamtenmentalität.

In their organizational norms and codes of behavior, the unions show striking similarities to the employers' associations. Similarities are also induced by the fact that the representatives of capital and labor are in a constant process of negotiation on wages and fringe benefits: tariff autonomy is a vital component of SME. Thus, terms of reference and agenda have been standardized.

The tariff wages in various sectors are fixed by representatives of the employers' associations and the trade unions. While in the past, tariff wages were increased irrespective of the economic situation, the crisis of the early 1990s has changed the modalities of tariff negotiation. For the first time, wage increases have been pegged to the growth rate. A comparison with former tariff increases in recessionary periods illustrates this point:

- In 1974, during the first oil recession, wages increased by an average of 13 percent in spite of a growth rate that stagnated at 0.2 percent.
- In 1982, during the second oil recession, with -0.9 percent growth, tariff wages were increased by 4.1 percent.
- In 1994, with growth at over 2 percent, wages increased by only 1.5 percent.[16]

Conflict situations reveal the mentality of Germany's unions. One case in point was a crisis within the steel industry of the Saarland in the late 1970s. Faced with the collapse of one of the region's major sectors and the closure of major factories, the IG Metall union plan of action involved concrete suggestions for improving the industry's structure. Trade unionists cooperated with management in organizing retrenchment as humanely as possible.

On the one hand, IG Metall went through the rituals of protest: these included well-organized public demonstrations and workers' meetings that the union itself referred to as being "disciplined and orderly!" Polemical statements were made against the industrialists, seen as being job killers, and reference was made to them as former supporters of Hitler, who had in the past contributed to Germany's downfall. This rhetoric contrasted with active trade union cooperation in all phases of crisis management, including strategic concepts for the future of the steel industry. Thus, aggressive posturing masked a constructive, trouble-shooting approach.[17]

RITES OF CODETERMINATION

Trade unions represent workers in various sectors, while works councils ensure Mitbestimmung—codetermination—within companies. The works council law passed in 1920 institutionalized codetermination: workers were given codified rights of intervention in corporate affairs. New arbitration mechanisms established a degree of self-regulation between employers and workers. Disputes were arbitrated by parity committees—and if necessary mediated by independent personalities. Works councilors became members of the supervisory boards of public-limited companies. Consensus mechanisms of this kind account for the high degree of cohesion within companies, described in the chapter on business mentality.

Siegfried Kracauer, the famous sociologist whose book on German cinema, *From Caligari to Hitler*, is required reading for all film buffs, described the activities of the works councilors in the 1920s in his study, *The White-collar Workers*. He was impressed by the fact that they had their own offices but pointed out that they were often manipulated or outmaneuvered by management. Their formal rights of membership in the supervisory board did not really upset power mechanisms in the companies.

This basic situation has remained the same: in contemporary Germany, works councilors rarely challenge corporate structures and mechanisms. On the contrary, codetermination has enabled modern methods of production and organization to be carefully integrated into the working environment.

Codetermination laws passed in the 1970s have consolidated employee participation within corporations. Parity on the supervisory board level is one component: corporate supervisors have—as seen in the chapter on business mentality—the power to elect members of the board of directors, who need a two-thirds majority in order to be confirmed in their positions. Thus, constructive cooperation between top management and employees' representatives is imperative.

Opinion surveys indicate that codetermination is positively judged by the majority of entrepreneurs and managers: it is seen as furthering democratization and "social peace." In one survey, 60 percent of all entrepreneurs considered the works councilors as being managers responsible for working conditions. This positive attitude is all the more remarkable because Germany's companies foot the bill for codetermination, estimated at thirteen billion marks a year.

The links between works councils and trade unions are indirect. Two-thirds of all councillors belong to DGB. However, they act autonomously and—particularly in the crisis of the early 1990s—they have directly negotiated compromises with management. Some compromises involve wages lower than the tariff minimums. This is particularly the case in East Germany, where competitiveness is strongly impaired by high wage levels. Such compromises have relativized the power of the trade unions as the negotiators of tariff agreements.

CODETERMINATION AS A GERMAN SUCCESS STRATEGY: BMW AND BERTELSMANN

Two examples illustrate codetermination's contribution to corporate success. In 1959, the luxury car maker BMW was in a catastrophic situation. Its liquidity problems had deepened and the company was on the point of being taken over by Mercedes Benz. The crisis reached its climax at the annual general meeting and the company was saved by a group of share-holders led by the industrialist Herbert Quandt. Quandt invested his own capital to stabilize the finances of BMW.

One of Quandt's major allies in the years to come was a man called Kurt Golda, a simple locksmith who had become president of the works council in 1956. Golda admired Quandt's courage and supported him. Quandt on the other hand was keenly aware of the need for a general consensus between management and labor. Under Golda's influence, BMW developed generous employee participation schemes and an ambitious project to integrate foreign workers. As the workers' representative, Golda even advized Quandt on whether the contracts of members of the board of directors should be renewed or not.

As Horst Mönnich points out in his vivid chronicle of BMW: "Golda never overstepped his competences in all the actions influenced by him. However, he used his influence in such a way that Quandt in his role as entrepreneur realized how closely entrepreneurial decisions were linked to social policies."[18]

The Bertelsmann story by contrast shows how an industrialist can develop a social conscience and continue to be successful. Reinhard Mohn inherited a provincial publishing house after returning home from the Second World War. He had spent two years as a prisoner of war in Kansas and had used the time to learn both English and the rudiments of U.S. management methods.

Complying with his father's wishes, Mohn qualified as a book seller and founded a book club, Bertelsmann Lesering, in 1950. Shrewd market research and aggressive sales methods made the book club a runaway success. Skillfully capitalizing the profits, Bertelsmann under Mohn systematically acquired an empire of publishing houses, including Bantam Doubleday Dell in the United States.

At the same time, Mohn is a pioneer of *Success through Partnership*, a term coined by him. He has integrated the works council into the decision-making process and practices his own form of participative management. In the meanwhile, Bertelsmann has become one of the world's largest media empires.[19]

Mohn's success shows that coopting employees is a strategy that supplements conventional organizational skills and results in a greater degree of employee commitment. Because of Mohn's coopting strategy, trade unions have failed to gain influence among the Bertelsmann employees. Thus, the efficient practice of codetermination weakens the scope for representation.

BMW and Bertelsmann demonstrate that *German companies can achieve entrepreneurial success with management techniques that differ profoundly from those practiced in the United States and Japan.* Because of their reliance on organizational skills rather than leadership charisma, most German companies are well equipped for codetermination. Organizational cohesion and reliance on consensus—the two major qualities analyzed in the chapter on business mentality—make entrepreneurs and managers accessible for codetermination. Far from challenging management's authority, trade unions and works councils commit the workforce to entrepreneurial success.

WEIGHING THE PARTNERSHIP'S COSTS AND BENEFITS

The balance of responsibility between management and the workforce is a form of social engineering. The dangers of overengineering apply here as well—too many issues and forums for discussion and negotiation, a blurring of distinctions between petty and crucial issues. Trade unions and works councils are as susceptible to the dangers of pettiness as large corporations: they too are staffed by Beckmessers, pedantic officials of the kind we encountered in connection with the Meistersinger of Nuremberg.

In the early 1990s, trade unions have lost more than a million members, approximately 10 percent of total membership. In the context of high unemployment, trade unions are seen as representing the haves—those with jobs—rather than the have-nots. Their power has diminished commensurately: few observers are now likely to echo the conservative historian Golo Mann's statement in the early 1970s that the trade unions were now the strongest social force in Germany. Speculation is rife that the trade unions will have to foresake their "socially conservative" attitudes. They remain, however, a powerful interest group with the same legitimation as the business associations.[20]

Representation and codetermination have indeed endowed the workforce with a sense of responsibility: the strike rate for instance is far lower in Germany than in other countries. Between 1970 and 1991, strikes accounted for an average of thirty days per 1000 employees, as against sixty-four in Japan and 216 in the United States Beyond this, corporate loyalty in Germany matches that in Japan, though lifelong employment is not guaranteed by German companies: the average employee remains 10.4 years in the same corporation, as against 10.9 years in Japan and 6.7 years in the United States.

Germany's trade unions have been coopted into support of SME. Their legal and administrative responsibilities extend to general issues such as vocational education, where they interact with government bodies. This institutional role has made them seem like "sheep in wolves' clothing," as the U.S. sociologist Clark Kerr sarcastically pointed out as far back as the 1950s. It seems however fairer to regard them as part of a well-organized economy.

Just as Germany's economic policies have been portrayed as being between the Anglo-Saxon free-market and French planification models, so also do its trade unions differ from the more fragmented organizations in the Anglo-Saxon countries and the syndicalist bodies in the romanic countries. The German unions are more unified than their Anglo-Saxon counterparts, less ideological than their French or Italian equivalents—and far richer than the unions in all the other countries.[21]

In Japan, on the other hand, trade unions have traditionally been suppressed and the workforce is correspondingly docile. Trade unions organize a privileged minority, mostly in large corporations: 70 percent of all employees in Japan lack representation. Like the AFL-CIO in the United States, Japan's central union Rengo lacks the grass-roots support and the organizational competence that distinguishes Germany's DGB. The much-vaunted harmony at the workplace in Japan is mostly imposed and contrasts starkly with the complex codification of workers' rights in Germany.[22]

The costs of the German model of industrial partnership are high: the country's wage levels and the indirect costs to employers—insurance, pensions and so on—are, as mentioned in this book's introduction, the highest in the world. The real benefits of representation and codetermination are indeed qualitative rather than quantitative. *Without industrial partnership, Germany's SME would lack a vital source of support*. Without vocationally oriented trade unions, Germany's Mittelstandsgesellschaft, its estate-oriented community, would equally lack a foundation.

THE CLICHÉ OF THE HARDWORKING, DISCIPLINED GERMAN

In the chapter on business mentality, we discovered that the German success recipe is not individual excellence but rather organizational cohesion and consensus. Similarly, Germany's industrial success derives from success factors such as quality-orientation and specialization—and from representation and codetermination.

Traditional clichés about hard-working and disciplined Germans need to be revized in the light of both quantitative and qualitative evidence. Absenteeism for instance is far higher in Germany than elsewhere: 8.8 percent as against 2.9 percent in the United States and 1.6 percent in Japan. Germans work fewer hours per year than their colleagues in other countries and they have more holidays.

In addition, various surveys show that the traditional work ethic has now been replaced by a mixture of individualistic and communitarian values. Average German employees expect an agreeable corporate culture in addition to job security and old age benefits. They consider their family life to be at least as important as their profession.

An international survey, *Jobs in the 1980s* discovered that between 1950 and 1980, work satisfaction in Germany had declined, while preference for leisure as against work had increased. In contrast to other countries like the United States and Great Britain, Germany's workforce seemed more critical in their attitude to work and more avid in the pursuit of pleasure.[23]

Evidence of this change in working attitudes has been interpreted as the end of the Protestant ethic in Germany—Chancellor Helmut Kohl provoked a major controversy when he disparaged the "leisure park" attitudes of his countrymen. However, Germany's competitiveness in world markets did not decrease: it in fact increased during the time span of the thirty years covered by the survey.

In his interpretation of the *Jobs in the 1980s* survey, industrial sociologist Burkhard Strümpel explained this discrepancy by pointing out that German employers had eliminated unproductive jobs and replaced potentially disruptive German workers by machines and foreign workers. This argument overlooks the many restraints on management decisions that, as we have seen, make behavior of the kind mentioned above virtually impossible. Beyond this, the results of the survey indicate that a broad cross-section of the employed shared a sense of dissatisfaction. Thus, those employed hardly seem to belong to "those workers least affected by postmaterialist values," as Strümpel puts it.

The real paradox is that Germany's industrial position as against the United States and Great Britain improved perceptibly during a period when its working ethic apparently declined. Efficiency increased in spite of an apparent lack of personal motivation. Evidently, the business environment played a stronger role in determining success than the motivation of the individual worker.

There is a deep schism in the Anglo-Saxon perception of the homo oeconomicus. On the one hand, the talented individual as an entrepreneur has always been the symbol of wealth creation. On the other hand, Tayloristic working methods and the Fordist "paradigm" have made the average employee into a substitutable industrial resource.

In recent years, a succession of management experts—most prominently Tom Peters—have preached the efficacy of upgrading and empowering the individual employee, making him or her less of a tool and more of a creative asset. In spite of this humanization however, *the Anglo-Saxon ideology of capitalism remains predominantly mechanistic, while the German perception of the working environment is organic.* Organic in the belief that individual skills and personal effort can only flourish in a supportive context. Thus, in the survey cited above, individual Germans could afford to disparage the work ethic and still achieved more than their apparently more committed counterparts in the Anglo-Saxon countries.

Individual commitment is in fact powerless without supportive environmental factors such as social security and the regulation of industrial relations. Individual achievement is doomed to remain an isolated phenomenon if infrastructure—in terms of education, financial stability and other ancillary factors—is insufficient. The Anglo-Saxon glorification of the charismatic individual (whether entrepreneur or manager)—and its corresponding disparagement of the average employee—neglects the importance of a supportive context for stable wealth creation.

In the long run however, talented individualism has no chance against a judicious mixture of individual autonomy and a supportive context. This mixture is not put together by an "invisible hand"—it needs to be grasped, defined, codified, implemented.

Tradition and legally prescribed structures—the guilds, the trade unions, the works councils—have formalized the constant search for a quid pro quo between capital and labor in Germany. But the real explanation for Germany's unique balance of responsibility lies deeper. *In spite of occasional frictions, the classic antithesis of capital and labor has evolved into a synthesis: a community of interest.*

Writing as far back as 1929, business economist Heinrich Nicklisch envisioned the individual worker as part of a "Betriebsgemeinschaft," a working community, capable of making "an organism out of the working mechanism."[24] Contemporary Germany's workforce is a part of this organism, committed to the same basic socioeconomic goals as the entrepreneurs. *The egalitarian nobility of a working community is the German ethos. This is also the moral quintessence of the Social Market Economy.*

SECTION 4: COHESION AND CONSENSUS IN THE MITTELSTANDSGESELLSCHAFT

Business associations, trade union activities, the state's socioeconomic priorities: they all contribute to social cohesion. Cohesion does not result from specific policies, nor is it a question of personal choice. Its specific nature in Germany can best be highlighted by a comparison of the reformist ideas of John Stuart Mill with the perceptions of the famous German sociologist Ferdinand Tönnies.

Mill was not only one of the nineteenth century's most talented economists, he was also unusually humane. At the time, classical economics was qualitative rather than mathematical, oriented toward the human experience rather than to statistics. Both the wealth and the misery caused by the industrial revolution in England were visible—and Mill strongly reacted to the misery.

Mill linked the principles of political economy—in other words of the causes of national wealth—with questions of social philosophy. His famous prophecy of the attractiveness of communism for the common man culminated in the often quoted statement that "if therefore, the choice were to be made between Communism with all its chances, and the present state of society with all its sufferings and injustices.... All the difficulties, great or small, of Communism would be but as dust in the balance."[25]

This statement is illuminating in various ways. Mill evidently believed that free market mechanisms could be threatened by social unrest. He tried to reconcile laissez-faire with social justice and went so far as to point out that "mankind are capable of a far greater amount of commitment than the present age is accustomed to suppose possible."[26] In today's terms, he was a socially conscious liberal—and very Anglo-Saxon in his perceptions. His humanitarianism was Christian-Utilitarian: love thyself as the first step toward loving thy neighbor.

Mill's point of departure was the two Englands of the Victorian period: the rich and the poor being tightly segregated in terms of norms, values, and expectations. Seen retrospectively, he misinterpreted the dogmatic egalitarianism that communism sought to impose; Mill evidently believed that communism could ensure the "commitment" of the individual and the "general benefit of the community."

The real problem however seems to have been—and continues to be—that England's class-bound society did not, and does not, constitute a unified community. *Neither communism nor any other imposed system of values can achieve the subtlety of bonds that identifies a true community.*

In Germany, the fateful distinction between Gemeinschaft and Gesellschaft—community and society—made by the sociologist Ferdinand Tönnies created a theoretical duality belied by the effective coexistence of both community and society in late nineteenth century Germany. As we have already seen, state policies, the influence of the guilds, and liberal social ideas made Bismarckian Germany both traditional and modern, both a proud community and a forward-looking society, both spiritual and materialistic.

This balancing act was fraught however with a number of dangers. Tönnies himself for instance unduly glorified and mystified Gemeinschaft, which for him was something "real and organic," as against Gesellschaft, seen as being "ideal and mechanical." He contrasted and polarized instead of searching for a synthesis: city culture for instance belonged to the Gesellschaft side, while language, ethics, belief was Gemeinschaft. Thus, modern society was automatically artificial, and correspondingly negative.[27]

Though Tönnies rejected the ideology of National Socialism, his glorification of Gemeinschaft helped legitimize the primitive "Volksgemeinschaft" populism of the Nazis. However, both before and after the Third Reich, German society was cohesive in a way that English society could not emulate. As the welfare economist Gosta Esping-Andersen points out, the German approach to economic development can be perceived "as a way to uphold traditional society in the unfolding capitalist economy; as a means to integrate the individual into an organic entity, protected from the individualization and competitiveness of the market, and removed from the logic of class opposition."[28]

As we have seen in the context of business mentality, Germany's economic steadiness lies in an imposed equilibrium between organized capitalism and organized socialism. Equally, *cohesion derives from the fact that Germany is both a community and a society.* This duality characterizes the Mittelstandsgesellschaft, a society with strong elements of an estate-oriented community. The predominance of the Mittelstand—both in economic terms and in terms of social values—has made Germany a society oriented toward the middle rather than toward elitist aspirations.

DARWINISM OR COHESION: THE SOCIAL QUESTION

In England, even reformers like Mill expected the "lower classes" to prosper mostly through self help. Later, social legislation was espoused by humane representatives of the upper classes: members of the Fabian society, literary figures like H.G. Wells and George Bernard Shaw. Thus, though Britain implemented social security in 1911 that went beyond Bismarck's legislation—it provided unemployment insurance before Germany did—the German reforms were more profound, because they did not just represent charity on the part of the privileged toward the deserving poor. Social Darwinism in England could survive the welfare state—it expanded vastly after the Second World War on the recommendations of the Beveridge Commission—and reassert itself in the guise of Thatcherism in the 1980s.

Similarly in the United States, the New Deal provided a large measure of social welfare and seemed to reflect a commitment made in Franklin Delano Roosevelt's memorable inaugural address statement of 1932: "I see one third of a nation ill-housed, ill-clad and ill-nourished." However, the pioneer ethic could survive Great Society policies and other rallying calls. Writing some sixty years after Roosevelt's statement—and after the effects of Reaganomics—the political economist Robert B. Reich could portray an America divided into high- and low-income communities and point out ironically that a common area code had become the best definition of community.[29]

In America as in Britain, a profound difference to German traditions and attitudes can be perceived. Society was "commodity-oriented" rather than community-oriented. Human needs were commodified, just as production factors like labor became easily replacable commodities. Social Darwinism has remained the prevailing ethos, despite the Democratic party politics of Roosevelt, Johnson, and Clinton in the United States and Labor party policies implemented by Attlee, Harold Wilson and Callahan in Britain.

The insight that this comparison reveals is simple: the substance of social legislation cannot survive without the spirit of cohesion. *Without cohesion, wealth creation is socially divisive*: it creates schisms rather than integrating large sections of society and thus providing a stable foundation for economic development. The highly publicized decline of the U.S. middle class in the context of an economic upsurge in the early 1990s is a symptom of these schisms.

In Germany on the other hand, cohesion has enabled an egalitarian Mittelstandsgesellschaft to develop and to survive recessions. Cohesion has also promoted the business emphasis on organization rather than on leadership, on a high middle level of achievement rather than an individualistic search for excellence that assigns the less-gifted to marginal roles.

The Mittelstandsgesellschaft is closely linked with the social state: an egalitarian estate-oriented community needs both vocational training and a high subsistence level for the individual. For the architects of the SME like Walter Eucken, social policies were not mere appendages of economic policies. They were an intrinsic part of these policies and Eucken points out: "There is nothing which can be considered socially unimportant."[30]

The German state ensures the well-being of its citizens with an intricate mesh of social insurance and aid, covering employment, sickness, and old age. All employees are compulsorily coopted into social insurance and receive state pensions to the extent of their contributions to the pension fund.

This puts immense budgetary pressure on the state: the social budget totals more than 1,000 billion marks, representing roughly a third of GNP. Pensions and health insurance are the major cost factors, accounting for approximately 30 percent and 20 percent, respectively, of the social budget.

The German state's dominating welfare role can best be perceived by a multicountry comparison of private life insurance: the average life insurance per head in Germany is estimated at 25,000 marks as compared with 60,000 marks in the United States and 174,000 marks in Japan. It also means a high degree of taxation: the average German pays around 44 percent of his salary in taxes and social insurance, as compared to around 31 percent in the United States and 29 percent in Japan. Thus, the German employee is automatically protected and taxed accordingly, while in the United States and Japan, he is freer to provide for his own security—and faces correspondingly greater risks.

THE CRISIS OF THE WELFARE STATE

The German social state is now facing a crisis caused by an aging population and large-scale unemployment. In the context of unfavorable demographics—16 percent of the population is over sixty years of age and the percentage is calculated to rise to 24 percent by the year 2030—the "pension crisis" is a perpetual issue. Budgetary strains are augmented by a drastic rise of persons in need of nursing: their number rose from 260,000 to 540,00 between 1970 and 1990. To cope with these burdens, the government has imposed a new nursing insurance, which further increases the tax burden of the average employee.

Unemployment is a more immediate problem. The number of those without work increased steadily during the 1970s and 1980s in the context of layoffs in "rust-bowl" sectors like steel and coal-mining. Germany's reunification in 1990 drastically increased unemployment: entire sectors in East Germany were effectively closed down or rigorously restructured. With approximately four million unemployed and a further two million kept from the dole statistics by means of training programs and other schemes financed by the state, the welfare state is increasingly burdened by the volume of unemployment benefits. Here, the negative side of SME and the Mittelstandsgesellschaft can be perceived: *an economy oriented toward equity rather than dynamism and a society tightly organized in vocational groups lack the structural flexibility to dynamically generate jobs.*

Reunification confronted the social state with enormous challenges. Millions of East German pensioners, who had not paid into the West German pension funds, were nonetheless given pension benefits almost as high as those given to West Germans. The general standard of living in East Germany has improved dramatically in the space of five years: in terms of disposable income, own housing and savings ratios, East and West have virtually merged.

The social reunification of Germany is an enormous achievement, but it has delayed the reform of the social state. In terms of the Gini coefficient, which economists use to measure income inequality, the average German in the mid-1990s lives in a far more egalitarian environment than the average U.S. or Japanese citizen. Social equity has extended the Mittelstandsgesellschaft into the East.

Germany has now started reassessing its commitments toward the recipients of pensions and unemployment benefits. This reassessment needs to be extended to all areas of social aid. The original SME emphasis on solidarity and subsidiarity was a sound policy priority, later subverted by the headlong expansion of social benefits in the 1960s and 1970s. The welfare state has thus become a kind of universal insurance company, guaranteeing benefits that have little to do with ensuring a basic subsistence level for all its citizens. Increasingly however, social benefits are being linked to market conditions, just as wage increases are now more closely pegged to the growth rate and to productivity gains.

The first signs of success are visible. Budgetary requirements for state-financed health insurance in West Germany dropped in 1993 as compared to the previous year. But much needs to be done. The normal employee's health insurance automatically covers his or her entire family. Similarly, pension funds are utilized to pay for all kinds of contingencies dating back to World War II. A large percentage of social aid is administered by autonomous non governmental organizations that have developed enormous bureaucracies. Here too, there is great potential for reforms.

In the United States, the backlash against the social state started in 1980. The number of those earning more than 500,000 dollars a year increased by 985 percent during the 1980s and early 1990s. Simultaneously, the median family income for workers and for a broad cross-section of white-collar employees steadily declined. Household savings have dropped radically and the economic foundations of the middle class are disintegrating. As Robert Frank and Philip Cook point out in their book, *The Winner-Take-All Society*, "The top earners are richer now than ever before, but few among them can feel proud of the social environment we have bequeathed to our children."[31]

Wealth creation in America is still broad-based, wealth distribution however is beginning to resemble that of developing countries. In the context of rank social inequity, the potential for populism and for social disruption has increased. The "Brazilianization" of the United States would however ruin the social foundations of the U.S. economy.

Japan on the other hand has never been a social state in the Western definition of the term. The general standard of living—in terms of housing, medical care and so on—is far lower than in Germany. The overwhelming majority of the Japanese consider themselves as belonging to the middle class, but they are actually part of what one perceptive observer has called the "ritual harmony" of a feudalistic system.[32]

Neither the United States nor Japan can thus serve as models for the reform of social aid. Germany needs to draw on its own experience as a pioneer in social welfare to restructure its social state.

COHESION AND THE RITUALS OF THE "ENERGIEKONSENS"

Cohesion, coupled with a constant search for consensus, have accounted for Germany's success in sectors like trade fairs and eco tech, as seen in the chapter on business mentality. An energy consensus on the other hand has not yet been achieved. However, the constant search for a consensus on energy issues reveals the German approach to tackling a complex issue and achieving a modus vivendi.

Since the early 1970s, the energy sources issue has been intensively negotiated by the energy industry, the state, trade unions, and ecological pressure groups. Each participant has clearly defined interests:

- The energy industry is interested in retaining the mix of coal and atomic energy, each of which contribute approximately one-third of Germany's electricity supply.
- The state is interested in reducing the subsidies of approximately 10 billion marks, and for the coal industry, accorded in the interests of employment. It is also considering the deregulation of the monopolistic energy sector and a progressive reduction of atomic energy.
- The trade unions have a vital interest in job security for coal miners and agitate for the continuation of state subsidies.
- The ecological pressure groups stress energy saving, the banning of atomic energy and more subsidies for solar, wind, and water energy sources.[33]

The general consensus of the early 1970s on the need to reduce oil consumption and increase Germany's energy autonomy by supporting both coal and atomic energy dissolved in the context of falling oil prices, budgetary strains, and increasing public criticism of atomic energy.

The energy industry lobby succumbed to the pressure of public opinion in voluntarily desisting from reprocessing atomic residues, but still proclaims the need for atomic energy. Political parties have been divided on this issue, with the Social Democrats and Greens demanding an immediate stop to atomic energy, as compared to the phased-out restructuring favored by the Christian Democrats. The trade unions have successfully pressurized both Social Democrat and Christian Democrat governments toward providing stable subsidies and thus guaranteeing a reasonably high rate of employment in the coal sector.

The "Energiekonsens" has become a catchword in the German media. It symbolizes the constant and difficult search for harmony in the context of changing economic realities and social attitudes. It is also the name of a working group that has met periodically over a period of years. The endless negotiations have a symbolic character. Unlike tariff negotiations, where the opposing viewpoints of capital and labor are well-defined and the outcome can easily be predicted, the rituals of energy consensus are protracted, their results uncertain.

However, public expectations of a consensus ensure a constructive attitude toward finding a quid pro quo. The formalization of the consensus process encourages the negotiating parties to compromize behind closed doors while publicly assuring their respective clienteles of steadfastness. Beyond this, business decisions depend on the consensus: Germany's energy industry has indicated that it will not build any new atomic reactors before a broad-based consensus has been reached.

Business decisions taken on the basis of a consensus obviously have a sound foundation. Thus, both the energy corporations and the large cluster of enterprises that serve the sector have profited from the energy discussion. Beyond this, public discussion has stimulated consciousness of the need to economize on energy: it is certainly no coincidence that Germany is a world leader in energy-saving techniques, consuming approximately 30 percent less per capita than the average consumption in the industrialized world.

The German approach to searching for a consensus on controversial issues can best be visualized as a ballet that features a series of soloist pirouettes on the part of major protagonists (in this case eco groups, trade unions, and industry). But the choreography varies the improvizations of these prima ballerinas with the well-orchestrated performances of the corps de ballet (in this case the negotiators and specialists from industrial associations and central ministries, who generally stay in the background). Both the improvizations and the group performances are well-rehearsed.

German society has brought forward a series of gifted choreographers of consensus: politicians with academic backgrounds like Karl Schiller, with trade union roots like Georg Leber, or with business experience like Kurt Biedenkopf, all of whom have successfully mediated on various issues. In the context of Germany's egalitarian society, leadership consists more of coordinating different viewpoints than of imposing personal convictions.

However long-winded and futile the consensus negotiations may seem, they fulfill a vital role in defining and restricting the parameters of dissent. They represent a potential for harmonious change and absorb the shocks of unforeseen events. *The search for a viable consensus strengthens cohesion.* Through cohesion, the state, trade unions and society constitute a supportive environment, which provides business with stimuli and correctives.

The number and efficiency of consensus mechanisms determine a country's cohesion. *Cohesion provides Germany with a far more stable social basis for wealth creation and distribution than is the case in the United States and Japan.*

BALANCE AND COMMITMENT

This chapter has explored the impact of the Business Environment on wealth creation and revealed the central importance of commitment:

- an *official* commitment to both economic and social priorities, concretized in the Social Market Economy and implemented by the public administration,
- an *autonomous* commitment to shared responsibility for economic success on the part of the business community and the trade unions,
- a *broad-based* commitment to the social state and the need for social equity in the Mittelstandsgesellschaft.

The complex nature of commitment in the German context contrasts with the more individualistic understanding of the term in the Anglo-Saxon countries. Harvard Business School professor Pankaj Ghemawat for instance, author of a book on commitment, defines it as a management focus on key strategic issues. For him, commitment consists of "constraints imposed by past choices or present ones." Thus, commitment is a barrier to change, the dead-weight of the past that needs to be recognized and tackled.[34]

An influential group of philosophers and social scientists in the United States considers commitment to communities to be a valuable social attitude. Communitarianism has in fact rivaled postmodernism as a fashionable topic of intellectual discussion in most Western countries since the early 1980s. U.S. theorists like Michael Walzer and Richard Rorty have challenged the premises of an atomistic society and postulated the need for a closer connection between the individual and the community. However, despite the efforts of Amitai Etzioni and other communitarian activists, U.S. society has continued to drift apart in the late 1980s and early 1990s.[35]

Communitarian ideas are warily discussed in Germany, because of the Nazi emphasis on Volksgemeinschaft, on racial community. *The Mittelstands-gesellschaft is however innately communitarian: society as an amalgam of vocational communities rather than a civil society in the Anglo-Saxon mold.*

Commitment in the German context is clearly defined and tightly organized, not idealistic and individualistic. Few individuals would qualify to be called "aristocrats of commitment," to use a term coined by Wilhelm Röpke, a neoliberal economist. These aristocrats are largely unnecessary, when social policies are systematically conceived and inequities are clearly identified. In the context of the many inequities connected with the reunification of Germany, a group of prominent East and West Germans has called for a return to frugality and solidarity—in other words, the old communitarian virtues that have made Germany's lasting economic achievements possible.[36]

Commitment belongs to these old virtues, just like a sense of order. As one comparative study of the relationship between the individual and the community in four Western countries discovered, freedom in Germany is strongly associated with responsibility. The "social code" requires an identification of the individual with the welfare of all. This code, rather than personal altruism, commits the individual to contribute constructively to the common welfare by fulfilling a vocational role. [37]

Beyond the vocational role that the individual plays in the context of guilds and trade associations (Verbände), he also contributes to cohesion by becoming a member of a Verein, a private association. Fifty-eight percent of all West Germans and 55 percent of all East Germans are members of some 250,000 private associations. The range of Verein activities covers sports, church aid and charitable work, music, and animal protection. Like the Verbände, the Vereine have codified statutes. They are however mostly run by honorary officials. The same formalism and pride in holding titles characterize the functioning of private and professional associations alike.

Like the trade unions, the Vereine have lost membership in recent years. However, they continue to rope in a sizeable cross-section of the population into social activities and charitable work.

Commitment is thus linked to the estate order of the Mittelstandsgesellschaft. The individual participates through professional and private associations in the res publica. His vocation and his affiliations provide him with an assigned social role.

Order, the central quality analyzed in connection with the business mentality, and commitment are a formidable combination of virtues. Together, they often form a collective corset, inciting an inner rebellion in individuals that can lead to militancy and violence. Leftist terrorism and neo-Nazi agitation in Germany can be seen in this light. They are as much a form of brutal self-assertion as one of political affiliation, a revolt against what some critics have polemically entitled the "structural violence" of the German set-up. They are also a revolt against the leveling pressure of the Mittelstandsgesellschaft. The emergence of new interest groups such as the Greens, the Anti-Atomic-Energy, and the Peace movements has been of therapeutic value to German society, because it allowed for a constructive ventilation of dissatisfaction.

Germany's distinctive sociocapitalism is poised between the United States and Japan. It incorporates the univeralism of an Anglo-Saxon Protestant culture, with appropriate value attached to covenants—and to the rights and duties of the individual. At the same time, it has elements of the particularity of a Japanese-style symbiotic community with carefully defined roles for the individual.

Germany's economic wealth, its social welfare, and the well-being it provides to the individual all depend on its ability, in a constantly changing world environment, to inspire and harness commitment without stifling self-will.

NOTES

1. Quoted in Ernst Engelberg, *Bismarck—das Reich in der Mitte Europas* (Berlin: Siedler, 1991), p. 396.

2. Harold James, *A German Identity* (London: Weidenfeld & Nicholson, 1989), p. 3.

3. Alfred D. Chandler, Jr., *Scale and Scope* (Cambridge, MA: Harvard University Press, 1990), p. 11; see also E. Klein, "The U.S./Japanese HR Culture Clash," in *Personnel Journal*, November 1992, pp. 30ff.

4. R. J. Berling, "The Emerging Approach to Business Strategy: Building a Relationship Advantage," in *Business Horizons*, July-August 1993, pp. 16ff.

5. Quote from the article by Wilhelm Bleek and Stefan Machura, "Ministerialbürokratie," in Uwe Andersen and Wichard Woyke (eds.), *Handwörter-*

buch des politischen Systems der Bundesrepublk Deutschland (Opladen: Leske + Buderich, 1993), p. 346.

6. Bleek and Machura, "Ministerialbürokratie," p. 346.

7. Thomas Luber, "Amtsschimmel auf Trab gebracht," in *Capital,* 12/1992, pp. 278–284.

8. Werner Jann, "Öffentliche Verwaltung," in Werner Weidenfeld and Karl-Rudolf Korte (eds.), *Handbuch zur deutschen Einheit* (Bonn: Bundeszentrale für politische Bildung, 1993), pp. 526–538; see also Klaus von Beyme, *Das politische System der Bundesrepublik Deutschland nach der Vereinigung* (Munich: Piper, 1991), pp. 314–318.

9. Jürgen B. Donges et al. (Kronberger Kreis), *Reform der öffentlichen Verwaltung: Mehr Wirtschaftlichkeit beim Management staatlicher Einrichtungen* (Frankfurt: Frankfurter Institut für wirtschaftspolitische Forschung, 1991).

10. Viktor Vanberg, "Ordnungstheorie as Constitutional Economics—the German Conception of a Social Market Economy," in *ORDO,* 1988, p. 19.

11. Alfred Müller-Armack, *Wirtschaftsordnung und Wirtschaftspolitik* (Freiburg: Rombach, 1966), pp. 243–245, 257–259; see also Alfred Müller-Armack, *Genealogie der Sozialen Marktwirtschaft* (Bern: Haupt, 1974), pp. 132–135.

12. Walter Eucken, *Grundsätze der Wirtschaftspolitik* (Hamburg: Rowohlt, 1967), pp. 191–195; see also from the same author, *Nationalökonomie wozu?* (Godesberg: Küpper, 1947), pp. 50–51, 66–67, 74–75.

13. Quoted in Dieter Schmidtchen, "German Ordnungspolitik as Institutional Choice," in *Zeitschrift für die gesamte Staatswissenschaft,* 140/1984, pp. 54–70, particularly p. 69.

14. See among others Rainer Hübner, "Rosa Brille," in *Capital,* 4/1991, pp. 113–114.

15. See an interview with Karl Schiller in the *Süddeutsche Zeitung,* December 4, 1992; see also the review of Karl Schiller's book, *Der schwierige Weg in die offene Gesellschaft* (Berlin: Siedler, 1994), in *Die Zeit,* January 14, 1994, and Helmut Schmidt's book *Handeln für Deutschland* (Berlin: Rowohlt, 1993), pp. 24–25.

16. See "Immer mehr auf Tuchfühlung," in *IWD,* March 17, 1994; see also "Innovationsfähig," in *IWD,* April 7, 1994.

17. Described in Josef Esser and Wolfgang Fach, "Korporatistische Krisenregulierung im Modell Deutschland," in Ulrich von Allemann (ed.), *Neokorporatismus* (Frankfurt: Campus, 1981), pp. 167–179.

18. Horst Mönnich, *BMW: eine deutsche Geschichte* (Wien: Zsolnay, 1989), p. 571.

19. Reinhard Mohn, *Erfolg durch Partnerschaft* (Berlin: Siedler, 1996); see also the portrait of Reinhard Mohn in *Münzinger-Archiv,* 15/1994.

20. Golo Mann, "Einführung," in Karl Heinrich Herchenröder, *Soziale Marktwirtschaft* (Düsseldorf: Handelsblatt, 1974), p. 17; see also Dagmar Deckstein, "Den alten Einheitsbrei mag niemand mehr," in *Süddeutsche Zeitung,* February 25, 1994.

21. For a cross-national comparison, see Klaus von Beyme, *Interessengruppen in der Demokratie* (Munich: Piper, 1991), pp. 75–79.

22. Tokunaga Shigeyoshi, "German and Japanese Industrial Relations: Similarities and Differences in a Historical Perspective," in Joachim Bergmann and Tokunaga Shigeyoshi (eds.), *Economic and Social Aspects of Industrial Relations* (Frankfurt: Campus, 1987), pp. 19–33 and Hirosuke Kawanishi (ed.), *Japan im Umbruch* (Düsseldorf: Bund, 1989), pp. 23–34.

23. Burkhard Strümpel, "Work Ethics in Transition," in Günter Dlugos et al. (eds.), *Management under Differing Labour Market and Employment Systems* (Berlin: de

Gruyter, 1988), pp. 121–132, see also for other studies Hans Christian Altmann, *Motivation der Mitarbeiter* (Frankfurt: Frankfurter Allgemeine Zeitung, 1989), pp. 118–131.

24. Heinrich Nicklisch, *Die Betriebswirtschaft* (Stuttgart: Poeschel, 1929), pp. 294–296.

25. John Stuart Mill, *Principles of Political Economy*, Volume 1 (New York: The Colonial Press, 1900), pp. 204–205.

26. Mill, *Principles of Political Eeconomy*, p. 202.

27. Ferdinand Tönnies, *Gemeinschaft und Gesellschaft* (Berlin: Curtius, 1926), p. 3.

28. Gosta Esping-Andersen, *The Three Worlds of Welfare Capitalism* (Cambridge, GB: Polity Press, 1990), p. 40.

29. Robert B. Reich, *Die neue Weltwirtschaft: das Ende der nationalen Ökonomie* (Frankfurt: Ullstein, 1993), pp. 301–310.

30. Walter Eucken, *Grundsätze der Wirtschaftspolitik* (Hamburg: Rowohlt, 1965), p. 179.

31. See publisher's draft of Robert Frank and Philip Cook, *The Winner-Take-All Society* (New York: Martin Kessler Books, 1994), p. 5; see also Jack Beatty, "Who speaks for the Middle Class?" in *The Atlantic Monthly*, May 1994, pp. 65–78.

32. Florian Coulmas, *Das Land der rituellen Harmonie* (Frankfurt: Campus, 1993), pp. 22–23, 37–39; see also Itsuko Teruoka, *Armes Japan: die Schattenseiten des Wirtschaftsgiganten* (Hamburg: Rasch und Röhrung, 1991), pp. 28–30.

33. For the standpoints of the interest groups see Heinz Jürgen Schürmann, "Suche nach einem neuen Konsens—Nationale Optionen sind begrenzt," in *Handelsblatt*, December 29, 1988, "Ohne Energie-Konsens keine Lösung des Klimaproblems," in *Die Welt*, August 13, 1991, "Energiekonsens," in *Handelsblatt*, March 3, 1994.

34. See an interview with Pankaj Ghemawat, "Commitment," in *The McKinsey Quarterly*, 3/1992, pp. 121–137.

35. For the German reception of communitarianism, see Thomas Gil, "Moralische Kontext—die Individualismuskritik des Kommunitarismus," in *Die neue Ordnung*, December 1993, pp. 462–467; Walter Reese-Schäfer, "Kommunitärer Gemeinsinn und liberale Demokratie," in *Gegenwartskunde*, 42/1993, pp. 305–317; Günter Rieger, "Wieviel Gemeinsinn braucht die Demokratie?" in *Zeitschrift für Politik*, 3/1993, pp. 304–332.

36. Marion Dönhof et al., *Weil das Land sich ändern muß* (Hamburg: Rowohlt, 1993), pp. 10ff; see also Helmut Schmidt, *Handeln für Deutschland* (Berlin: Rowohlt, 1993), pp. 20–21.

37. Werner Schiffauer, "Die civil society and der Fremde—Grenzmarkierungen in vier politischen Kulturen," in Friedrich Balke et al. (eds.), *Schwierige Fremdheit* (Frankfurt: Fischer, 1993), pp. 195–198.

CHAPTER 4

The Socioeconomic Foundations of Wealth

> The sovereign has not been placed in his high position and endowed with the highest power so that he can be lazy and suck the blood of his people. He is the first servant of the state. He is well paid, so that he can maintain the honor of his position, but for this he must work like all servants of state for the common good.
>
> —Frederick the Great, King of Prussia

In his political testament of 1752, quoted from above, Frederick the Great set the standard by which the rulers and administrators of Prussia would since be judged.[1] The many administrative changes carried out during his reign were well planned, modified to suit regional needs and efficiently implemented by a committed bureaucracy.

Frederick's father, the "Soldier King" Friedrich Wilhelm I, had laid the foundations for Prussia's meteoric rise from a provincial territory to a major power in Europe. The Soldier King's own father, Friedrich I, was a typically extravagant and pretentious potentate, who lived in a world of diamonds, trumpet-calls, and Spanish wigs. Friedrich Wilhelm buried him with all appropriate ceremony—and then "downsized" the establishment. He sacked most of the courtiers, delegated a large percentage of his personal staff to the army, radically reduced the royal life style and balanced his budget by selling unnecessary possessions. Most important of all: he personally supervised the administration.

Despite his youth—he acceded to the throne at the age of 25—the Soldier King quickly grasped the rudiments of wealth creation. He was no saint. The French historian Pierre Gaxotte describes him as "suspicious, brutal, stingy, despotic and pedantic." But he laid the basis for a certain attitude, which guided Prussia and later Germany through enormous catastrophes and allowed the country to recover with uncanny resilience.[2]

This attitude can best be described as a passion to serve the state, a willingness of those in high positions to work at least as hard as those they rule and with a high degree of compulsive perfectionism. It also meant that the monarch assumed responsibility not only for financial and military affairs but also for trade and transport—in short for all economic policies. Taxes were high and were used to improve agriculture and crafts.

Frederick the Great, as much a philosopher and musician as a statesman, inherited his father's dedication to state duty. He reformed the public service by reducing nepotism and emphasizing the importance of education. He was equally attached to the need for financial stability, though the state finances at the time were mostly expended in the upkeep of the army. In economic terms, his regime can be seen as both mercantilistic and cameralistic, favoring both a financial surplus reached through trade restrictions and state welfare achieved by a dedicated bureaucracy.

Prussian monarchs combined military strength with financial rectitude: "I am the field marshall and financial expert of the King of Prussia," said the Soldier King of himself. In other words, he was not only the first servant of the state: he served a higher ideal, that of a committed monarchy. "Travailler pour le roi de Prusse," working for the king of Prussia, was synonymous with an ascetic ethos: hard work, low salary.

This commitment has served as a model for administrative leadership in Germany ever since. Former Chancellor Helmut Schmidt, for instance, liked to speak of himself as the "leading employee in the country." He too has personified the ascetic, old Prussian virtues of efficient administration. The Prussian ethos will be examined in the chapter on cultural roots, compulsive perfectionism in the context of psychological roots.

THE KEY TO WEALTH CREATION: INFRASTRUCTURE

The Anglo-Saxon commitment to public service and welfare is more equivocal. Adam Smith certainly prescribed the state's "duty of erecting and maintaining certain public works and certain public institutions, which it can never be for the interest of any individual, or small number of individuals, to erect and maintain." Equally, the reformist John Stuart Mill differentiated between necessary and optional state functions. Significantly, for Mill, basic education belonged to the optional category.[3]

The individualistic slant of the classical school of economics led to the belief that free markets ensured public welfare. Though basic education now belongs to the necessary state functions, Great Britain and the United States have continued to relegate public-sector involvement to a residual role.

Figure 4.1
The Stable Deutsche Mark: Purchasing Power of Currencies

Index
1950 = 100

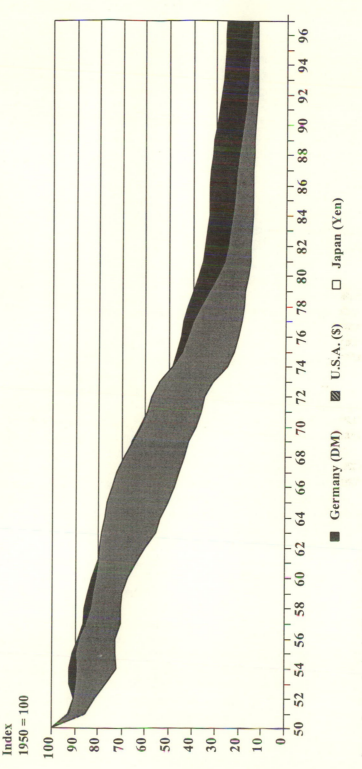

■ Germany (DM)   ▨ U.S.A. ($)   □ Japan (Yen)

Sources: Prognos, Institut für Wirtschaft und Gesellschaft

restricting credit in 1924, just as he later helped finance Nazi industrial policies with special bond issues.[9]

The Bundesbank officials are as cautious and consensus-oriented as their colleagues in government and private sector positions—and generally less outspoken than Pöhl, whose career started in journalism. While proclaiming the merits of Germany's "stability culture," the country's central bankers have often praised the fundamental consensus that supports the Bundesbank's policies. Thus, they also stress the social backdrop to stability.[10]

Nothing characterized the difference between the two Germanies before reunification as much as the roles of the two central banks. The Staatsbank in East Germany had a dual role: it was obviously subservient to government directives, though it did point out weaknesses in confidential reports. East German citizens yearned for a stable, convertible currency at least as much as for political freedom. The imposition of financial stability in reunited Germany has curbed growth in the East, while ensuring a uniform framework for development in both parts of the country.[11]

A GENERAL COMMITMENT TO STABILITY

The Bundesbank ensures monetary stability, while the federal government is responsible for measures to balance the budget. Though the recent rise in public debt resulting from reunification has seemed alarming in Germany, it is comparatively mild in international terms: the budgetary deficit in 1993 for instance represented 47 percent of gross domestic product, as against 65 percent in the United States and 66 percent in Japan.

Germany's banks are, as we have seen, important members of the "stability community." Both the private banks, which profit from the country's universal banking system, and the saving banks, who mostly finance small business, subscribe to stability rather than profitability at any price. Significantly, only two German banks belong to the twenty-five largest in the world, while thirteen are rated in the list of the world's twenty-five stablest banks.

While large universal banks like Deutsche Bank make international headlines, Sparkassen constitute the real backbone of German banking. Around 700 of these savings banks dotted all over Germany offer a complete range of banking services. Together with regionally organized clearing banks, they account for a market share of 40 percent. In a business climate that values stability rather than volatility, Sparkassen offer ultimate security: their liabilities are guaranteed by the regional authorities that own them.

The financial solidity of the average German corporation or enterprise certainly profits from the long-term loan strategies followed by the banks, as discussed in the chapter on business mentality. However, it also derives from the high extent to which German companies reinvest their profits. In this respect, Germany's business world shows a great degree of continuity: Siemens-Schuckert for instance financed half its investments out of profits in the first two decades of this century, while in the chemical sector, the ratio lay between 33 and 50 percent. As a result of this investment emphasis, the insolvency rate is far lower in Germany than in other industrialized countries.

Germany's citizens support the stability commitment of the banking community through their personal behavior:

- Surveys show that 43 percent of all Germans save money regularly and 34 percent do so irregularly, major motives being saving for emergencies and providing for the future.
- A large percentage of those who save favor risk-free investments: around 90 percent hold savings accounts and 65 percent have their own life insurance policies (in addition to the pensions that all employees automatically gain on retirement). Only 4 percent on the other hand are shareholders.
- The younger generation of Germans—those aged between eighteen and twenty-seven—also favor solid forms of investment such as building society savings contracts, life insurance policies and savings accounts.[12]

Stable real estate markets in Germany are as responsible for the remarkable solvency of private households as the consistently low rate of inflation. Individual debts rose from an average of 500 marks per person in 1970 to 4000 marks in 1992, but they still represent less than 10 percent of the annual incomes of the borrowers, as against 114 percent in Great Britain and 115 percent in Japan.

The government, the banks, corporations, and individuals: together they create the "stability culture" lauded by Gemany's central bankers. The Bundesbank can only impose its rigorously monetaristic policies because it can count on a general consensus. This contrasts vividly with the discrepancy between individual savings and financial sector profligacy in Japan. The Japanese private savings ratio is higher than in Germany. Simultaneously, however, Japanese banks are faced with enormous debts in the aftermath of the bubble economy of the late 1980s. This inconsistency contrasts with the overall emphasis on stability in Germany.

THE PITFALLS OF STABILITY

Stability has its price: in the banking sector, for instance, it has inhibited international competitiveness. A McKinsey study of international banking shows that Germany lags behind both the United States and Japan in terms of operating efficiency.[13]

Lean banking has become a catchword in Germany and major banks are adopting stringent rationalization strategies. Their operating costs however remain distinctly higher than elsewhere. Their emphasis on safe investments rather than profitability and their lack of experience in investment banking have led to a high degree of provinciality. Except for the Deutsche Bank, no German financial institution is a major international player.

Similarly, Germany's stock exchanges are still dormant by world standards, in terms of both equity issues and derivatives. Trading in futures and options has increased since 1990 with the founding of the Deutsche Terminbörse and new insider legislation has tightened control of the stock markets. However, as one foreign banker has commented: "The reform process will be typically German—step by step, stone by stone."[14]

In financial affairs, as elsewhere, change in Germany is an incremental process. The views of various institutions and interest groups—the government, the Bundesbank, private banks, brokers, regional stock exchange authorities— are integrated into decision-making. All have a stake in avoiding risk. *The contrast to Anglo-Saxon banking is evident: no Big Bang is ever likely to happen in Germany—and no fiasco either.* Innovative financial deals—mergers & acquisitions, demergers, management buyouts, and so on—are relatively uncommon. Germany's large corporations rather consolidate their holdings than trade with them.

One of the most ludicrous episodes in the contemporary German business world—and one that best illustrates the pitfalls of stability—is venture capital. In the early 1980s, buzzwords like high-tech-financing, seed money and co-venturing entered Germany from the United States.

Germany's financial world responded by founding the Deutsche Wagnisfinanzierungs-Gesellschaft (literally: German Venture Capital Corporation, DWG). twenty-nine banks united to contribute a share capital of fifty million marks. However, since the proposition of supporting high-tech enterprises seemed risky, the federal government took over 75 percent of the risk.

After spending 35 million marks of the taxpayer's money, the government refused to carry on subsidizing seed money. Upon this, the banks jettisoned the idea of supporting high-tech, wrote off all real and possible losses with the aid of the subsidies and forthwith applied their conventional principles of risk analysis to all new ventures. The "venture nothing financiers," as they were satirized in Germany, quickly retreated into the safety of traditional banking, which they had only half-heartedly left.[15]

DWG is the role model followed by a number of venture capital companies founded by banks and insurance companies. Thus, though thirty venture capital companies with seed money of 700 million marks have been founded, the list of innovative projects is tiny. The German stability mentality has proved disastrous to those involved in new ventures. The German approach to venture capital is in fact absurd, a parody of what this kind of financing is supposed to achieve.

FINANCIAL STABILITY AS A GLOBAL PRIORITY

Financial stability is of existential importance for Germany's economic order. Inflation or widespread speculation in the German context could lead to a radicalization of group conflicts, which the state—because of institutional arrangements such as tariff autonomy—would not be able to control or resolve.

The economist Alfred Müller-Armack, who coined the term "Social Market Economy," once pointed out that a country cannot remain a "stable island." It needs to be part of a "Stabilitätsgemeinschaft," a community of stability. The

European Union (EU) is predestined to be the Gemeinschaft that Müller-Armack called for. Monetary union and a European single currency are designed to achieve broad-based stability.

Significantly however, Germans lack faith in the EC's—more recently, the EU's—capability to guarantee monetary stability. As surveys have shown, public attitudes to a single European currency, the euro, are mostly skeptical. On the other hand, 90 percent of all Germans have great confidence in the Deutschmark.[16]

The siting of the European Central Bank in Frankfurt was not only a prestige issue for the EU's most powerful economy. For most Germans, it represents "a concept of stability that can be seen," as former Economics Ministry State Secretary Horst Köhler pointed out.[17]

Germans trust the Bundesbank more than any other monetary institution. The bank has also quietly accumulated enormous international prestige. Its severe monetary policies have been periodically criticized—the phrase "dictat allemand," for example, aptly characterizes French fears of Teutonic domination—but its persistence and reliability have gained widespread respect.

In recent years, the Bundesbank has become a role model for other central banks in the world:

- The Banque de France has recently achieved a greater amount of freedom from government intervention on the lines of the Bundesbank and is specifically committed to ensuring price stability.
- The Banca d'Italia has achieved more independence from the Italian government and closely cooperates with the Bundesbank.
- The Bank of England has also emulated the Bundesbank by emphasizing monetary stability and calling out for more central bank autonomy.[18]

Similar declarations of intent have been made by countries as different as Japan and Denmark. Whether this represents a cultural revolution (as Bundesbank president Hans Tietmeyer once pointed out) or whether countries like France are going through a process of cultural evolution (in the words of the French banker Jacques de Larosière) is a question of definition. Undisputable is that the Bundesbank has become a beacon of financial rectitude, and a role model for other central banks.[19]

German norms of financial stability have penetrated into the consciousness of decision-makers in different parts of the world on a deeper and more permanent basis than products or services could ever achieve. And the country that sets the norms is generally able to fulfill them better than the countries that follow them. However, as the decline of Great Britain—the country that pioneered and set the norms for the industrial revolution—has shown, the norm-setter's role can be transient, if it ignores danger signals and has a myopic or insular view of the world.

Individual sectors and companies in all countries are subject to a constant process of change and short-term economic growth is often affected by unpredictable and uncontrollable factors: the price of oil or a stock market crash, to name only two of the shocks suffered by the world economy in the

1970s and 1980s. While no economy can escape the consequences of future shocks, financial stability can help it resist, recover and readjust. *Monetary and fiscal solidity are in fact the foundation of balanced development—and a guarantee for the sustainability of economic policies.*

SECTION 2: EDUCATIONAL EGALITARIANISM

Formation and education: the breadth and depth of the word "Bildung" is the key to understanding Germany's unique educational infrastructure. Bildung involves far more than educating individual—it forms their characters and their views of the world.

Education in Germany seems like a paradox at first sight. On the one hand, Germany's uniquely practical system of vocational training is widely admired. On the other hand, its excessively theoretical type of university education based on the Humboldt legacy seems irrelevant and counterproductive in the contemporary world. One seems well adapted to the needs of business, while the other appears to be a quaint relic of a different epoch.

The epoch was that of the enlightenment and of romanticism. Educate and form thyself—"Bilde dich selbst"—demanded the pioneer pedagogue Wilhelm von Humboldt. This motto became an ethic for generations of scholars and scientists, comparable in its programatic implications to the "know thyself" dictum of the Oracle of Delphi. Kant and other philosophers of the enlightenment had linked education with ethics. The sheer quest of knowledge was not enough. Hegel deepened the amplitude of Bildung, requiring that it be a form of thought permitting reflection. Rather than acting on the basis of inclinations and desires, the individual ought to act according to general principles.[20]

All this sounds highly idealistic and unattainable. However, Hegel's emphasis on general principles—and on the importance of considering the general good rather than the particularity of personal interest—was imbibed by the higher echelons of the Prussian bureaucracy at the University of Berlin and elsewhere. In the chapter on business environment, the public service's vital role in wealth creation and distribution has been described. Administrative efficiency derived in Germany from the Prussian ethos of serving the common good—and from high educational standards.

At the same time, the schism between humanistic and practical education deepened. Humboldt considered hard work as anathema to Bildung. He approved of slavery because it released the free from the toils of monotonous activity. These were reactionary ideas even at the beginning of the nineteenth century. Humboldt had first-hand exposure to the industrial revolution during his stay in London as a Prussian diplomat in 1818–19, but he ignored the profound changes in the character of economic activity.

For Hegel, on the other hand, work was something real and a "positive formation of outside things," dialectically linked with the inner world of the individual. However, Hegel still favored theoretical as against practical Bildung. The one was organic, the other mechanistic. While favoring

Allgemeinbildung—general cultivation—these thinkers refused to consider technical, economic, and social aspects of education.

By contrast, vocational education fulfills ideas that were radically opposed to the humanistic elitism of Bildung. One vocational pioneer, Eduard Spranger, proclaimed that the way to Allgemeinbildung passed through, and only through, vocational education. According to him, the vocation of an adult crystallized his interests and gave him honor and consciousness, it created community and authority.

Spranger and vocational education's leading thinker, Georg Kerschensteiner, were canny enough to endow their educational ideas with a communitarian focus well suited to Germany's Zeitgeist in the early twentieth century. Kerschensteiner emphasized the need for community studies in addition to specialized and general knowledge. During a trip to America, he was inspired by the ideas of embryonic community life expressed by John Dewey. Later he sought to create structures of responsiblity within the vocational schools—various forms of self-administration—that would equip young people with the civic sense needed for their participation in a civic community.[21]

The reforms initiated by Kerschensteiner and others improved the curricula utilized by vocational schools. However, the civic community concept could not be fulfilled during the Republic of Weimar, though civic studies was added to the curriculum in all schools. Republican ethics could not be communicated in a largely reactionary atmosphere. And for obvious reasons, the spirit of civic responsibility was later anathema to the racial communitarianism preached and practiced by the Nazis. But the insight that vocation is the road to true education has gained general acceptance in Germany since Spranger and Kerschensteiner.

The struggle against the elitism of academia continued after the Second World War. One of Germany's leading vocational educationalists, Friedrich Edding, protested against the "Totalitätsanspruch des Akademischen," the totalitarian claims of academic education. Achieving a more egalitarian meeting ground between the academically and vocationally qualified remains a perennial priority for vocationalists.

VOCATIONAL EDUCATION: ORGANIC RATHER THAN MECHANISTIC

The Prussian welfare states of the Soldier King and Frederick the Great had already laid the foundations for a high general level of education. Compulsory schooling was introduced in 1717 and educational policies can best be described as both enlightened and concrete: designed both to improve the characters of Prussia's subjects and the quality of agriculture needed to nourish a large army.

By the beginning of the nineteenth century, the Germans were already the best-educated people in the world, as the historian Immanuel Geiss points out. The rate of literacy increased by 1870 to practically 100 percent, at a time when

England had just begun with its education act to impose compulsory schooling. Thus, education in Germany developed ahead of industrial progress, just as in England it lagged behind.

The roots of the Anglo-Saxon education problem—superb facilities for an elite coupled with mediocre or practically nonexistent training for broad sections of society—can be traced back to Adam Smith and to basic attitudes toward education and national wealth. In *The Wealth of Nations*, Smith applies his logic of selfish interest to vocational training: "The institution of long apprenticeships has no tendency to form young people to industry. An apprentice is likely to be idle, and almost always is so, because he has no immediate interest to be otherwise."[22]

The fatal consequences of this logic—Bernard Avishai very rightly refers to "the terrible genius of Smith's contract" in his *Harvard Business Review* article on business's educational role—are evident today. Neither the business community nor the state feels particularly responsible for vocational education and training in the United States and Great Britain. The logic of the division of labor involves simplified work skills for specified tasks. Why then, according to this logic, should the "people" (or rather the lower classes) be taught more than they reasonably need to know?

Beyond this, the classical school of economists and policymakers sees companies as artificial entities, as market players with a mission to maximize profits. The Anglo-American approach thus emphasizes mass production and low skills. Avishai quotes an auto supplier south of Detroit: "We send a $250,000 machine to a GM plant, and in six weeks it is trashed—it is like sending a Mercedes to Zaire."[23]

In Germany, on the other hand, vocational education has always been a national resource. As we have seen, Germany never adopted the division of labor as profoundly as the Anglo-Saxon countries. The guilds and their emphasis on craftsmanship exercized a profound influence on industrial labor. The worker played a vocational role in the workplace, he was not a cog in the wheel of industrial activity. The German approach to vocational education was thus organic rather than mechanistic.

During the nineteenth century, the vocational training that has contributed toward making the Mercedes and a multitude of other high-quality products was slowly developing. Manufacture and commerce was liberalized. Though this loosened the guild monopolies, vocational training still aimed at educating the "efficient journeyman." It was modeled on traditional craftsmanship training.

Slowly, the training horizons were enlarged. In 1821 for instance, regulations in the state of Sachsen-Weimar required the master craftsman to allow his journeyman further education in writing, drawing, and mathematics. Later, vocational schools systematically broadened the horizons of the average worker. These were the origins of Germany's unique dual system of vocational education: practical training at the workplace plus theoretical education at an outside school.

THE DUALITY OF PRACTICAL TRAINING AND THEORETICAL EDUCATION

The present system prescribes one or two days of obligatory state-financed schooling each week in addition to the hands-on training at the workplace. The schooling includes both specialized knowledge and a general introduction to other fields such as foreign languages and economics. After three to four years, the apprentice faces extensive examinations and then qualifies as a skilled worker or journeyman. Two-thirds of all Germans in employment have been through this rigorous training program.

This process gives young people early exposure to the working environment:

- They have to apply for apprenticeships in the same way that they later apply for jobs.
- They are soon expected to assume responsibility for various tasks in the companies they work for.
- They are provided with general knowledge to enable them to cope with the world outside the workplace.

This combination of competences integrates the individual and imbues him with a sense of responsibility. As one of Germany's leading vocational experts, Friedrich Edding, put it: "Praxis bildet," the practice of a profession forms the personality as much as it educates. And though 40 percent of all apprentices criticize the fact that they are often used as cheap labor, around 80 percent have positive attitudes toward their training.[24]

Standards vary in different sectors: most industrial companies and trading organizations have a written training plan, as against 54 percent of the craftsmanship enterprises. However, the craftsmen can guarantee the prescribed completion of the apprenticeship programme to a greater extent than the industrial and trading firms: only 6 percent of the apprentice-craftsmen fail to complete the prescribed curriculum as against 11 percent of the other apprentices. There are professions that excel in training such as the engine fitters and the bank and insurance clerks, while the training of other vocational groups—bakers, masons, and joiners—is considered substandard.

The general picture of vocational training in Germany is extremely positive, but has its price: the German state pays approximately thirty billion marks a year toward vocational education, while the business world faces a bill of around forty billion marks.

Vocational education ensures Germany's industries, trade, and service enterprises of a regular stream of qualified employees. As one U.S. observer has recently remarked: "The purpose of German training methods is not to turn out geniuses but to raise the ordinary talent of average people to a level of extraordinary competence."[25] This is the foundation for the high medium level of achievement, commented on in connection with business mentality.

Thus, while the United States has the largest percentage of workforce with university or equivalent qualifications—36 percent, as against 22 percent in

Germany and 17 percent in Japan—the Germans have a larger cross-section at the medium qualifications level of vocational training and school-leaving certificates: 61 percent, as against 48 percent in Japan and 46 percent in the United States.

More impressive than the statistics is the fact that most German companies have resisted slashing their vocational programs in spite of the serious recession in the early 1990s. The business community's commitment to providing qualified vocational training can be construed as a constructive approach to corporate citizenship. It represents an attitude of enlightened self-interest: former trainees often remain as employees. The apprentice system creates bonds of loyalty. The personnel fluctuation level in German banks, for instance, is only one-third as high as in the United States.

Upward mobility is also possible: approximately 10 percent of those with vocational qualifications study further in specialized schools and polytechnics. 15 to 30 percent of vocationally educated employees have later attained managerial positions: the CEOs of leading companies like the Deutsche Bank, Mercedes Benz, and Bosch all did apprenticeships before starting their careers.

Germany's business community considers training in general to be a top priority. The World Leadership Survey conducted by *Harvard Business Review* in 1991 revealed that German managers considered workforce skills to be their key success factor. For U.S. business leaders, customer service was paramount, for the Japanese, product development took first place.[26]

In recent years, vocational education has faced some challenges:

– In 1990, the number of students at Germany's universities surpassed that of apprentices for the first time: 1.8 million as against 1.5 million. This reflects the increasing academization of society.
– Large corporations in some sectors—for instance in the metal and electrotechnic industries—have been considering the reduction of their apprenticeship programs, because only 35–45 percent of apprentices stay in the companies as employees. These companies are moving toward appointing the graduates of polytechnics, whose education has been paid for by the state and who have often passed through apprenticeship before studying. This is however an exceptional phenomenon.
– The vocational schools lack qualified teachers and have been criticized for being too theoretically oriented.

The reunification of Germany has brought new challenges. On the one hand, the structure and substance of vocational education in East and West were similar. On the other hand, subjects like costing and marketing were ignored in East Germany for obvious ideological reasons. Seventy percent of East Germany's vocational schools were run by the companies in which apprentices worked. Their training was therefore strongly oriented toward the specific needs of the companies they worked for. This has impaired workers' flexiblity in adapting to the restructuring of entire industrial sectors. Significantly, however, craftsmanship skills are as well developed in East Germany as in the West.

Despite these problems, vocational education continues to thrive. Because of Germany's federal setup, state responsibility for education is partially national, regional, and communal. The business community codetermines policy through its trade associations, its chambers of commerce and chambers of craftsmanship. Employees' works councils also participate in policymaking.

The coordination of vocational education highlights the organizational efficiency of the German economy. The true value of Germany's vocational education is however not its operating efficiency but its contribution to social cohesion. By the time they finish apprenticeship, qualified workers are coopted into the working community. Characteristically, surveys show that some apprentices have complained that "secondary" virtues like punctuality and orderliness are stressed more than individualistic qualities like a sense of initiative and critical consciousness. However, the overwhelming majority had a positive attitude to their training.

The system of Meisters, journeymen, and apprentices ensures that the "ordo socialis" of the guilds lives on. *The individual gains a vocational identity through work and adheres to a social order based on commitment to vocation.* This is the fundament of the Mittelstandsgesellschaft, the estate-oriented society that has given contemporary Germany an unparalleled degree of shared prosperity and social stability.

UNSPLENDID ISOLATION AT THE UNIVERSITIES

The coherent structure of vocational education and its seasoned mixture of theory and practice contrast with a university setup that many observers consider close to catastrophic. The unsplendid isolation of the Humboldtian universities has provided public opinion with a succession of catch-words: educational emergency, teacher surfeit, student explosion. At Germany's universities, masses of students spend an inordinate amount of time in gaining degrees, but lack practical experience and a pragmatic focus toward the working world.

In the context of contemporary Germany's communitarian focus, the universities are odd dinosaurs. Their organizational structures and the privileges enjoyed by German professors—life-long tenure, high salaries, and light obligations—are contradictory to the tenets of an egalitarian society. In a country where responsibility is clearly defined and performance is severely monitored, the academic elite is absolved from these constraints to a great extent.

The academic performance of Germany's professors is mostly mediocre, a far cry from the days when German scholarship was renowned all over the world. Ironically, the inefficiency of the universities confirms the efficacy of the order through control ethos, which respected German institutions like the TÜV and the Bundesbank reflect. Lack of control has in fact led to substandard performance.

The management consultancy Kienbaum has repeatedly analyzed the situation at the universities and called for professional academic management on U.S. lines: sharper control and more emphasis on service. Similarly, the former president of Johns Hopkins University, Steven Muller, has called

Germany's universities the country's "Achilles' heel," also recommending restructuring according to the U.S. model.[27]

Such recommendations ignore both the cultural and structural weight of the German university tradition and the specific role that German universities play in the socioeconomic environment. Neither professors nor students are motivated to achieve excellence. Examination gradings are collective rather than competitive and university rankings of the kind carried out in the United States are virtually unknown. The emphasis is less on competitive achievement and more on passing through a process.

In the context of a business community characterized by impeccable mediocrity and of an egalitarian society—both aspects were analyzed in the course of the last two chapters—German universities play a logical role. They provide a growing supply of reasonably well-qualified graduates, capable of a middle level of achievement. *Since in the German context, it is the many that count and not the few, the universities unwittingly fulfill their role better than they are discerned as doing.*

Germany's polytechnics, which now educate roughly one-quarter of all students in Germany, are more pragmatic. Almost half the students at polytechnics have passed through vocational education before starting their studies, in contrast to 10 percent of all university students. The polytechnic graduates are obliged to do stints of practical training in the course of their studies and their education is well suited to business needs, as the results of one survey indicate. Thus, the polytechnics partially close the gap between eminently practical vocational education and ivory-tower Humboldtian universities.

LIFELONG LEARNING—ALIGNED TO MIDDLE LEVELS OF ACHIEVEMENT

In Germany, education is a continuing process for a broad cross-section of society. Each year, approximately one-third of all Germans participate in further education, up from one-quarter of all Germans in the late 1970s.

German companies account for almost half of all further education. Many corporate programs are aligned to teaching employees how to utilize new technologies. Beyond this, there are regional focuses: in East Germany, employees need to catch up with Western aptitudes, particularly in information technology. In the "rust bowl"—Germany's Ruhr region—education is aligned toward the structural change from coal mines and steel to high-tech and services. Corporate investment is massive: in 1992, German business spent over thirty-six billion marks on further educating staff, up from two billion marks in the early 1970s.

Parallel to this, a huge number of "People's Universities" (Volkshochschulen) dotted all over Germany—in cities, towns, and villages—cater to general interests, in particular the desire to learn foreign languages. The broad-based, regionally organized Volkshochschulen are particularly adapted to the needs of women, who represent approximately 70 percent of all participants. Subsidized to a great extent by the regional administrations, they provide a forum for various interests and promote lifelong learning.[28]

Here again, the accent is not on producing excellence but on roping in a large cross-section of the population into constructive activities. Typically for Germany's consensus approach to tackling policy issues, a "Concerted Action Lifelong Learning" is regularly organized on a national level. It coordinates educational activities and periodically redefines their focus. Contemporary Germany constantly attempts to adapt learning activities to technological, economic, and social changes—and to ensure a high level of general knowledge.

All this is not new. The famous soldier-philosopher Helmut von Moltke, chief of general staff during the wars that led to German unification in 1871, once pointed out: "Germany's strength is derived from the homogeneity of its population and true homogeneity cannot be induced by outside influence. It can only be brought about by what constitutes the mental and moral foundations of community life—by the education of the people."

As we have seen, Germany constitutes a working community rather than an anonymous labor market. Similarly, contemporary Germany is an educational community. Through vocational and lifelong education, Germans learn how to tackle work in an organized and systematic way.

The educational homogeneity in Germany has traditionally been far greater than the racial homogeneity, which the Nazis stupidly and brutally enforced. This is unsurprising in a centrally located country that has absorbed various waves of migration while retaining a continuity of social and educational norms.

Germany is a highly homogenous country both in social and educational terms. It is neither a "melting pot" nor a "salad bowl"—two common metaphors used to characterize U.S. society—and it is also not a community with strongly stressed ethnic ties as in Japan. *Germany is a secular, normative community, and education merges with familial socialization in ensuring cohesion. Education is in fact the deepest foundation of Germany's wealth.*

SECTION 3: TECHNOLOGICAL INCREMENTALISM

Just as the German word Bildung represents both education and formation, so also does the word Wissenschaft mean more than mere science. In Germany, science has traditionally been associated with the enlightenment, with the ideal of "Bildung durch Wissenschaft," literally: education through science. Science was not only intended to produce inventions and discoveries, but also to edify the individual.[29]

In contrast to the epoch-making founding of the University of Berlin, the early polytechnics and professional schools developed in the shadow of France's École Polytechnique. They were closer to craftsmanship than to scholarship. In the mid-nineteenth century however, Ferdinand Redtenbacher gave engineering a more theoretical and mathematical focus, while the Association of German Engineers (Verein deutscher Ingenieure, VDI) demanded equal rights and privileges for the technical institutes, which soon became universities. The technical universities were progressively equipped with mechanical and electrotechnical laboratories. However, U.S. universities were better equipped at the turn of the century and VDI lobbied for more investment in this area.[30]

Machine building could count on traditional craftsmanship skills. Progress in the more abstract natural sciences on the other hand was mostly achieved by a new type of research-oriented corporation. The chemical industry is a case in point. Companies like BASF and Hoechst started in the 1860s as small laboratories: BASF with a staff of thirty, Hoechst with six employees. These enterprises excelled by employing highly qualified and specialized personnel.

Through a constant process of specialized innovation, the German companies attained commanding positions on world markets. Progress was most dramatic in the dyes sector: in the early 1860s, BASF, Hoechst, AGFA, and the other German companies were insignificant market players. By 1870, they controlled 50 percent of the world market for dyes; by 1900, their market share increased to 90 percent.

At the turn of the century, scientific quality belonged as much to the national ethos as academic excellence. German was an international scientific language and scientific careers depended on research success. "Discover or perish" is an albeit exaggerated characterization of this ethos, just as "publish or perish" sums up the U.S. competitive ethos.

EMPIRICAL RATHER THAN ORGANIC

This ethos of scientific achievement has been replaced in present-day Germany by the medium level of achievement already described in economic and social contexts. *The spirit of discovery has been domesticated by the comfortable monotony of an egalitarian society.*

The social sciences in particular have lost their identity. The famous historic-hermeneutic approach followed by Max Weber, Werner Sombart, and many others has not been succeeded by any equivalent after the Second World War. *Germany's aptitude in organic thought, in perceiving the wholeness of economic and social endeavor, has declined.*

Contemporary social scientists have mostly copied and adapted Anglo-Saxon empiricism, just as the economists tend to be epigonic Keynesians and monetarists. They lack the historical understanding and universalist focus of their predecessors. Apart from Ralf Dahrendorf, none have international reputations. In the absence of the insights that an interdisciplinary approach can provide, social sciences in Germany seem trapped in a vicious circle of banality: uninspired questions as the point of departure to equally uninspiring research findings.

This is not an exclusively German problem. Peter L. Berger has criticized the undue abstraction and the pettiness of sociology in the United States However, the disappearance of the German "mandarins," as the great scholars and thinkers were called, and their replacement by mediocre empiricists, has been far more dramatic than in the United States.[31]

The natural sciences have retained a relatively high level of achievement. Germany's research orientation is long-term rather than utility-oriented: 20 percent of all R&D expenditure is for basic research, as against 13 percent in the United States and 12 percent in Japan.

Business already finances around 85 percent of all research carried out in Germany. Significantly, 20 percent of the corporate R&D budgets is invested in process innovations and a further 18 percent in production planning. This illustrates an incremental approach to innovation. The R&D director of Siemens, Germany's most innovative corporation in terms of patents registered, has pointed out that the country excels in "status quo" rather than in change-oriented innovations.[32]

Corporate R&D policies have come in for an increasing amount of criticism. Comparative studies of research strategies in the United States, Japan and Germany have come to the following conclusions:

- German researchers are too technology-driven and lack market orientation.
- German management shuns risk-taking and favors secure rather than innovative projects.
- State support for R&D, in particular subsidizing procedures, is bureaucratic.[33]

Such deficits are of course easily explainable in the context of a business mentality marked, as we have seen, by incremental improvement and formal perfectionism and a business environment that favors stability, cohesion, and consensus rather than dynamic risk-taking. Over-engineering rather than time-to-market strategies affects research as much as production. R&D departments possess the same specialized hierarchies as other departments.

Beyond this, German companies are slow to translate inventions into marketable products. Siemens developed the world's first fax machine, AEG the first flat screen for computers. However, Japanese companies successfully implemented and marketed the inventions.

Criticism in recent years has centered on the patent statistics: only 35 percent of all patents registered in Germany are of local origin, in contrast to 64 percent in the mid-1970s. Whereas the total number of patents registered has increased sizeably in both Japan and the United States, stagnation has been registered in Germany.

This stagnation is particularly dramatic in microelectronics. The number of patents registered yearly at the Patent Authority by local inventors decreased from 210 in 1980 to 170 in 1991, while those registered by Americans increased from 203 to 517, and those by Japanese inventors from 154 to 831.

Thus, even in its home market, Germany seems vanquished by its major competitors. Since the early 1980s, the German weaknesses in microelectronics, electronic data processing, and telecommunications have led to fears of a "high-tech crisis."

HIGH-TECH HYPE AND HYSTERIA

It is characteristic of the mental confusion of our age that the term high-tech has acquired a magical flavor without being convincingly defined. In German as in English, the term high-tech is a symbol for state-of-the-art, for the "technologies of the future." The question is: which technologies?

Answers vary widely, depending on the origin and interests of the observer. For many commentators, microelectronics is a synonym for high-tech and the chip serves as the symbol for a quantum leap in technology. Others include electronic data processing and telecommunications as being typical high-tech fields, yet others extend the purview of the word to bio and gene tech, new materials, laser technology, and so on The various technologies listed by think tanks like Battelle, Stanford Research, and Prognos vary as widely as their definitions of high-tech.[34]

More relevant seem definitions that include all technologies with a high percentage of R&D or with a great impact on economic success and social change. Broad parameters need to be defined for high-tech. Our own definition is that it constitutes state-of-the-art product and process technology in sectors with a sizeable impact on national wealth and social welfare (see Figure 4.2).

Since the early 1980s and the publication of Bruce Nussbaum's book on the high-tech explosion and its consequences, *The World after Oil*, Germany has lived in an almost constant state of high-tech hysteria. Nussbaum argued plausibly that Germany was lagging behind both the United States and Japan and would soon be eclipsed as an industrial power, because its strengths lay in nineteenth century technologies.[35]

In actual fact, while Germany clearly lagged in the spectacular high-tech sectors described by Nussbaum—robots, computers, telecommunications, gene tech—it excelled in other sectors like electronic process technology, medical technology, energy, traffic and ecological technology. These sectors tend to be less spectacular but are at least as important for the wealth of a nation. In fact, the futuristic hype about robots and gene tech, which finds prominent mention in the German media, is not matched by their tangible impact on national wealth. The impact of artificial intelligence and of experiments in outer space were for instance grossly overestimated in the 1980s.

The Germans excel in equipping state-of-the-art factories, in supplying medical equipment for hospitals, and in installing traffic control equipment. *Germany in fact revels in "communitarian" rather than individualistic technologies, in technologies that are evolutionary rather than revolutionary.*

In the introduction to this book, the reasons why Germany is an ecological champion and an electronic laggard were briefly explanied. Ecology, with its evolutionary approach to solving specialized problems, is well attuned to Germany's economic identity. Like energy production, another area in which Germany excels, it thrives on consensus. Electronics on the other hand, with its individualistic dynamism, thrives on cutthroat competitiveness.

High-tech deficits in Germany can be traced back to the business environment and to operating procedures in companies:

Figure 4.2
High-Tech Rankings: Germany Excels in "Communitarian" Technologies

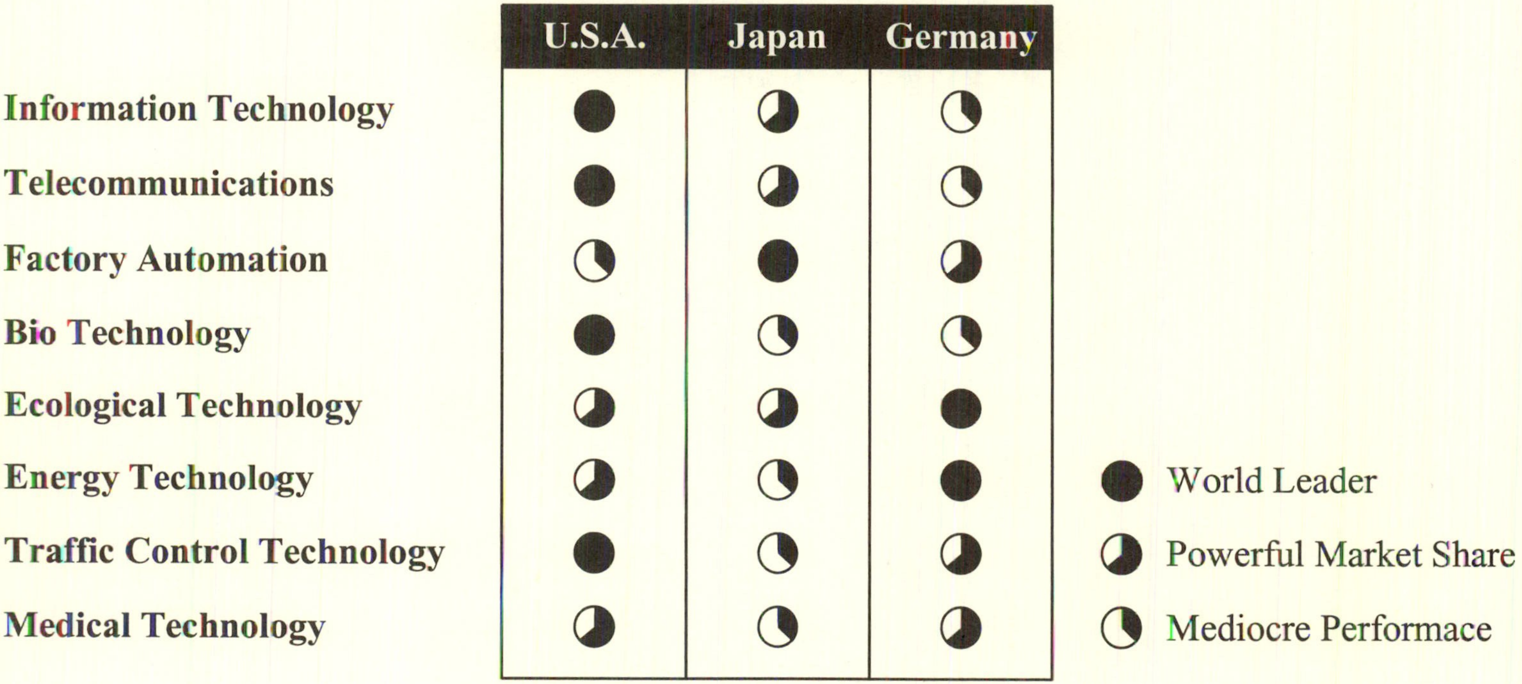

	U.S.A.	Japan	Germany
Information Technology	●	◑	◔
Telecommunications	●	◑	◑
Factory Automation	◔	●	◔
Bio Technology	●	◔	◔
Ecological Technology	◑	◑	●
Energy Technology	◑	◔	●
Traffic Control Technology	●	◔	◑
Medical Technology	◔	◔	◑

● World Leader
◑ Powerful Market Share
◔ Mediocre Performace

Sources: Prognos, Press Reports

Both trade unions and society have reacted reservedly to microelectronics, computers, and telecommunications, though attitudes are slowly changing.
- The German state has restricted research and applications in genetic technology for ethical reasons.
- The organization of German companies favors continuity rather than change: time-to-market in Germany tends to be three times as long as in the United States and Japan.

The SAP success story proves that German high-tech producers can make it internationally if they are properly focused and capable of dynamically expanding. SAP has become a world leader in standardized information systems that run on mainframes. Founded by a team of former IBM Germany employees, it focused on providing instant accessibility to all computerized data on orders, supplies and production. It expanded rapidly internationally and has in the meanwhile outfitted U.S. companies like Chevron, Intel, and Microsoft with broad-based information systems.

SAP is however the exception to the general rule: most of the other internationally successful German software producers have concentrated on products like sales software for Internet vendors, data transmission security systems, and graphic cards. Like the Mittelstand entrepreneurs in traditional technology areas like machine building, Germany's electronics enterprises have occupied market niches.

Media criticism of the German lag in cutting-edge technologies and public appeals to the business community to be more innovative tend to be superficial and short-sighted, because they ignore the socioeconomic and psychological roots of technological incrementalism. As we have seen, venture capital is a farce in Germany. Entrepreneurs are powerless without the initial loans provided by banks. The country's banks are interested in a stable return on investments and public opinion expects them to respect the norms of financial stability. This "virtuous circle" of mutual security is an intrinsic barrier to innovation.

High-tech does not exist in a vacuum. *A country's industrial profile reflects its economic Gestalt.* Thus, neither the hype nor the hysteria about high-tech deficits are justified.

Germany will continue to gradually assimilate rather than boldly adopt new technologies. In the short term, it will lag behind more technologically dynamic countries like the United States and Japan. In the long term, it will excel in specific applications of new technologies that are attuned to the specialized markets most German manufacturers compete in. It will also play a leading role in advanced technologies that suit the communitarian priorities of SME.

SECTION 4: CONTRASTS IN MOBILITY—THE TRANSPORT CONSENSUS AND THE COMMUNICATION GAP

The creation and distribution of national wealth are inconceivable without mobility. The physical movement of human beings and goods coupled with the mechanical or electronic movement of information constitute the backbone of economic exchange. The efficiency and imagination with which a country masters mobility is an integral part of its economic identity.

Neither efficiency nor imagination were visible in early nineteenth-century Germany. Werner Sombart poetically describes the rudimentary road conditions in the many German states of the time, emphasizing that travelers needed "a good constitution and Christian patience." The whole of Prussia only had 500 miles of paved roads and in cities like Berlin, there were only a few coaches. Public lighting was virtually nonexistent.[36]

In terms of mobility as much as in general economic terms, the German states were far behind England and France. While the quality and quantity of roads increased radically in the course of the nineteenth century, real progress came with the railways. As in the United States, industrialization and modern management methods were closely connected with railway transport.

The historian Alfred Chandler points out with regard to the railways: "In the 1870s the salaried managers in Germany perfected, even earlier than did their counterparts in the United States, the operating and organizational procedures needed to assure a steady, fast, regularly scheduled flow of goods over the new national, and increasingly international, network."[37]

The railways were pioneers of industrial organization. They were also symbols of public services. In the United States, their decline in the context of the automotive revolution reflected the triumph of individualism over community-oriented services. In Germany by contrast, railway services have been steadily improved, though their share of passenger traffic and goods transport has decreased in recent decades.

Punctilious efficiency characterized the administration of both Germany's railways and its postal services. Werner Sombart spoke of these services as constituting the "civil sections of the army" and one account of the postal services published in 1907 describes how the postmen worked with military discipline, responding to bells that signaled "Ready to march off."[38]

The reunification of Germany in 1990 revealed conditions in the East that were reminiscent of the early nineteenth century:

- 22 percent of the highways, 40 percent of all regional roads, and 68 percent of local roads were defective.
- 39 percent of all road bridges and 33 percent of all rail bridges were in a derelict state.
- 11 percent of all inhabitants were equipped with telephones, as against 50 percent in West Germany.
- A large percentage of the telecommunication switches dated back to the 1920s.

One report on telecommunications in East Germany was fitting entitled "A message from the dark side of the moon." Local area codes varied, depending on the area of the caller. Connections were so bad that it took four to five hours to send off a fax.

Meanwhile, East German telecommunications have radically improved. More than 25 percent of all inhabitants are equipped with telephones. The reliability of communications has been vastly improved through the laying of a fiberglass network. Fax and mobile telephones have integrated East Germany into the Western world of communication.

On the other hand, the attempt to introduce electronic mail to East Germany revealed a mindset that is typical for both parts of the country. As one pilot project showed, the East Germans were quick to learn how to operate the hardware and software. The key problem was that they mistrusted the medium and doubted its utility.[39]

A PEASANT-LIKE APPROACH TO MODERN COMMUNICATION

In their fears and apprehensions, the East Germans have followed in the footsteps of their West German countrymen. Electronic mail has been an enormous flop in West Germany, ever since its introduction in the early 1980s. The number of users both for professional and for private applications has lagged far behind countries like the United States and Great Britain. The invisibility of electronic mail—as against the visibility of telex and telefax— has militated against its use. Most Germans have found it difficult to understand and to trust a medium where messages are distributed by a computer into electronic boxes, which the receiver is supposed to empty.

Electronic mail is used to a greater extent in international companies, where corporate culture is more attuned to an open exchange of messages. But the specific creativity and flexibility needed to implement innovative e-mail applications are missing in Germany. As we have seen, the German corporate culture is too formalistic to encourage a free flow of electronic messages.

The same deficits are visible in the use of other value-added services such as online databases, videotex, and voice mail. Except for the banks, 75 percent of which use online databases both to quickly acquire market information and to offer their customers information brokerage services, use of these electronic libraries in Germany is sluggish. In spite of a growing number of databases, German business still relies on conventional forms of information and documentation.

Most companies complain of lacking information and advice on the various value added services. This reflects the technology-push rather than the demand-pull marketing strategies of most online vendors. As in the other sectors analyzed in the context of business mentality, German service-providers are more preoccupied with technical perfection than with pleasing customers.

By far the best example of this incapacity to operate customer-friendly value-added services is videotex. Germany introduced this interactive medium of information and communication at the same time as France. The French evinced brilliant marketing skills—the telecom authority distributed one cheap and user-friendly terminal free of charge to millions of households and offered an electronic telephone book as basic service. This stimulated a host of private services as varied as databases, games, and erotic correspondence. Videotex became an attractive form of information and communication for users of all age groups and professions.

The Germans on the other hand concentrated on perfecting the CEPT norm and on devising complex color graphics. They confused the potential user by offering a variety of different technical configurations and by changing the name of the service several times. Though in the meanwhile, basic applications like the electronic telephone book are also offered in Germany, the private market has remained sluggish. With approximately the same capital investment, the French achieved five million subscribers in the course of ten years, as against 500,000 in Germany. Thanks to telebanking, the number of videotex users in Germany more than doubled between 1993 and 1996. However, videotex usage remains restricted to specialized applications.[40]

Germany's telecom utility, which was responsible for the videotex flop, is substandard in terms of functional efficiency. As one comparative study shows, Deutsche Telekom lags behind both the Japanese NTT and deregulated U.S. utilities like Ameritech and Bell Atlantic in terms of personnel productivity (turnover per employee). With regard to capital productivity (turnover as against fixed assets) its performance is inferior to privatized utilities like British Telecom and the U.S. telecom companies on the one hand and to state-held utilities like France Telecom and the Swedish telecom authority on the other hand.[41]

The level of digitalization of both national and regional switching also lags behind other industrialized countries. In the old analog days, Germany's telephone system was considered one of the most efficient in the world, reflecting high standards of network maintenance. However in the context of digitalization, manual maintenance has become outmoded.

Germany's slow digitalization has proved to be a costly mistake: though telephone tariffs in Germany are higher than in many other industrialized countries, turnover per telephone connection is lower than in the United States, Japan, Britain, France, and Sweden. Statistics also show that it has more maintenance employees per installed telephone than the countries mentioned above.

The privatization of Deutsche Telekom is expected to increase efficiency and customer-friendliness. The state monopoly on voice and data transmission has already been curtailed to a great extent and a number of powerful private-sector consortiums are competing for lucrative market segments in digitalized networks and value-added services.

However, it remains to be seen whether liberalization can drastically improve the present situation: the inefficiency of telecom providers is in fact paralleled by the conservative attitudes of telecom users in Germany. Long after fax machines had spread across the corporate worlds in Japan and the

United States, German business held onto telex, while Deutsche Telekom made a futile attempt to promote teletex.

Telecom services do not exist in a vacuum: they react to business requirements as much as they create new potential applications. Above all, they reflect deeply rooted social values and attitudes.

Private usage of Internet has made sluggish progess. The vast majority of Germans have no interest in the "net of nets." The percentage of those who log onto Internet at least once a week is four times as high in the United States.[42]

Germans are avid users of telecommunications when initial distrust has been overcome and when the communication process is simple, as with mobile telephones. In terms of mobile telephone installment, Germany has expanded enormously in the early 1990s, catching up on the European market leader Great Britain. It is a pioneer-developer of the international GSM transmission standard for mobile communication. The business world has also efficiently implemented procedures like electronic banking and electronic booking systems, which basically rely on standardized machine-machine communication.

Technologies that on the other hand require an interactive input on the part of the users, like online databases, or that feature novel forms of communication, like electronic mail, tend to fail in Germany, because they repudiate established procedures and organizational parameters. They also demand a zest for experiment, for trial and error, that is painfully lacking in Germany.

Thus, Germany can fittingly be described as a peasant communication culture. The German saying, "what the peasant doesn't recognize, he doesn't eat," seems well applicable to the communication habits of the country at large. Managers and specialists use sophisticated equipment without having grasped what modern communication is really about. *Communicative behavior mirrors the German emphasis on stability rather than dynamism.*

A PROFESSIONAL APPROACH TO TRANSPORT ORGANIZATION

Germany's inaptitude in communications contrasts with a high degree of professionality in the transport sector. The country's central location in Europe and the needs of an advanced economy have created a critical situation both on the highways and for the regional road networks. In the past four decades, road traffic has expanded exponentially. An increasing number of Traffic Information and Navigation systems (TIN), such as Park & Ride terminals and motorway signs are helping city planners cope with traffic jams and reroute vehicles.

The most productive aspect of traffic control is the cooperation between auto producers like Mercedes Benz and BMW, car component manufacturers like Bosch and electronics producers like Siemens and AEG. These corporations interact with various institutions in the public sector and experts at universities and research institutes.

Traffic management has become an issue on which ecological considerations, the promotion of efficient mobility and market potential merge. German business has a vested interest in improving road transport: alone in terms of TIN-equipped cars, market potential is estimated at forty billion marks. On the other hand, since traffic jams are estimated to cost as much as twelve billion marks a year, efficient traffic management is a public issue. Beyond this, Germany's Automobile Manufacturers Association has pledged to reduce gasoline consumption by 25 percent until the year 2005. Thus, the automobile industry and its suppliers are under pressure to produce tangible improvements.

In effect, both financial and ecological considerations favor the coordinated use of advanced technology rather than the construction of new roads. Germany's central government is investing six billion marks in an attempt to improve traffic capacity on the existing road network by 15 to 30 percent through TIN systems. In particular the harmonization of road, rail, air, and ship transport is an official priority in Germany.

Germany's impressive traffic management schemes have less to do with futuristic technology and more with the combination of organizational skills and technical proficiency that is at the core of its business mentality. Down-to-earth innovations in regional traffic like the "Stadtbahn," for instance, bring more tangible results than spectacular technological projects like the "Transrapid."

The Karlsruhe Stadtbahn involves a specially constructed city-tram that runs on both tramlines and railway lines. The tram-train, which switches between the different energy sources, communication equipment, and security precautions of local and long-distance transport, was built by ABB in cooperation with the local traffic authority and with a subsidy from the Federal Ministry of Research. State-of-the-art electronics ensures automatic switching in the tram-train.

The tram-train is a path-breaking link between local and long-distance travel. Commuters can travel through the city of Karlsruhe and then reach destinations in the region around the city without changing vehicles.

The Stadtbahn project is successful: five times as many passengers use the new facilities. Project manager Dieter Ludwig, Karlsruhe's director of transport, emphasizes that the Stadtbahn is a "Gemeinschaftsaufgabe," a communitarian task. Indeed, the real achievement lies in the cooperation between a private company, the Bundesbahn, the regional transport authority, and public administration at the central, state, and local levels.[43]

By contrast, the "Transrapid" project is a highly controversial example of "techno-euphoria." The first model of a planned magnetic train network was presented as early as 1971. In the 1980s, the Transrapid system was built by leading corporations like Siemens and AEG. It reached speeds of around 400 kilometers an hour on test routes. In 1993, the federal government accepted the industry's proposal, whereby the state is to construct the rail infrastructure, while a consortium of industrial companies and banks finance train manufacturing.

Investments in infrastructure for the Transrapid will be massive, since an entirely separate network of rails and platforms has to be constructed. The incompatibility of the magnetic trains to the existing railway system is a serious deficiency. The fact that Germany is apparently ahead of the United States and Japan in magnetic technology hardly justifies the expenditure.

As the chief economist of a leading automobile corporation points out: "The Transrapid project has nothing to do with infrastructure. It is clearly designed to demonstrate German technological excellence." Thus, its function is that of a "made in Germany" showcase, rather than a constructive improvement of transport facilities.[44]

The Transrapid is a typical example of a technology-driven rather than community-oriented project. It ignores the true priorities of improving existing infrastructure, in particular coordinating the logistics of passenger and freight transport by road and rail. Fortunately, it is an aberration rather than a typical project.

Germany has continuously invested in transport infrastructure, in roads and bridges, railway lines and logistic centers. The overall quality of its infrastructure is far superior to that of the United States, where interstate highways and mass car production led to a decline of the railroads. More recently, official neglect has allowed roads and bridges to deteriorate, most prominently in the country's capital. Tokyo's roads and bridges are in far better condition than Washington's. However, regional transport in Japan is substandard, whereas in Germany, the entire country enjoys the same high standards of transport services.

TRANSPORT CONSENSUS AND COMMUNICATION CONFUSION

Germany has made vast strides toward developing a coherent approach to the transport issue. Partisan interests are slowly retreating into the background. Ideological debates are being steadily replaced by pragmatic policies.

Automobile corporations openly advocate the synchronization of private and public transportation. As one automobile corporation executive points out, traffic jams are a sign of bad organization. Self-interest is prompting companies like BMW and Mercedes Benz into traffic coordination and other projects that have little to do with their core business.

Similarly, the Automobile Manufacturers Association has founded a transport round table with the intention of integrating all relevant interest groups into a constant discussion of transport policies. So far, the way to a consensus has been blocked by maximalist demands on the part of the ecological associations, but traffic optimization rather than transport restrictions will ultimately prevail.

The beneficial effects of the eco consensus—air pollution has been reduced, though energy consumption has risen—will be paralleled by those of a new transport consensus. It seems likely that Germany will progressively reduce both traffic jams and pollution in spite of an increased volume of transport.

Advances in road security indicate that such achievements are possible: in spite of the lack of speed limits on Germany's highways and of rising traffic volume, the total number of accidents on Germany's roads has decreased from 530,000 injured and 19,000 dead at the beginning of the 1970s to 450,000 and

8,000, respectively, in the late 1980s. The "social costs" of traffic, as they are entitled in Germany, are constantly being reduced.

A social consensus already exists on the need to optimize traffic: one survey indicates that 80 percent of all Germans would welcome improvements in public transport and in traffic coordination. Two-thirds of those interviewed favor electronic information and navigation systems and half would be ready to install electronic apparatus in their own cars. Another survey indicates that half of all West Germans—but significantly only 39 percent of all East Germans—feel that for ecological reasons, cars should be abolished.[45]

Thus, public opinion exerts pressure on the protagonists of interest groups to arrive at a consensus. Here again, there are obvious parallels to the eco and energy consensus mechanisms described earlier. As we have seen in the chapters on business mentality and business environment, the search for a consensus represents a gradualist approach to economic progress, one aligne:d to the technological incrementalism described earlier in this chapter.

The success of the consensus approach depends on the sector involved. Transport is inevitably consensus-oriented, since infrastructure capacity is limited and traffic jams visibly affect all concerned. *Traffic management is in the German context a means of imposing order.* The consensus on policies and procedures of traffic management relies on private sector commitment reinforced by pressure from the state and from public opinion. This basically is the same success recipe as with ecology.

Communication on the other hand is a dynamic sector favoring individualistic solutions. *Germany's lack of creative dynamism, its nearness to a craftsmanship rather than a mercantile ethos inevitably makes it a me-too user of communication technologies and applications pioneered elsewhere.*

Germany's unique skills in planning, organizing, and coordinating complex processes predestine it to excellence in synchronizing highways, railways, and airways, but nothing in its economic history or its social norms favors telecommunication. Seen in a larger context, the one is as inevitable as the other: instinctive excellence and epigonic mediocrity.

INFRASTRUCTURE: THE BACKBONE OF BALANCED DEVELOPMENT

Order and commitment, the two major qualities that characterize Germany's business mentality and business environment, are closely linked to the stability of socioeconomic foundations:

- Financial stability results from the order established by the Bundesbank and the "stability commitment" of Germany's financial lobby, corporations, and private citizens.
- Educational stability builds on the complex organization of vocational education and the commitment of the participating corporations, associations and individuals.
- The quality of Germany's transport infrastructure derives from the commitment of city planners, car manufacturers, and environmental activists.

Equally, we have discovered the limits of order and commitment in sectors like telecommunications, where dynamic, individualistic strategies and actions are necessary. Information highways and value-added networks upset the existing order inside and outside corporations. They stimulate a free flow of communication rather than an orderly succession of messages. Thus, user strategies lack commitment and are ineffective.

Order and commitment favor the solid rather than the spectacular, the weaning of collective potential rather than individual brilliance, of gradual progress rather than dynamic growth. *The "spirit of Germany" is that of infrastructure rather than suprastructure, of productive potential rather than headlong growth.*

Why did Germany, a late-comer to industrialization with neither the home market, the natural resources, nor the immigrant potential of the United States, succeed so spectacularly with its industrial revolution at the turn of the century, surpassing the industrial pioneer, Great Britain? Why did it rise like a phoenix from the ashes in the 1920s and 1950s after two ruinous wars?

A succession of individual achievements cannot explain the collectivity of a nation's wealth and the continuity of economic progress. *The infrastructure of a country is the foundation of its collectivity and a mirror of its continuity, of its capability to build brick upon brick and to patiently reconstruct the destroyed and refashion the decayed.*

Infrastructure in Germany is not just capital invested in public works and utilities. It is a moral imperative, the symbol of a basic commitment to wealth's foundations. Financial stability supports the policy balance of economic and social priorities, while educational egalitarianism is a precondition for the balance of responsibility between the business community and organized labor. *Germany's continuing commitment to infrastructure is the backbone of balanced development. Its mastery of balance is closely linked to its fixation with wealth's foundations.*

NOTES

1. Cited in Otto Hintze, "Das politische Testament Friedrich des Großen von 1752," in his book, *Geist und Epochen der preussischen Geschichte* (Leipzig: Koehler & Amelang, 1943), p. 474.

2. Pierre Gaxotte, *Friedrich der Große* (Frankfurt: Propyläen, 1974), p. 13; see also Theodor Schieder, *Friedrich der Große* (Frankfurt: Ullstein, 1986), pp. 300–302.

3. Smith, Bentham and Mill quoted and cited in Thomas Schulze, *Infrastruktur als politische Aufgabe* (Frankfurt: Lang, 1993), p. 83.

4. For Hirschman, see Schulze, *Infrastruktur als politische Aufgabe*, p. 41; see also Egon Matzner, *Der Wohlfahrtsstaat von morgen* (Frankfurt: Campus, 1982), p. 126; for Jochimsen, see Reimut Jochimsen, *Theorie der Infrastruktur* (Tübingen: Mohr, 1966), pp. 100–101.

5. Walter E. Diewert, *The Measurement of the Economic Benefits of Infrastructure Services* (Berlin: Springer, 1984), pp. 128–130; see also Michael Reidenbach, *Verfällt*

die öffentliche Infrastruktur? (Berlin: Deutsches Institut für Urbanistik, 1986), pp. 11–13.

6. Adam Smith, *An Inquiry into the Nature and Causes of the Wealth of Nations* (Oxford: Clarendon Press, 1976), p. 320.

7. The arguments mentioned here are gleaned from a revealing paper by Charles P. Kindleberger, "A Structural View of the German Inflation," in his book *Keynesianism vs. Monetarism and Other Essays in Financial History* (London: George Allen & Unwin, 1985), pp. 247–266.

8. Kindleberger, *Keynesianism vs. Monetarism and Other Essays in Financial History*, p. 255.

9. Pöhl is quoted in David Marsh, *Die Bundesbank* (Gütersloh: Bertelsmann, 1993), pp. 224–225 (Marsh gives several examples of governments that were toppled by Bundesbank policies); for Schacht, see Harold James, "Did the Reichsbank Draw the Right Conclusions from the Great Inflation?" in Gerald D. Feldman (ed.), *Die Nachwirkungen der Inflation auf die deutsche Geschichte, 1924–1933* (München: Oldenbourg, 1985), pp. 211–231.

10. See in this connection the speech of Ottmar Issing, "Standortfaktor Stabilität," published in *Deutsche Bundesbank: Auszüge aus Presseartikeln*, January 30, 1992; see also Hans Tietmeyer, "Geldpolitik der Bundesbank und Zinsen," in *Deutsche Bundesbank: Auszüge aus Presseartikeln*, October 29, 1993 and a statement from Tietmeyer in *Börsen-Zeitung*, April 5, 1995.

11. David Marsh, *Die Bundesbank*, pp. 268–271.

12. For statistics, see Statistisches Bundesamt (ed.), *Datenreport 1992* (Bonn: Bundeszentrale für politische Bildung, 1993), pp. 131–133; see also the survey *Debit and Credit* (Hamburg: Spiegel Verlag, 1993), pp. 9–16.

13. Heino Fassbender, "Die schlanke Bank der Zukunft erreicht mehr Kundennutzen bei weniger Kosten," in *Handelsblatt*, May 13, 1993.

14. Quoted in Wendy Cooper, "The Finanzplatz Fairy Tale," in *Institutional Investor*, May 1992, p. 36; see also Allan Saunderson, "Germany: Financial Powerhouse Starts to Take Shape," in *Euromoney* 12/1992, pp. 74ff.

15. See in this connection "Venture Capital—Spin Off und Buy Out," in *WirtschaftsWoche*, November 9, 1984.

16. See "IFO-Umfrage: Die Akzeptanz sinkt," in *Handelsblatt*, October 9–10 1992; see also Alfred Müller-Armack et al., *Stabilität in Europa* (Düsseldorf: Econ, 1971), pp. 17–21.

17. Quoted in Rolf Obertreis, "Am Main steht für die Euro-Zentralbank alles bereit," in *Der Tagespiegel*, October 12, 1993.

18. For France, see David Buchan, "France Gets its Bundesbank, But a Gallic One," in *Financial Times*, May 12, 1993; see also Jean-Pierre Robin, "Vers l'indépendance de la Banque de France," in *Le Figaro*, January 22, 1993; for Italy, see "Banca d'Italia wird unabhängiger," in *Börsen-Zeitung*, August 10, 1993; for Britain, see Peter Norman and Richard Lambert, "A Steady Hand at the Helm, in *Financial Times*, July 1, 1993, and Gavyn Davies, "Accountable Old Lady," in *The Independent*, June 28, 1993.

19. Tietmeyer quoted in "Kulturrevolution," published in *Frankfurter Allgemeine Zeitung*, March 26, 1994; Larosière in Peter Gumbel, "French Bank Steers Course for Autonomy," in *Wall Street Journal*, January 20, 1993; see also comments on Japan in David Marsh, *Die Bundesbank*, p. 23, and on Denmark in David Marsh, "Something Agnostic in the State of Denmark," in *Financial Times*, July 16, 1993.

20. See in this connection a short extract from Hegel, "Erziehung und Bildung," in Albert Reble (ed.), *Geschichte der Pädagogik*, Dokumentationsband II (Stuttgart: Klett,

1971), pp. 325–326; G.D. Schlossarek, *Wandlungen des Bildungsbegriffs im 19. und 20. Jahrhundert* (München: Bergstadtverlag, 1957), pp. 20–25.

21. Fritz Blättner, *Geschichte der Pädagogik* (Heidelberg: Quelle & Meyer, 1968), pp. 296–299.

22. Adam Smith, *An Inquiry into the Nature and Causes of the Wealth of Nations*, Volume 1 (Oxford: Clarendon, 1976), p. 139.

23. Bernard Avishai, "What is Business School's Compact?" in *Harvard Business Review*, January-February 1994, pp. 38–48; for quotes see pp. 42, 44.

24. Jürgen Baumert et al., *Das Bildungswesen in der Bundesrepublik Deutschland* (Hamburg: Rowohlt, 1990), pp. 344–345.

25. Peter Roma, president of a New York investment bank, quoted in *Fortune*, April 22, 1991, p. 61.

26. Rosabeth Moss Kanter, "Transcending Business Boundaries: 12,000 World Managers View Change," in *Harvard Business Review*, May-June 1991, p. 155.

27. Sabine Etzold, "Mißwirtschaft an der Uni," in *Die Zeit*, May 29, 1992; Steven Muller, "Vergessene Bildung," in *Die Zeit*, September 10, 1992; Dirk Horstkötter and Melanie Volberg, "Prinzip Hoffnung," in *Capital*, 5/1993, pp. 101–103.

28. Helmuth Dolff (ed.), *Die deutschen Volkshochschulen* (Düsseldorf: Droste, 1979), pp. 11–16.

29. Ludwig Huber, "Bildung durch Wissenschaft—Wissenschaft durch Bildung," in Heinrich Bauersfeld and Rainer Bromme (eds.), *Bildung und Aufklärung* (Münster: Waxmann, 1993), pp. 163–173.

30. Lars U. Scholl, "Die Entstehung der Technischen Hochschulen in Deutschland," in Walter Twellmann (ed.), *Schule und Unterricht als Feld gegenwärtiger interdisziplinärer Forschung* (Düsseldorf: Schwann, 1985), pp. 700–713.

31. Peter L. Berger, "Sociology: A Disinvitation?" in *Dialogue*, 4/1993, pp. 38–42.

32. Rainer Nahrendorf, "Bessere Standortbedingungen können die Gefahr der Zweitklassigkeit bannen," in *Handelsblatt*, June 16, 1993; see also Renate Mayntz, "Förderung und Unabhängigkeit der Grundlagenforschung im internationalen Vergleich," in *Berichte und Mitteilungen 1/1992*, Max-Planck-Gesellschaft, Munich.

33. See "Die großen Drei im Test," in *Manager Magazin* 10/1988, pp. 185–197; "Die Triade im Test," in *Manager Magazin* 10/1988, pp. 218–229; "Die Zeitfalle," in *Manager Magazin* 1/1989, pp. 84–94; see also "Die große Flatter" in *Manager Magazin*, 6/1993, pp. 163–170, and Jürgen Berke et al., "Todesurteil auf Raten," in *WirtschaftsWoche*, October 22, 1993.

34. Thomas M. Kabierschke, Battelle, *Die zehn wichtigsten Schlüsseltechnologien der 90er Jahre* (manuscript of a talk held in Bonn on May 4, 1988); see also the Prognos study, *International High Tech Report* (Basel, March 1990), and details of a Stanford Research Report published in *Manager Magazin* 3/1990, pp. 188–193; see also the Fraunhofer ISI-Institute's definition in Heinrich Revermann, *Schlüsseltechnologien* (Berlin VDE, 1987), p.9; the new definition was developed by the author in the course of a book on high-tech, see Kaevan Gazdar (ed.), *High-Tech Handbuch* (Bonn: Economica 1992), pp. 9–14.

35. Nussbaum's views have been rehashed and placed in the perspective of the 1990s by Konrad Seitz, *Die japanisch-amerikanische Herausforderung* (München: Bonn Aktuell, 1994); Seitz also wrote the introduction to the German edition of Nussbaum's "The World after Oil."

36. Werner Sombart, *Die deutsche Volkswirtschaft im 19. Jahrhundert and im Anfang des 20. Jahrhunderts* (Darmstadt: Wissenschaftliche Buchgesellschaft, 1954), pp. 3–4, 18–19.

37. Alfred D. Chandler, Jr., *Scale and scope* (Cambridge, MA: Harvard University Press, 1990), pp. 411–412.

38. Johannes Bruns, *Das Postwesen—seine Entwicklung und Bedeutung* (Leipzig: Teubner, 1907), p. 89.

39. Klaus Richter, "A Message from the Dark Side of the Moon," in *Information Management,* 3/1991, pp. 60–65.

40. Detailed information on German experience with value added service features in a book written by the author, see Kaevan Gazdar, *Informationsmanagement für Führungskräfte* (Frankfurt: Frankfurter Allgemeine Zeitung, 1989).

41. See Torsten J. Gerpott and Rudolf Pospischil, "Internationale Effizienzvergleiche der DBP Telekom," in *Zeitschrift für betriebswirtschaftliche Forschung,* 4/1993, pp. 366–389.

42. See "Neue Kommunikationsmittel werden noch kaum genutzt," in *Blick durch die Wirtschaft,* September 17, 1996, and "Die Mehrheit der Deutschen nicht am Internet interessiert," in *VDI Nachrichten,* May 17, 1996.

43. Roland Kirbach, "Schienen in die Zukunft," in *Die Zeit,* May 6, 1994.

44. This observation was made in a personal conversation with the author on May 17, 1994; for criticism of the Transrapid project, see Winfried Wolf, *Eisenbahn und Autowahn* (Hamburg: Rasch und Röhring, 1992), pp. 479–486, and Rolf Kreibich, "Flop statt Knüller," in *Die Zeit,* April 22, 1994.

45. See the survey Auto, *Verkehr und Umwelt* (Hamburg: Spiegel Verlag 1993), pp. 26–30.

CHAPTER 5

The Cultural Roots of Order and Commitment

Men are born to work, just as the birds are born to fly.

—Martin Luther

Germany has often been characterized as a country lacking a revolution: a drastic change of the old order as in the French and American revolutions or a more evolutionary change as in England's Glorious Revolution. In actual fact, Germany's religious Reformation was less spectacular but more profound. Its great Reformer, Martin Luther, founded a work ethic that the sentence quoted above sums up.

Luther's profound importance for German history lies in his fateful distinction between the power of the state and the freedom of the soul. "The laws of worldly rule do not cover more than bodies, properties, and other worldly things. God will not tolerate anyone other than himself to rule over the soul," he observed in his tract on the "Legitimation of Worldly Authority," published in 1523. He thus founded two worlds: that of the outside and of the inside. The inner world of the soul—Innerlichkeit—is the key to German cultural identity.

Worldly authority should not dictate the life of the soul. Conversely, the reformer calls on believers to accept and support worldly power—and if necessary to suffer injustice without actively resisting.

No state could ask for a better distribution of responsibility. Luther's revolution established an inner community of faith, firmly committed to supporting state-imposed order. *The Lutheran faith created the spiritual foundation for the Prussian ethos.*

Adhering to this logic, Luther supported the rulers against the peasant revolt, calling on state authority to exterminate the peasants like vermin. His own mission was a "peasant revolt of the spirit," as the philosopher Friedrich Nietzsche pointed out. The Lutheran credo was seriousness rather than sophism, service rather than self-enrichment.

Its emphasis on substance rather than ceremony was far removed from Italy's mixture of the easygoing, the cynical, and the corrupt. Luther detested the Roman Catholic style of Christianity because he was himself a peasant. Instinctively, he loathed Latin urbanity with its ornate ceremonies and its wise sense of relativity—and struck a chord in his equally peasant-like countrymen.

CULTURE RATHER THAN CIVILIZATION

Lutheran Protestantism is an important source of "Kultur." In his impressive study of the process of civilization, Norbert Elias observes that the German word for culture emphasizes the differences between nations, so that the question "What is typically German?" can be answered. The English word "civilization," on the other hand, concentrates on factors that link groups or nations.[1]

Elias discerned the link between civilization and countries with established national traditions like England and France. Germany on the other hand, lacking this natural sense of nationality, has constantly explored its own cultural identity.

This has consequences for culture's importance. Helmuth Plessner, like Elias a perceptive observer of cultural identity, once observed that the word Kultur cannot be translated by words like civilization, cultivation and so on. According to him, these terms are too sober, too flat, too "Western": "They lack the heaviness, the pregnant meaning, the soulful pathos that German consciousness in the nineteenth and twentieth centuries has associated with the word Kultur and that makes its emphatic usage understandable."[2]

Today, Germany's pride in being a "Kulturnation" is played down for understandable reasons. It is associated with the distasteful arrogance of former times. However, cultural events and issues enjoy a great amount of prestige and are taken very seriously. Contemporary Germany subsidizes culture—in particular classical music, theaters, and museums—to a greater extent than elsewhere.

Beyond this, Germany's ordoliberalism is more culturally oriented than neoclassical economics—or Keynesianism for that matter. Its theorists considered economic order to be a cultural achievement. The economist Alfred Müller-Armack in particular, who invented the term Social Market Economy (SME), stressed the interconnections between religion and national economy. Similarly, Kurt Biedenkopf, one of Germany's prominent politicians, has highlighted the importance of a high level of education and a high degree of consensus for the achievement of economic order.

SECTION 1: THE PRUSSO-PROTESTANT MOLD AND THE RHENISH-CATHOLIC FULCRUM

Protestantism was the cultural foundation of the Prussian state's moral mission. Though the Prussian kings were Calvinists rather than Protestants and though Frederick the Great mocked Luther's wildness, he adhered to the reformer's belief of the will's lack of freedom, opposing Voltaire on this issue. The compulsive passion to serve the state already described in connection with the socioeconomic foundations of wealth is rooted here. Equally so, the success—as also the severity and inflexibility of Prussian order—are derived from the Calvinistic energy of its rulers and the Lutheran loyalty of those ruled.

The more Calvinistically influenced Anglo-Saxon countries have always emphasized the representation of interests rather than the achievement of higher goals. Thus, their polities have automatically been more civically oriented, aligned to the rights and interests of their citizens as individuals. Germany on the contrary has remained tol the present day more a moralistic community than an urbane society.

In his famous analysis *The Protestant Ethic and the Spirit of Capitalism*, Max Weber stresses the relationship between the inner asceticism of the Calvinists and their economic rationality. Earning a living became a primary duty for the individual.

Lutherans also had a sense of calling. However, their work was dedicated to helping others in the community. Weber points out that "in almost grotesque contrast to Adam's Smith's precepts, Lutherism postulates that the division of labor forces the individual to work for others."[3]

Weber's "Protestant ethic" is in reality a study of the Calvinist ethic. He concentrated on Calvinism's achievement orientation, ignoring the Lutheran emphasis on loyalty to the state and the community. *Thanks to Luther, German economic endeavor gained a different focus.* It was religiously endowed with a communitarian ethos. The work ethic was enhanced by social commitment.

Luther was in fact an anticapitalist: he attacked the trade monopolies of the Fugger dynasty and Jewish moneylending. While attacking the mercantile flair of early capitalists, he supported the norms of craftsmanship, norms that are still valid for Germany's Mittelstandsgesellschaft. Vocational loyalty is a vital element of Lutheran behavior: the individual serves his employer as he serves the state, instead of using him to gain an income. Since Luther, the individual has played his vocationally assigned role in wealth creation.

Prussian tolerance allowed the Pietist movement, which emphasized human qualities like asceticism and selflessnes,to flourish. Lutherism had deteriorated by the eighteenth century into pedantic dogmatism and the Pietist emphasis on helping the poor influenced Prussian attitudes to welfare. Social responsibility became a priority for Prussia's bureaucrats and the state became a world pioneer in welfare policies.[4]

Pietist thinkers emphasized duty, rather than Lutheran obedience. They propagated Vernunftsrecht, law based on reasoning rather than on absolutist authority. This gave state officials an independent ethos: they served a higher ideal rather than a monarch.

As Hans Hattenauer remarks in his history of German officialdom, Pietism's role in making administration in Germany both efficient and humane has yet to be fully acknowledged. The social commitment of Prussia's bureaucracy owed a great debt to the "praxis pietatis," a practical motivation to serve the community as strong as the more individualistic economic rationality of the Calvinists.[5]

Prussian Protestantism was thus a blend of Lutheran loyalty, Calvinist dynamism, and Pietist idealism. Lutheran loyalty was "staatstragend"—literally state-supporting. Prussian subjects were commited to state order as much as to religious discipline. Sabotage was as unthinkable as venality was inexcusable.

CATHOLICISM AND BALANCE

In contrast to Prussia and its strident Protestanism, the Rheinland—often considered to be the heart of Germany—was always weaker and of more equivocal religiosity. Mostly Catholic in terms of population, its influence became suddenly apparent after the Second World War, when Prussia was abolished.

In the German context, Catholicism is ideally oriented toward balance because it lacks Protestantism's imperious search for perfection. Michael Novak tries in his study, *The Catholic Ethic and the Spirit of Capitalism*, to construct an alternative model to Max Weber's Protestant work ethic. However, apart from highlighting social justice and attempting to reposition it in a civic society, Novak lacks the evidence he would need to prove Catholicism's economic efficacy. The world's Catholic countries, whether in Southern Europe or Latin America, still trail the Protestant countries of northern and Western Europe and North America.[6]

However, modern German Catholics—in particular the Jesuit Oswald von Nell-Breuning, author of Pius XI's papal encyclical "Quadragesimo Anno," published in 1931—have helped define the social element of the market economy. Unlike the Lutheran church, the German Catholics have a codified social doctrine to fall back on. The two pillars of this doctrine, solidarity and subsidiarity, have defined social policies in contemporary Germany. Solidarity has made social aid a moral commitment. Subsidiarity on the other hand has restricted state intervention by emphasizing that "Gemeinwohl"—common well-being—is not only the legitimation but also the limit of state power.[7]

These principles have contributed to a humane collectivization of German society in the context of SME, to a relaxed communitarianism that constantly weighs the balance between the individual with his rights and duties on the one hand, and the need for social order on the other hand.

Catholicism has also relativized the importance of Innerlichkeit, the inward orientation that Lutherans exalt. The established church has always emphasized group worship rather than exaggerated inwardness. The Lutheran legacy on the other hand is radically uncompromising: the individual in effect faces salvation or damnation! *Thus, the pious ritualism of the Catholics has proved a healthy corrective to the exalted asceticism of Germany's Protestants.*

A Machiavellist Founding Father

The Catholic influence on contemporary Germany was intensified by the country's first postwar chancellor, Konrad Adenauer. Adenauer had principles. However, he mocked politicians like Ludwig Erhard, "who even believed what they said." His legendary quote, "What does the rubbish I said yesterday bother me!," sums up his attitude to the relativity of truth. This again is profoundly anti-Lutheran.

In Protestant terms, Adenauer was a Machiavellistic figure—a master of the art of subtle manipulation, of maneuvers and malice. An entire book has been dedicated to describing *Adenauer's Collected Malevolence*. He far more effectively relativized Prussian traditions and Protestant convictions than the regulation abolishing the state of Prussia passed by the Allied military administration in 1947.

Adenauer's impressive success—as lord mayor of Cologne and chancellor of West Germany—can be traced to a peculiar combination of Rhenish flexibility and Prussian accuracy. His British biographer Terence Prittie mentions both his "Roman clarity and logic" as also the more Protestant quality of self-discipline.

Adenauer's administrative strategies were Catholic rather than Protestant:

- The general emphasis lay on achieving a consensus through compromise, on coordinating policies from the background rather on declarations of conviction and open confrontations.
- Adenauer recognized the importance of associations for the German environment and broke with established practice by personally dealing with representatives of interest groups like the employers' association BDI.
- His social attitudes showed a valuable sense of proportion and reflected Catholic principles of solidarity and subsidiarity. Under his leadership, the government embarked on ambitious welfare programs.

Many of the specific success factors examined in the chapters on business mentality and business environment—consensus mechanisms, business cooperation, social cohesion—grew to their importance because of the chancellor's worldly wiseness. His style of government was profoundly restorative without being Prussian. His famous election slogan of 1957 consisted of two words: "No experiments." This is what the average German was hungering for and Adenauer's genius was that he constantly satisfied the country's need for paternalistic authoritarianism, while tempering this traditional medicine with a kind of benevolent venality.

Public expectations were Protestant, Adenauer's methods however were Catholic: string-pulling behind the scenes, an emphasis on personal loyalty rather than competence. *Postwar Germany became more tolerant and less implacable, more relaxed and less idealistic. Catholicism became a strong cultural source of balanced development.*

The Adenauer legacy sustainably changed the Prussian ethos. Chancellor Helmut Kohl for instance, whose term of office exceeded that of Adenauer, echoes his predecessor's benevolent venality.

The French historian Joseph Rovan has emphasized Kohl's Rhenish-Catholic background and indeed, Kohl's often-cited claim to be Adenauer's "grandson" is supported by his political style: manipulation rather than open discussion, functional efficiency rather than an ethos of service. Without Adenauer's normative influence on Germany, a man with Kohl's temperament and accomplishments could never have attained the chancellorship.

Kohl's success—notably with the reunification of Germany—has seemed to fulfill his belief in the "normative power of the factual," a restatement of Realpolitik. His leadership style fits well into the medium level of achievement category that, as we have seen in several contexts, characterizes contemporary Germany. Kohl's power derives from the fact that he personifies the Mittelstandsgesellschaft.

On the other hand, the traditional Prusso-Protestant archetype has lived on in the person of Kohl's predecessor, Helmut Schmidt. As we have seen, Schmidt's self-image as the "leading employee of the Federal Republic" echoed the service ideal of the Prussian monarchs.

A born leader in terms of intelligence, competence and eloquence, Schmidt personified the Protestant virtues of commitment and seriousness. His power derived from factual authority rather than from manipulation. His ethic was that of secular achievement, as against Machiavellistic maneuvering.

ADMINISTRATORS OF SOCIAL JUSTICE

In a memorandum published in 1991, the Lutheran church lauded the flexibility and "social symmetry"—defined as the balance between achievement and solidarity—of the German economic system. The church also pointed out: "The Social Market Economy is not a static creation. It can only be understood as a dynamic process, in which continuity and contradiction, path-breaking fundamental decisons and complex, diverging developments each have their own effect." Beyond this, the Lutherans demanded that codetermination—a specifically German form of industrial partnership seen in the context of the business environment—be protected from the effects of EU legislation.[8]

Both churches have grasped that a judicious dose of self-interest—and not an artificial distinction between self-interest and social welfare—is the key to German prosperity. Both have a stake in the status quo, since they are largely funded by church taxes, compulsorily deducted from the salaries of all Catholic and Protestant employees by the German state.

The German churches, both the Catholic and the Protestant, belong to the richest in the world. Their constitutional right to levy church taxes from all registered Catholics and Protestants earns them an estimated seventeen billion marks yearly. The accession of East Germany, whose population is largely atheist, and large-scale church withdrawals in West Germany have somewhat weakened the financial foundations of the churches, but other sources of income—like state contributions and interest earnings on real estate—remain awesomely high.

Both churches play a major social role: 60 percent of all kindergartens and 30 percent of all hospitals in Germany are church-run. The churches receive separate state funds for their charitable organizations Caritas and Diakonisches Werk.

Priests receive handsome salaries and enjoy life-long tenure like Beamten. Hierarchies and organizational structures resemble those of the state. Though the churches stress their spiritual missions, they in fact resemble bureaucracies manned by Kirchenbeamten—church officials. These officials have recently started to professionalize their services, using terms like marketing and lean management. The churches are increasingly being compared with large corporations, since they face the same need to allot funds, control costs, and restructure.

The churches are thus as much a part of order as the state and the business world. Religious thought has also supported commitment in different ways: the Lutheran tradition obliges the individual to respect authority while retaining inner convictions. The German Catholic heritage integrates the individual into society, committing him both to a vocational role and to the norms of solidarity.

SECTION 2: ENLIGHTENED ORDER AND ROMANTIC COMMITMENT

The philosophers of Germany's Age of Enlightenment were the architects of an inner sense of order. The leading dramatist of the epoch, Gotthold Ephraim Lessing, propagated the idea that the ideal society is not a choir singing in unison but an orchestra playing in harmony. Lessing's distinction between synchronization and harmony is valuable: a synchronized economy and society cannot change organically. Germany's economy today, with its associations and trade unions, guilds and Mittelstand, banks and cartels, is rather like a huge orchestra with strings, woodwinds, brass, and percussion, which functions harmoniously in spite of occasional frictions.

Lessing attempted to reconcile metaphysics and rationality, revelation and reason. A similar mixture between religious metaphysics and rational arguments characterized the mindset of the German Enlightenment's greatest thinker, Immanuel Kant.

For Kant, pure consciousness became the highest principle. Man should dare to know rather than automatically obey the powers-that-be. However, while Kant's ideas were intellectually revolutionary, he and his fellow Aufklärer argued on a level of abstract reflection that supported rather than threatened the Prusso-Protestant establishment. The Prussian philosophers of the Enlightenment accepted state-imposed order and concentrated their efforts on mental order, just as Luther bowed to worldly power while emphasizing the freedom of the soul.

It was however not Kant but Georg Wilhelm Friedrich Hegel, who provided the Prussian state of the early nineteenth century with its raison d'être. Hegel, whose lectures at the University of Berlin influenced an entire generation of Germany's intelligentsia—in particular the bureaucratic elite— saw the state as the reality of concrete freedom and as the incorporation of the Volksgeist, the spirit of the people.

In Hegel's world, the individual serves a higher cause: the Prussian polity. Nationalist thought in Germany could forthwith base its arguments on Hegel's ideas. But Hegel also propagated the need for a society, in which public administration and private associations would together guarantee order and a parity of interests. Thus, he was closer to Lessing's "orchestral" ideas of social harmony than might appear at first sight.

Here were the rudiments of a specifically German authoritarian communitarianism, a complete contrast to Anglo-Saxon concepts of liberalism and individual freedom. The German individual was wedged between the state and the guilds, urged both by the Lutheran church and the philosophers of the Enlightenment to contribute to order rather than to assert himself. The compulsiveness derived from these constraints will be examined in the next chapter.

In England on the other hand, utilitarian philosophers like Locke and Hume provided the setting for a civic society. As social scientist Karl de Schweinitz points out: "Nothing is more un-German than the philosophy of John Locke and the atomistic notions of individual welfare based on it."[9]

Similarly, American pragmatic philosophers like Charles Peirce and William James were empirical rather than speculative. Both were highly critical of German idealism. William James in particular could not stand Hegel's "through-and-through universe" with its "infallible impeccable all-pervasiveness." James makes no secret of his aversion to Hegel's world: "Its necessity, with no possibilities; its relations, with no subjects, make me feel as if I had entered into a contract with no reserved rights, or rather as if I had to live in a large seaside boarding house with no private bed room in which I might take refuge from the society of the place."[10]

James's disquietitude is understandable: Kant and Hegel were absolute perfectionists, as much "made in Germany" as the country's products. In the complexity of their thought, they were unrivalled. Similarly, Germany as an economic nation revels in the complexity of sectors like eco tech and Anlagen-bau, the construction of entire industrial installations. The ideal of perfection in the context of complexity is a challenge that German technological expertise and organizational skills are particularly attuned to. Thus, the more complicated a factory installation is, the more it stimulates the energies and imagination of the technicians and organizers involved with its construction.

In their comparison of economic culture in seven industrialized countries, Charles Hampden-Turner and Alfons Trompenaars remark on Germany's "labyrinthine mind which seeks to upgrade entire manufacturing processes."

Thus, the "higher order" of philosophy is reflected in the "lower order" of the machine.[11]

Philosophical order also lies at the roots of SME. The complexity of economic order—in particular the delicate balances between social and economic priorities, the partially autonomous negotiation processes on issues ranging from tariff agreements to ecological improvement described earlier in this book—can only be visualized in a broader and more abstract context. *Thus, the German capability to think in abstract terms is a valuable economic asset.*

ROMANTICISM AND THE ORGANIC

The philosophical order of the Enlightenment was challenged in the nineteenth century by a romantic movement that spread through poetry, drama, and philosophy to profoundly influence public life.

German romanticism has often been described as reactionary—and indeed, it reacted against the rationality of the Enlightenment. The romantics emphasized wholeness and emotionality rather than rationality and order. As Friedrich Schiller contended: "Reason has achieved what it can, when it finds the law of conduct and installs it. The fulfillment can only be carried out by the courageous will and the living feeling."[12]

Goethe and Schiller were both admirers of Kant, but they rejected the rational corset. Romanticism's leading philosopher, Friedrich Wilhelm Joseph Schelling, was a lover of nature, in company with poets like Novalis and Eichendorff. His philosophy is full of an enthusiastic yearning for wholeness and harmony. Romantic writers harked back to the Middle Ages and were firm supporters of the guilds. Thus, the craftsmanship ethos discussed in connection with the Mittelstand was culturally supported by romanticism.

The romantic love of nature is also the spiritual impulse behind the environmental movement in Germany. One reason why Germany is a world leader in the ecological sector is this deep inner commitment to forests, seas, and the soil.

The German forest crystallized this longing for fulfillment and purity in nineteenth century Germany. "O Wald, O Waldeinsamkeit, wie gleichst Du dem deutschen Gemüt," O forest, o forest solitude, how similar thou art to the German temperament, runs an often-quoted line of the romantic poet Julius Hammer.

A hundred years later, fears of Waldsterben, the death of forests, erupted in the early 1980s. Waldsterben rapidly became the rallying call for Germany's ecologists. Seen in retrospect, both the diagnoses of forest decay and the prognoses of imminent forest extinction were grossly exaggerated. But they prodded the German government into an ambitious forest-conservation program that cost a billion marks and radically reduced air pollution. The percentage of endangered trees decreased from 25 to 20 percent between 1991 and 1996. Air pollution laws stimulated a spurt of innovations in eco technology.[13]

ANTAGONISM OF THE TWO ADAMS: SMITH AND MÜLLER

Reverence for craftsmanship and a love of nature were symptomatic of romanticism's alternative vision of economic development. The pinnacle of economic thought during the romantic epoch was Adam Müller's repudiation of Adam Smith.

The apparent pragmatism of classical economics disguises the fact that Adam Smith was a moral philosopher rather than an economist. As the editors of an edition of Adam Smith's collected works point out: "Stoic philosophy is the primary influence on Smith's ethical thought. It also fundamentally affects his economic theory."[14]

The stoic concept of natural harmony was the basis of Smith's conception of economic harmony. Beyond this, stoic metaphysics postulated that good could come out of evil. This perception guides Smith's belief that the rich are led "by an invisible hand" to help both the poor and society at large.

Müller, in characteristically German fashion, emphasized a more concrete kind of harmony. In his masterpiece, *The Elements of Statesmanship*, published in 1809, Müller highlights the importance of the "visible hands" of state officials. He describes a symbiosis between institutional policies and personal aims: "Thus it is clear that every state can be to that extent truly rich, in which each individual is actively committed to an interest in the polity."[15]

Here lie the roots of a specifically German commitment to the whole, an organic rather than atomistic sense of responsibility. Citizens in Germany grow up with an instinctive sense of commitment—and with an equally instinctive perception of the state, which symbolizes the whole.

Adam Müller integrated individuals, society, and the state into his concept of national economy. Thanks to Müller and his many successors of the historic and ordoliberal schools, the German economy has remained integrated within a larger context till the present day.

While acknowledging the quantitative advantages derived from the division of labor, Adam Müller poses the rhetorical question: "What happens to the communitarian aspect of business transactions, which the guilds, where every person was so fittingly related to the needs of all, ensured so well?"[16]

Why indeed was the communitarian aspect divorced from the business process in England? The rapaciousness of Smith's butchers and bakers, who felt accountable to none, stimulated business while disrupting social bonds. *Here lie the deeper roots of the Anglo-Saxon malaise: wealth creation results in social divisiveness rather than integration. Seen today, Müller's prescience shows that romantics are sometimes the greater realists in their perception of what constitutes the real wealth of a nation in the long term.*

CONTEMPORARY COMMITMENT

German philosophy today is traditionalist rather than hedonist, more attached to the "Projekt der Moderne"—the modern project of the Enlightenment—than to fashionable postmodernism. Two schools of thought have vied for preeminence after the Second World War: the "critical theory" founded by Theodor Adorno and Max Horkheimer of the Frankfurt school; and the "critical rationalism" developed by Karl Popper. The negative idealism of the "Frankfurter," who attacked the supposed dogma of the Enlightenment without providing a viable alternative, contrasts with Popper's deductive focus, his attempt to falsify theories by trial and error, a critical process of rational argumentation. Popper's tenets of "trial-and-error" and his emphasis on "piecemeal engineering" and his faith in irrefutable logic are recognisably Anglo-Saxon. They fit in well with contemporary Germany's preoccupation with U.S. management methods and neoclassical economic theories.

However, we have seen that in many respects, Germany is not a society but rather a series of partly self-administered communities. The various private and professional associations, the vocational education councils, the trade unions, and the TÜV are far more tangible for the individual than free competition or abstract participation in a larger entity could ever be. In not recognizing this, most intellectual Germans seem to be victims of their own history, of an enormous mental blackout after the Second World War.

The free association of free citizens in the context of an open society is an edifying and exalting illusion. *The reality of social injustice and general disaffection in Great Britain and the United States indicates that any society— whether civic or communitarian—needs both support and guidance through institutions and autonomous associations.*

A country that merely offers its citizens possibilities of participation and welfare is simply not doing enough. It needs to coopt its citizens into autonomous activities and to coordinate the entire process. With its many mechanisms of assocation, contemporary Germany is a far more coherent and cohesive entity than either Britain or the United States. At the same time, it is freer and less feudalistic than Japan.

The critical theory and critical rationalism have both failed to provide Germany with a new intellectual orientation. Order and commitment—the heritage of the enlightenment and of romanticism—continue to influence the economy and society. Hermeneutics, best described as the art of historical understanding, provide insights into these influences. This is an unassuming kind of practical philosophy, concentrating on the object rather than postulating the need for theories or methods.

Hans-Georg Gadamer, Germany's leading hermeneutic philosopher, highlights the importance of commitment, explaining how the humanistic term sensus communis entered the Age of Enlightenment. While in the Anglo-Saxon countries, the term was construed as "common sense," the German interpretation was more abstract. The corporatist structure of German society favored the development of commitment rather than common sense.[17]

The historically derived distinction between common sense and commitment explains the basic difference between the two Adams: Smith's appealingly pragmatic precepts and Müller's deeper view of the individual's connectedness to a larger collectivity. It simultaneously reveals the gulf between Anglo-Saxon and German perceptions of wealth.

As we have seen, economic order is the quintessence of Germany's SME. The ordoliberal school of economics conceived SME as a synthesis of two worlds. They united a word from scholastic metaphysics—"ordo"—with principles of modern liberalism. Ordo remains an unreachable ideal, but the state is committed to striving for it, while equally striving to ensure liberal conditions of competition.

As one commentator points out: "The state is made by men—to achieve something however that reaches the metaphysical: to bring the order of this world closer to the ORDO of the world of ideas."[18] The protagonists of ordoliberalism—in particular Walter Eucken, Franz Böhm, and Alfred Müller-Armack—were sober scholars of economics and law who, however, had retained a perception of the metaphysical. Their ideas reflect Germany's philosophical and social traditions.

Contemporary German philosophy as a whole is widely seen as having deteriorated into mediocrity. Assiduous interpretation and pseudo-profound formulations have replaced originality. The philosophers of today seem the victims of the ghosts of the past. As Hans-Georg Gadamer has been quoted as saying: "We Germans are drowned in history."[19]

However, philosophical mediocrity needs to be seen in the context of the middle level of achievement that this book describes in the context of business, bureaucracy, and academia. It is in tune with the salutary banality of a stable society. In contemporary Germany, as we have seen, it is the many that count, not the few. Many citizens participate in communitarian activities as diverse as debates on vocational reform and ecological improvements. Thus, commitment is canalized and given a concrete form.

Communitarian commitment makes a society malleable. Nobody stands really high in a community. Thus, individuals are ritually responsible for their actions rather than fatefully responsible. Careers end not with a bang but a whimper. Responsibility is positionally defined as part of a larger Order.

SECTION 3: THE PRUSSIAN ETHOS

The Prussian ethos is more a mindset than a cultural phenomenon. It is generally identified with the army, with drill and discipline, brutal command and blind obedience. But it also encompasses devotion to public service and enlightened social values, as we have seen in connection with the business environment and the socioeconomic foundations of Germany's wealth. The Prussian bureaucracy is still a role model for both the public and private sectors in Germany.

The social archetype that the upper class in Prussian Germany aspired to was the "Reserveoffizier," the officer of the reserve. When Bethmann-Hollweg became Germany's chancellor, he appeared at the Reichstag in a reserve-major's uniform. Similarly, the Weimar Republic's last Chancellor von Papen was inordinately proud of being an officer of the guards.

The qualities that led to Prussia's military preeminence were however those of the "Generalstab"—and not of Reserveoffiziers, military parades, and fancy uniforms. The General Staff was the mind behind the Prussian victories against Austria and France. Its style was old Prussian rather than Wilhelmine Prussian. "Mehr sein als scheinen" was the motto: It was more important to be than to seem to be. Intelligence and modesty distinguished the Generalstab.

Without a General Staff, wrote Colonel Christian von Massenbach in a memorandum in 1795, an army was like a powerful but blind lion. Massenbach showed great foresight in prescribing criteria like intellectual ability, objectivity, and creativity for the selection of General Staff officers. These qualities ran contrary to the conventional leadership ideal, best symbolized by Marshall Blücher of the Prussian cavalry with his battlecry "Forward, Children!" Blücher triumphed in Waterloo together with Wellington against Napoleon's grande armée—and indeed he symbolized operative leadership as against strategy. The Generalstab, by contrast, united the intellectuals in the German army.

The instrument for training a new breed of staff officers was the War Academy, founded in 1801. Like the University of Berlin, the War Academy adopted precepts of general education. It too was a product of the Age of Enlightenment. The army's great philosopher-soldier was General Carl von Clausewitz, the founder of a specifically German school of strategic thought.

Clausewitz revoked mechanistic concepts of troop movements and attack formations. According to him, military leaders needed the same qualities as their peers in other fields: a mixture of Verstand and Gemüt, reason and temperament. Officers could not rely merely on carrying out commands punctiliously. They were neither technicians nor specialists: they needed courage and will-power to act responsibly under unforeseen circumstances. Clausewitz's observation that "in strategy everything is very simple but therefore not very easy," describes the seeming effortlessness that characterizes true mastery.[20]

THE SUPREME STRATEGIST

Clausewitz and other members of the military meritocracy enabled a non-Prussian outsider to became the supreme strategist: Helmuth von Moltke Moltke, who came from an aristocratic family in Mecklenburg, started his career as a cadet in the Danish army, and changed to the Prussian because it offered more opportunities. He is described as thin, with a high forehead, thin lips, and a fine profile—a typical intellectual. Prince Wilhelm, later the first German emperor, remarked on seeing him during a parade that the "Dane was not a good acquisition for the army."

At first sight, Moltke's intellectual interests hardly seemed to qualify him for his legendary role as the brain behind the German victories in the wars of unification. He was incredibly well-read, in subjects ranging from philosophy to natural sciences and national economy; he translated Gibbons' history of the Roman empire into German and spoke several foreign languages; he wrote novels and historic essays; and he was a lover of Mozart's music. Modest and unassuming, it was said of him that he "could be silent in seven languages."

But beyond all this, Moltke was a master of several disciplines with a direct impact on strategy:

- He had learned to analyze the political, social, and economic situations in other countries during a series of foreign assignments: as an instruction officer to the Sultan in Turkey, as an adjutant in Rome and during trips to England, Russia, and France.
- He possessed a profound knowledge of the railways and of their military and economic importance, having acted as a member of the supervisory board of the Hamburg-Berlin railway company as early as 1841.
- He also acquired an enormous expertise in cartography. After graduating from the War Academy, he taught military drawing, published a book on the subject, and carried out extensive fieldwork as a member of the topographic department of the Generalstab.

Moltke's profound grasp of geography and mathematics made him an active participant in the annual War Games organized by the army, which took place on the terrain of a historic battle and simulated the clash of forces. Here, he was in good company: four of the six chiefs of the General Staff between the Napoleonic wars and the First World War had a profound knowledge of topography.

Thus, it can fairly be said that the Battle of Sedan against the French in 1871 was won in the Cartographic Room of the Prussian General Staff, just as the Battle of Waterloo was—as the legend goes—won on the playing fields of Eton. The Generalstab excelled in "Fachwissen"—specialized knowledge of all areas relevant to strategy.

THE GENERALSTAB SUCCESS FORMULA

The German army excelled in efficiently implementing technoloy. It for instance optimized mobilization procedures during the wars against Austria and France by means of telegraphic messages. Cooperation with the civil administration ensured a high standard of organizational efficiency. Military organization featured the delegation of authority: local officers were given directives rather than commands and were thus empowered to act independently. Common operational procedures ensured a high degree of concurrence with strategic goals.

Moltke and his Generalstab colleagues embodied qualities that characterize managers in Germany today: *specialized knowledge, an international outlook, attention to logistics*. These quietly effective qualities are aligned to planning and coordination rather than to the more flamboyant task of leadership. As we saw in connection with business mentality, German managers are excellent organizers but mediocre leaders.

Military operations showed a high degree of functional efficiency. This was particularly true of mobilization plans. As Arden Bucholz points out in his analysis of Generalstab strategies: "The Military Travel Plan described large-scale 'transportation paths' for shipping the million-man army like so many units on a factory production line. This is very different from the cavalry regiment, the Junker noblesse de style, and the militarist ethos—brainless virility mixed with punctilious brutality—often said to dominate the Prussian army."[21]

One signal advantage of this systematic approach was the replaceability of the individual. General von Seeckt, who rebuilt the Reichswehr after Germany's defeat in the First World War, once pointed out that the General Staff did not try to produce geniuses—it concentrated on "healthy and efficient mediocrity."

The Leitmotiv of Impeccable Mediocrity, which we have already perceived in management and in society, pervaded the supposedly elitist army at its highest intellectual level. Here too, it was the many well-qualified Generalstab officers that counted, not the few truly gifted.

Germany's military success derived not from grand strategies but from the Generalstab's organizational skills—specialization, coordination, delegation of authority. A wise mixture of theory and practice and a constant process of incremental improvement based on modern technology and organizational innovations was the Generalstab's success formula.

This theory-practice mixture is also the secret of Germany's vocational education, while incremental improvement is, as we have seen, German industry's key to success. Thus, the Generalstab lives on, even if Prussia was declared extinct in 1947.

BUSINESS ARCHETYPES: RESERVEOFFIZIER AND GENERALSTAB

Business in contemporary Germany reflects the Prussian tradition in its entirety. Several surveys carried out in the early 1990s have shown that German managers are prone to command rather than delegate, in the manner of Reserveoffiziers. They tend to be authoritarian and overestimate their own capacity to communicate and motivate.[22]

These imperious and unreflected attitudes are derived from the past. Top managers reasserted themselves as "Mini-Führer" after World War II, revealing attitudes derived as much from the "Führer" principle during the Nazi period as from traditional military role models. According to the journalist Hans-Otto Eglau, they tended to be more authoritarian than the earlier generation of paternalistic entrepreneurs: "They made their decisions in noble solitude, like field marshalls on high horses."[23]

Eglau provides vivid portraits of corporate leaders in the 1950s:

- VW Chairman Heinrich Nordhoff rarely held board meetings. Instead, he communicated his decisions to one of the directors every Sunday, who then relayed the decisions to other board members the next day.
- Ulrich Haberland, CEO of the chemical corporation Bayer, only allowed high-ranking directors to enter his villa through the front door. Others used the back door, in company with tradesmen and domestics.

– Hermann Winkhaus, head of the Mannesmann engineering concern, was known to treat those who overstepped their authority like recalcitrant military cadets.[24]

These brusque Reserveoffizier attitudes were prevalent in the 1950s and 1960s and are not so common today. Occasional exceptions like Eberhard von Kuenheim, the remarkably successful CEO of BMW, only serve to prove the general rule. Kuehnheim belonged to the East Prussian landed aristocracy, started from scratch after the war as a worker on the assembly line at Bosch, and qualified as a mechanical engineer. He joined the Quandt group, which owns a major share in BMW, in 1965 and occupied responsible positions in the holding company before becoming BMW's CEO in 1970.

In the twenty-three years before he voluntarily stepped down in 1993, Kuehnheim steered BMW constantly higher, till it surpassed the annual production figures of its arch-rival Mercedes Benz. Kuenheim's leadership style has been described as "Prussian-Lordly." A series of talented managers left the company in the 1970s and 1980s, but Kuehnheim's success ultimately silenced his critics.[25]

The authoritarian postures of the past have now been succeeded by more restrained styles of leadership. Managers in the 1990s are closer to the Generalstab archetype.

Organizational procedures in German companies also reflect the Prussian ethos. The "Harzburg model" for instance exercized a seminal influence on business organization. Its quintessence: delegation of authority to employees on all levels within clearly defined boundaries and with a high degree of formalization. Written descriptions of tasks and a formalized method of rating employee achievement define the parameters of responsibility and decision-making. As one observer points out: "No other theory is so thorough, so hierarchic, so typically German."[26]

Reinhard Höhn, who invented the Harzburg model, saw it as a synthesis of functional requirements and autonomous responsibility. In actual fact, it was close to the Generalstab archetype: Moltke for instance issued directives rather than giving orders. Höhn himself was ultimately discredited because of his role during the Nazi period and the Academy he founded almost went bankrupt in the mid 1980s. However, the Harzburg precepts are still reflected in organizational norms and procedures in many companies.

The Generalstab legacy lives on in areas like project management and logistics, where careful planning and meticulous coordination prevail. When Munich's airport moved from one end of town to the other in 1992, a team of young management consultants—mostly former officers of the German army—supervized the operation. In the time span of one night, 600 installations of various sizes and shapes had to be transferred and installed by several thousand workers.

With fifteen months of preparation, the airport project team coordinated traffic control, telecommunications, and personnel management. The greatest problem was not technical: it consisted of convincing all service providers at the old airport to allow their installations be transferred by a single transport organization. The young consultants had no authority to force the 170 companies to cooperate. Their achievement was coordinating a deal by which a coalition of transporters offered favorable conditions in cooperation with the airport authority.[27]

Thus, as with the Generalstab, the unspectacular coordination of many tasks was the secret of organizational success. As seen in earlier chapters, Germany excels in processes with a high degree of complexity: coordinating the ecologization of the entire manufacturing process, connecting rail and road traffic and so on. *There is no magic to the coordination of processes. It requires specialized knowledge, organizational skills, and what can be called cooperative acumen.*

The Generalstab represents an evolution from feudally determined to rationally oriented organization. In a sense, a great many of the liberation-management, creative-decentralization concepts developed by U.S. writers like Tom Peters and John Naisbitt are reactionary: they hark back to the feudal days of bold decisions based on flimsy premises. The blind loyalty of former times has in these concepts been replaced by a kind of anarchic individualism.

In certain business sectors and situations—the high tech and service sectors, innovative phases of corporate activity—this kind of individualistic flexibility can prove highly effective. However, formalization and specialization (the "German virtues") are formidable accomplishments in the long term.

The Prussian ethos personifies traditional German virtues. Its legacy is not only administrative efficiency but also an internalized sense of order. The economy in contemporary Germany relies on the voluntary participation of individuals with specialized accomplishments, who integrate themselves within a larger whole.

SECTION 4: THE VOCABULARY OF ORDER AND THE RHETORIC OF COMMITMENT

German philosophy is literally unthinkable without the words used to express ideas. In particular, the philosophers of the enlightenment and of romanticism depended on word-constructions to express the complexity of their thoughts.

The exactitude with which both abstract ideas and the habits of the heart can be explained through word constructions and word combinations is uniquely German. One example is the word "Welt":

- The German dictionary edited by the Grimm brothers in the nineteenth century includes terms like "Weltgeist" (world spirit), "Welträtsel" (world riddle) and "Weltanschauung" (worldview).
- The romantic period introduced a large number of eloquent expressions such as "Weltgefühl" (the individual's feeling toward the world), "Weltschmerz" (world sadness), "Weltseele" (world soul) and "Weltverachtung" (contempt of the everyday world).
- In "Psychologie der Weltanschauungen," the twentieth-century philosopher Karl Jaspers explores the "Weltbild"—understanding of the world—of the individual.

In all the cases mentioned above, the English translations are pale travesties of the original German meaning: for this reason, words like Weltanschauung and Weltschmerz have been assimilated into the English language. Similarly, comparative studies have shown that the German language surpasses French in terms of flexible word combinations and precision.[28]

At its best, the German language has stimulated a quest for both complexity and wholeness, both Hegel's complex sublimation of the state and Adam Müller's emphasis on organic unity. Philosophers have often acknowledged their debt to the language. In the seventeenth century, the scientist-philosopher Gottfried Leibnitz emphasized the importance of German as a language of inner dialogue.

In the twentieth century, Theodor Adorno, one of the Frankfurt school's founders, pointed out that he returned to Germany from the United States after the Second World War not only for sentimental but also for linguistic reasons: "The German language has a special elective affinity to philosophy, and, to be sure, to its speculative moment." Elective affinity: the German word "Wahlverwandschaften," used equally by literary figures like Goethe, is infinitely more expressive than its English equivalent.[29]

ORDER—AND ORDERLINESS

On a more prosaic level, the German language reflects a constant search for orderliness. German is as much the language of bureaucrats as of philosophers. The complexity of SME, in particular its balanced priorities, are mirrored in the vocabulary used to discuss social and economic issues.

The many uses of the word "Leistung" (achievement) illustrate on the one hand Germany's achievement ethos and on the other hand SME's checks and balances. "Leistungsprinzip" describes the principle of achievement that is fundamental to SME, "Leistungsgesellschaft" a society attuned to these principles.

An enormous ideological debate has focused on the pros and cons of an achievement-oriented society and words like "Leistungsdruck" (the pressure of achievement) and "Leistungsverweigerung" (resistance to achievement) express dissatisfaction with contemporary Germany's work ethic. In the context of reunification, Leistung has become the rallying call for those who propagate traditional virtues. In 1992, some politicians called Leistung the word of the year.[30]

Leistung however means social benefits as much as economic achievements. Those in need of social aid receive "Sozialleistungen." Thus the word encompasses the specific nature of Germany's sociocapitalism.

Amtsdeutsch—administrative German—provides ample examples of an emphasis on orderliness rather than a philosophically inspired sense of order. In the vocabulary of bureaucrats, words lead their own functional lives, divorced from human experience. Nouns dominate over verbs, the passive over the active tense. Human beings rarely appear, and when they do, they are functionalized as "Leistungsträger" and "Entscheidungsträger," carriers of achievement and of decisions. Bureaucratic German is the language of files and filing cabinets.

Germany's private sector has to a great extent adopted a public-sector vocabulary in its search for a respectable identity. Business correspondence and terminology echo the abstraction and meticulousness of Amtsdeutsch.

This applies both to the formality and functionality of business affairs:

Formality. Business correspondence adheres to a precise form. Instead of "Dear Sir," German letters start with "Highly Respected Ladies and Gentlemen" (Sehr geehrte Damen und Herren). The form "Lieber Herr," Dear Mr., is only used when a certain intimacy of contact has been established between writer and addressee.

Even more important is the use of titles. Many managers hold doctorates and it is imperative that they are addressed as "Dr." This applies also to other titles such as honorary professorships. Beyond this, the exact designation of a person belongs to the title. One addresses, for instance, Herrn Direktor Dr. Johannes Meyer-Müller, Abteilungsleiter Finanzwesen. The man has the rank of a director and heads the department of finances.

Titles in Germany are important not only as status symbols, but also because they denote authority. Thus, even in a paltry Verein—a private association—titles are lavishly distributed and proudly flourished by the incumbents. Formerly, the wives of professors and other luminaries decorated their own names with their husband's titles: the widow of a university professor could call herself "Universitätsprofessorenwitwe!" However, this is now forbidden by law.

Functionality. German business administration features an unique emphasis on organization. Whereas the term "organization" in English covers the entire company, in German it means a system of regulations applying to the administrative process. Business economics (BE) differentiates between "Aufbauorganization" and "Ablauforganization":

- "Aufbauorganization" is the personnel aspect of organization and is connected with organizational potentials and hierarchies.
- "Ablauforganization" is the equivalent of operations management. However it also describes the process by which business is conducted.[31]

In reality of course, Aufbau and Ablauf are closely connected with each other. BE separates them in the interests of analytical clarity.

For the business world, organization is not a boring formality: it is the essence of existence. Linguistic exactitude mirrors perfectionism in working procedures. German is the language of organizers, not innovators. Innovations need an informal vocabulary and English, which is more open and laconic, more eclectic in the use of words, offers a fertile terrain.

The German language's formality and functionality block creative ideas and quick-fix innovations. It favors step-by-step improvements. *Contemporary German also reflects the impact of the ethic of positional responsibility mentioned earlier. It regulates the human element in the business process, thus ensuring functional efficiency and a medium level of achievement.*

A COMMITMENT TO FUNCTIONAL PESSIMISM: CONTEMPORARY RHETORIC

"Tritt fest auf! Machs Maul auf! Hör bald auf!" Martin Luther's advice for speakers could not be more cogent: Present yourself firmly! Open your mouth properly! Stop soon! The great religious reformer also reformed the German language. Luther's translation of the Bible is the core of modern German. Simplicity, depth, and emotionality characterized his writing style. His mighty eloquence founded a pastoral school of rhetoric that has strongly influenced public speeches in Germany until the present.

Rhetoric in Germany is less an art of persuasion, its classical function, and more the expression of commitment. Key words like "Bekenntnis" and "Gesinnung"—avowal, conviction—describe a tone of voice and a form of expression that owes much to the pulpit and little to the discussion of ideas among free people.

Public discussions and political debates in Germany often end in mutual declarations of faith, in sententious declamations of inordinate length. Speakers address imaginary audiences rather than directly communicating with those around them. The questions that members of the audience pose to the speakers often turn out to be "Befindlichkeitsbekenntnisse," avowals of feeling rather than the clarification of specific issues.

Rhetoric as such has always been considered crafty and underhand in Germany. Kant considered it to be a "deceitful art." Hegel and Schelling, Goethe and Schiller voiced equally negative opinions. The Prussian kings were poor orators: their language was one of military command, not of elegant urbanity. Bismarck, in his own way an accomplished orator though he had a piping voice, was proud to call himself a bad speaker. The word "Rhetor" still has a distinctly negative connotation in German.[32]

However, Prussian inarticulacy was coupled with social welfare, with a dutiful approach to providing the Untertan (subject) with adequate means of existence. Careful planning and administrative efficiency rather than eloquence characterized the Prussian ethos.

By the late nineteenth century, the average citizen in Germany was economically more protected than his counterparts in other countries like the United States, Britain, and France. Beyond this, he was less an atomized individual than elsewhere: he belonged to guilds, trade unions, and professional or private associations.

Public discourse in Germany correspondingly mutated into a "Funktionärssprache," the language of functionaries representing these guilds, trade unions, and associations. The legitimation of representing a cross-section of the community replaced the qualification that orators gained in other countries through the quality of their speeches.

In contemporary Germany, the salutary banality of a stable society is reflected in its rhetoric. Parliamentarians, public officials, businesspeiople, and church officials all speak like functionaries. As the cultural critic Hermann Glaser points out, members of Germany's economic, political, and social elite have the same vocabulary and tone of voice.[33]

The prevalent cultural ethos is one of heavy-handed pessimism, coupled with moralization about the causes and nature of problems. There is a consensus in the rhetoric of making demands and refusing them, in particular of preparing for worst-case conditions. Phrases like "Industriedämmerung," the twilight of industry, illustrate this kind of functional pessimism.

Everyone joins in the litany of pessimism: politicians, business leaders, trade union representatives, and also intellectuals. The campaign against Waldsterben, the death of the forests, has been criticized as a typical example of "Untergangsromantik," a highly Germanic romanticism of decline that characterized works like Oswald Spengler's *Decline of the West*. Cultural pessimism, the equivalent of the business community's functional pessimism, is a fine art in Germany. Its exponents express their opinions in leading newspapers and magazines. Thoughtful Germans have an instinctive revulsion to optimism: it is considered superficial and manipulative. Germany's elites thus revel in the rhetoric of pessimism.

On a meta level, the "Sonntagsreden"—so-called Sunday speeches full of moralistic pessimism, that hark back to the sermons of the past—constantly reassure the individual citizen that everything is in order. His representatives are earnestly and conscientiously perorating on various issues and action will ultimately be taken after a consensus has been achieved.

Aesthetes like Gerd Ueding, who holds Germany's only Chair for the Art of Rhetoric, bemoan the reduction of rhetoric to a social technology. The normal citizen however is used to speaking in his "Fachsprache," his specialized vocabulary. He therefore readily accepts the fact that the functionaries have their own rituals and jargon of communication.

Functional rather than personal articulacy is indeed the expression of Germany's sociocapitalism. Public speakers express commitment rather than individualistic viewpoints.

Shared commitment is the backbone of Germany's economic success in sectors like ecology, energy, and transport, which rely on a basic consensus between the representatives of business, the trade unions, private assocations, and government.

CULTURE AND BALANCED DEVELOPMENT

Culture gives economic activity its "Sinnstiftung," its sense of meaning. As we have seen, Germany's philosophical sense of order corresponds with economic order and administrative orderliness, rhetorical commitment with a basic commitment to economic stability and social justice (see Figure 5.1).

The interaction between cultural norms and economic functions is central to a country's wealth. Put drastically: A country that dwells on its ideals without taking action to fulfill them is as lost as a country that functions smoothly without ideals.

Germany's future wealth will depend on its capability to balance and tone down its idealism, to construct its economic edifice sensibly without losing its sense for the grandiose and the eternal. Its implicit search for the best of all possible worlds—in philosophy as much as in ecology, in economic order as much as in social legislation—is a powerful wealth creator that can however run haywire.

Mäßigung, a sense of proportion, is the call of the hour. Mäßigung is closely allied to Mittelmäßigkeit—mediocrity—and is thus constantly imperiled, since excellence is a far more attractive ideal. *But Germany would be wise to continue its cautious path toward a consensus, based on a medium level of achievement—and to allow other countries to excel with spectacular achievements. For the wealth of a nation in the long term is not the sum of its economic achievements but the extent to which the polity adjusts to the changes caused by achievements.*

If for instance the introduction of electronics results in the neglect of mechanical production methods and craftsmanship, a country will ultimately suffer, even if it profits from electronics in the short term. If however it manages to integrate electronics into the conventional industrial setting and to find a synthesis between electronics and mechanics, the country will prosper in the long term.

This in a nutshell is the difference between Japanese and German priorities. The Japanese have jettisoned their former traditions of craftsmanship in search of quick mastery of electronics production, while the Germans have integrated electronics into their predominantly mechanical context, thus retaining the link to their craftsmanship heritage.

Countries need economies that are attuned to their cultural heritages, so that their societies can digest rapid changes. They need to constantly question the real value of innovations rather than blindly assuming that innovations per se are positive.

Because of its cultural traditions, Germany asks cogent questions about innovations. Often it exaggerates the length of the questioning process and consequently trails other countries—in particular the United States and Japan—that have fewer qualms about adopting new technologies and subjecting their societies to abrupt changes. However, *in the long term, the questioning process is invaluable because it ensures balanced development. Economic priorities are balanced by social and cultural considerations.*

In contrast to the past—and to other Western countries—Germany is not a victim of transcendental illusions. Policies, attitudes, and postures in France for instance are still colored by the great illusion of a "grande nation." France's hostile attitude to the English language and its chauvinistic postures in the European Union are symptoms of "folie de grandeur," of an incapability to grasp the parameters of its actual role in the world. The planning process in both the public and private sectors—key positions in both sectors are held by "Enarchs," a select coterie from the elitist ENA school of administration—is in its own way a grand illusion, divorced from the realities of everyday life.

Figure 5.1
The German Economy and the Culture Link

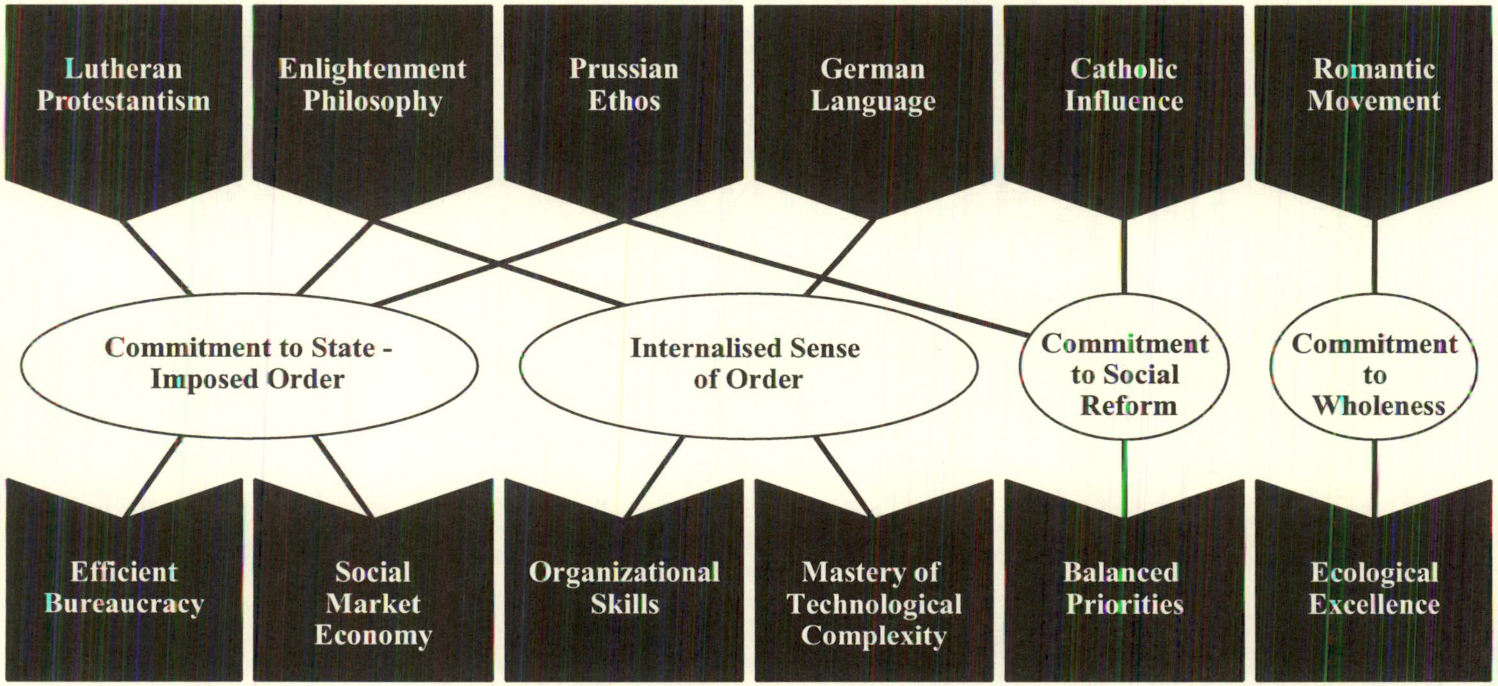

Colbertism has dominated economic thought since the eighteenth century and justified the state's preeminence.[34]

Equally, Great Britain suffers from the after-effects of past grandeur, of having possessed an empire on which the sun never set and of having been a land of hope and glory. It accordingly neglected its former industrial and mercantile talents and has failed to invest in social integration and infrastructure.

The United States is also a victim of its own illusions, of being God's own country, a country of Manifest Destiny, of having the American dream and an American way of life. For too long, Americans have perceived their economic primacy as a sign of excellence, rather than recognizing that the country profited from its natural resources, an influx of talented immigrants—and from the comparative weakness of its major competitors. These myths of goodness or greatness have made the Anglo-Saxon countries and France self-centered and self-satisfied, incapable of grasping their own vulnerability.

By contrast, Germany has no illusions to fall back on. It lacks the false comfort of supposed grandeur or self-righteousness. The Third Reich, frightful as it was, laid the foundation for a self-critical openness that characterizes contemporary Germany.

As we have seen, modern Germans have two souls in their breast: Protestant compulsiveness and a Catholic search for consensus by compromise. Compulsiveness is a powerful impetus, while consensus is an invaluable control mechanism. As the economist Joseph Schumpeter once pointed out, the speed of a car ultimately depends on the quality of its brakes, not the power of its motor.

The key to balanced development is to harness both energies: the compulsive perfectionism that guarantees the quality of "made in Germany" and the consensual aptitude that has led to a uniquely harmonious business environment. The psychological roots and implications of compulsiveness and consensus will be examined in the next chapter.

NOTES

1. Norbert Elias, *Über den Prozess der Zivilisation*, Book 1 (Bern: Francke, 1969), pp. 4–5.

2. Helmuth Plessner, *Die verspätete Nation* (Frankfurt: Suhrkamp, 1969), p. 73.

3. Max Weber, *Die protestantische Ethik und der Geist des Kapitalismus* (München: Siebenstern, 1993), p. 68.

4. Alfred Müller-Armack, *Religion und Wirtschaft* (Stuttgart: Kohlhammer, 1968), pp. 122ff; see also E.J. Feuchtwanger, *Preußen—Mythos und Realität* (Frankfurt: Atheaion, 1972), pp. 16–19.

5. Hans Hattenauer, *Geschichte des deutschen Beamtentums* (Cologne: Heymanns, 1993), pp. 166–170.

6. Michael Novak, *The Catholic Ethic and the Spirit of Capitalism* (New York: Free Press, 1993), pp. xvi–xvii, 62–67.

7. Oswald von Nell-Breuning, *Wirtchaft und Gesellschaft heute*, Book III (Freiburg: Herder, 1960), pp. 24–39, 99–102.

8. For the memorandum, see *Gemeinwohl und Eigennutz* (Gütersloh: Mohn, 1991), pp. 58, 134–135.

9. See Karl de Schweinitz, *Industrialization and Democracy* (London: Collier-Macmillan), p. 160.

10. Quoted in A. J. Ayer, *The Origins of Pragmatism* (London: Macmillan, 1968), pp. 186–187, see also pp. 13–21, 192–197.

11. Charles Hampden-Turner and Alfons Trompenaars, *The Seven Cultures of Capitalism* (New York: Currency Doubleday, 1993), pp. 207–213.

12. Friedrich Schiller, "Die Bestimmung des Menschen zum ästhetischen Leben" in Raffaele Ciafardone (ed.), *Die Philosophie der deutschen Aufklärung* (Stuttgart: Reclam, 1990), p. 113.

13. See "Die Bäume wachsen schneller," in *iwd*, published by Institut der deutschen Wirtschaft, Cologne, December 19, 1996; for a critical portrayal of the Waldsterben campaign, see Burkhard Müller-Ulrich, "Holzwege und andere Irrtümer," in *Süddeutsche Zeitung*, August 7–8, 1996.

14. Adam Smith, *The Theory of Moral Sentiments* (Oxford: Clarendon Press, 1976), p. 5.

15. Adam Müller, *Die Elemente der Staatskunst* (Meersburg a. Bodensee: F.W. Hendel Verlag, 1936), p. 235.

16. Adam Müller, *Die Elemente der Staatskunst*, p. 193.

17. Hans-Georg Gadamer, *Gesammelte Werke*, Book 1 (Tübingen: Mohr, 1986), pp. 24–35.

18. Otto Veit, "Ordo und Ordnung—Versuch einer Synthese," in *Ordo*, 1953, p. 32.

19. For the Gadamer quote, see Lorenz B. Puntel, "Zur Situation der deutschen Philosophie der Gegenwart," in *Information Philosophie*, 1/1994, p. 21 (the entire article is an excellent summary of contemporary trends, see pp. 20–30); see also Joachim Jung, "Die Eule der Minerva bleibt im Nest," in *Süddeutsche Zeitung*, July 11, 1994; for an analysis of philosophical directions ignored in this book, see Eckhard Nordhofen, "Schöne Rede—flacher Kopf oder: Skepsis macht munter," in *Die Zeit*, September 19, 1986.

20. Carl von Clausewitz, *Vom Kriege* (Bonn: Dummler, 1973), p. 347.

21. Arden Bucholz, *Moltke, Schlieffen, and Prussian War Planning* (New York: Berg, 1991), p. 3.

22. Brigitta Lenz, "Selbsttäuschung," in *Capital*, 9/1993, pp. 119–127; Hans-Peter Scherer, "Die Fetzen fliegen," in *WirtschaftsWoche*, March 11, 1994, pp. 70–75; Bolke Behrens, "Himmel und Hölle," in *WirtschaftsWoche*, December 24, 1992.

23. Hans Otto Eglau, *Erste Garnitur* (Düsseldorf: Econ, 1980), pp. 40–42.

24. Ibid.

25. See the portrait on Eberhard von Kuenheim in *Munzinger Archiv*, 32/1993.

26. See "Heldensagen," in *Capital*, 19/1988, p. 286.

27. See "Umzug des Flughafens gewürdigt," in *Süddeutsche Zeitung*, October 16, 1992; see also "Logistik: Fliegender Wechsel von Riem nach München 2," in *WirtschaftWoche*, April 17, 1992.

28. Bernard Nuss, *Das Faust-Syndrom* (Bonn: Bouvier, 1993), pp. 19–23 (see also his references to Malblanc's study on the French language).

29. For Leibniz, see Theodor Haering, *Das Deutsche in der deutschen Philosophie* (Stuttgart: Kohlhammer, 1942), p. 215; for Adorno, see Martin Jay, *The Dialectical Imagination* (London: Heinemann, 1973), p. 283.

30. Hans D. Barbier, "Leistung—das Wort des Jahres," in *Frankfurter Allgemeine Zeitung*, June 6, 1992; for a more general discussion, see Helmut Schoeck, "Leistung,"

in Martin Greiffenhagen (ed.), *Kampf um Wörter?* (Munich: Hanser, 1980), pp. 325–330.

31.Erich Frese (ed.), *Handwörterbuch der Organisation* (Stuttgart: Poeschel, 1992), pp. 1–4, 1589–1590; see also Erich Frese, *Grundlagen der Organisation* (Wiesbaden: Gabler, 1980), pp. 40–43.

32. For negative attitudes to rhetoric, see Dolf Sternberger, "Der Staatsmann als Rhetor und Literat," in *Merkur*, 1967, pp. 19–30; see also Walter Jens, *Von deutscher Rede* (Munich: dtv, 1972), pp. 16–45.

33. Hermann Glaser, "Wurzeldeutsch und andere affirmative Sprachmuster," in *Spießer-Ideologie* (Freiburg: Rombach, 1964).

34. Stephen Cohen, "Planung im französischen Kapitalismus," in Wolf–Dieter Narr and Claus Offe (eds.) *Wohlfahrtsstaat und Massenloyalität* (Cologne: Kiepenheuer & Witsch, 1975); see also Bernard Guetta, "L'Allemagne est désormais européenne par nature," in *Le Nouvel Économiste*, October 21, 1994, p. 6.

CHAPTER 6

The Psychological Roots of Order and Commitment

No other European nation has been affected to such a degree by the character and acts of one single man.

—Erich Kahler on Martin Luther
in his book *The Germans*

Martin Luther was indeed—as Erich Kahler states in his book, *The Germans*, quoted from above—a uniquely influential personality. Luther's religious reform was epoch-making. By translating the Bible into German, Luther simultaneously gave his fellow citizens a common language that had not existed until then.

His influence on the German mentality was even more profound. For centuries, Luther was a national hero. Generations of Germans revered his acts and personality.

In his fascinating psychoanalytic study entitled *Young Man Luther*, Erik Erikson highlights the seminal influences on Luther's personality. His socialization was brutal: both his parents beat him to an appalling extent and the process of chastizement continued in school.[1]

Even by the standards of the fifteenth century, the child Martin experienced an excessive amount of pain and helplessness. At school, Luther also experienced psychoterror: the teachers recruited schoolboys as spies ("wolves"). Speaking German instead of Latin, speaking in an excited way, the use of abusive language: all such "sins" were secretly registered and the culprits were publicly punished.

Many commentators praise Luther's childlike nature without however considering the devastating effects of his childhood. Luther indeed was a highly conservative revolutionary. His rebelliousness derived from his tormented, life-long search for authority.

In contrast to his great opponent Erasmus of Rotterdam, the German reformer lacked the intellectuality and the enlightenment that would have enabled him to perceive and reflect on his own victimization, though he often complained as an adult about his childhood. He was in fact an early example of what can be called the compulsive personality.

Compulsive individuals are, as Erikson points out, particularly susceptible to religious, racial, and social intolerance. Luther was certainly intolerant of those who were different: he denied his adversaries Erasmus and Zwingli their Christian legitimation and was equally contemptuous of Jews who refused to convert to Christianity.

All in all, Martin Luther was a German archetype. He incorporated human qualities that were later to be considered "typically German":

- His much-lauded "Innerlichkeit" (inwardness) reached the inwardness in the common man far more than Spinoza, Erasmus, and other intellectual reformers could ever achieve. Luther's robust, rabble-rousing rhetoric was the reverse side of this coin. Ever since, Innerlichkeit has become the key to both cultural and psychological identity.
- Luther was in his own way a great idealist, assuming others to be as interested in the life of the soul as he was. His absolutist search for eternal values denied compromise—and glorified inflexible attitudes.
- Luther remained hearty and unaffected till the end of his life: the very opposite of Catholic urbanity. The great reformer was wont to say: "I guzzle like a Bohemian and booze around like a German." "Fressen" and "saufen"—eating and drinking in a boorish rather than civilized way—were words used by Luther, words that later characterized the cliché of the peasant-like Germans.
- Above all, Luther was highly compulsive. His constant need to confess apparent sins is evidence of this "Zwanghaftigkeit." The German word covers, as we shall see later, a broad radius of compulsiveness.[2]

Inevitably, Luther's critics are more perceptive than the many who extravagantly praised him. Thomas Mann for instance points out that the German people have always been closer to Luther than to Goethe, though Goethe was a more urbane and civilized personality. The reason, though Mann does not mention it, is obvious: Luther was far closer to the common people, their forms of expression and their need for redemption, than Goethe, who had a privileged social status, a more exalted vocabulary, and a more refined emotionality. Mann associated instinctively with Goethe—and the common man equally instinctively with Luther.

Public glorification of Luther exalted human qualities that should have been recognized as signs of profound psychic imbalance. Luther's mixture of excessive obedience and equally excessive rebelliousness was an appalling role model for Germany.

Compulsiveness is closely connected with Germany's economic achievements, in particular its perfectionist approach to manufacturing and administration. As we shall see in this chapter, compulsiveness can however also be counterproductive. It exaggerates the need for exactitude and leads to over-engineering and over-regulation.

Compulsiveness is accentuated by Innerlichkeit. Since the Reformation, inner communion rather than outward communication has characterized German identity.

Compulsiveness remains a powerful archetype. Its grip on the German psyche has however been partially balanced by an increasing commitment to consensus rather than to the authoritarian communitarianism of the past. The psychology of consensus is aligned to negotiation processes that this book has analyzed in sectors such as ecology, energy, and transport. This chapter will examine how changing attitudes to work, consumption, and personal identity reflect a more balanced sense of priorities. *This is the inner foundation of balanced development, just as a zest for short-term profits is more aligned to growth and productivity.*

Consensus in the German context is not only an economic success factor: the constant dialogue necessitated by it balances Innerlichkeit. It domesticizes dissent and forces business leaders, trade union functionaries, and representatives of associations and other interest groups to express their viewpoints and reveal their interests.

SECTION 1: THE COMPULSIVE PERSONALITY

Luther was one of several seminal influences on the German mentality. Through him, but also through the guilds and the Prussian state, many Germans developed qualities that were admirable but not humane: in particular Gründlichkeit and Gehorsamkeit, thoroughness and obedience.

The country has often needed these qualities. As Friedrich List, the great nineteenth-century national economist pointed out, qualities like a sense of order, diligence and efficiency helped Germany survive the devastation after the Thirty-Years war, which ended in 1648. Similarly, they helped Germany recover from the devastation of two world wars in this century.[3]

The German character has traditionally included a large number of so-called secondary virtues ("Sekundärtugenden") and shown a dearth of primary virtues ("Primärtugenden") like tolerance and a sense of humanity. Is it however legitimate to refer to a "German character?" Like the term "mentality," defined in Chapter 2, national character has often been used to describe the collectivity of those who belong to a nation. It similarly covers norms and values, attitudes and convictions.

Particularly in times of war, character stereotypes of the enemy have been developed for propaganda reasons. During the two world wars, Germans have been pictured as "Huns" and "boches" and have in turn developed stereotypes both of themselves and of the others. The Nazi period witnessed the horrifying consequences of enemy stereotypes: the Jews and the Slavish races were seen and treated as "Untermenschen," subhuman beings.

Long before this however, German academics like Werner Sombart and Max Scheler contributed the following stereotypes during the First World War:

- The Germans: patient, tenacious, methodical, masculine.
- The French: enthusiastic, frivolous, ingenious, feminine.

German propaganda during the First World War reveled in such polarities: the "organic" character of Germany contrasted with the mechanical nature of France. Similarly, Germans were "deep," while the English were shallow, the Germans idealistic and the English materialistic.[4]

These stereotypes hold an element of truth. As we have seen, German business is strong because it is "organically" connected with its environment. German philosophy and the German language provide evidence of a specific depth, both in the creation of ideas and their formulation.

Human qualities are not invalidated because they are exaggerated and misused in the context of propaganda. Stereotypes, however, ignore the roots and nuances of the collective psyche.

German identity changed perceptibly during the nineteenth century. In the first half of the century, the Germans were often pictured, most prominently by the French emigrant Germaine de Staël, as the country of "Dichter and Denker"—of poets and thinkers. The typical German was old-fashioned, sentimental, and self-effacing.

This image changed radically in the context of German industrialization. By the year 1900, Germany was the leading industrial nation in continental Europe, richer and more powerful than its neighbors. The typical German was seen as being orderly, hard-headed, and arrogant. This cliché has persisted ever since and shades of it appear in contemporary descriptions of German character.

The English novelist Aldous Huxley paid an ironic tribute to Germany's new powerful image: "How appallingly thorough these Germans always managed to be, how emphatic! In sex no less than in war—in scholarship, in science. Diving deeper than anyone else and coming up muddier." Similarly, Mrs. Munt, the aunt of the Schlegel sisters in E. M. Forster's *Howard's End*, seems to echo the author's views in pointing out: "The Germans are too thorough, and this is all very well sometimes, but at other times it does not do."

This indeed is the psychic quality most often identified as typically German. A Japanese observer in postwar Germany has called them "gründlich bis zur Graumsamkeit," thorough to the point of being gruesome. Quite evidently, Germans are perceived as being excessively thorough. However, the country's philosophical thought, its economic and technological achievements owe a major debt to this quality. "Made in Germany," the legendary quality of German products, derives from thoroughness in every phase of the manufacturing process.

Thoroughness in itself is a positive quality, the opposite of sloppiness or erratic behavior. When coupled however with the quality of obedience (a quality that German socialization after Luther emphasized), thoroughness became excessive. The combination led during the Kaiserreich and the Third Reich to "Kadavergehorsam": blind or slavish obedience (Kadaver means corpse).

Kadavergehorsam is one example of compulsiveness. *Because of compulsiveness, Germans have lacked the inner balance that leads to Anglo-Saxon virtues like fairness and common sense, or attributes like savoir vivre and empathy, associated with countries like France and Italy.*

COMPULSIVE OR AUTHORITARIAN?

In the context of National Socialism, political psychologists like Erich Fromm developed the concept of the "authoritarian personality." People with these personalities were unable to be independent and to use their individual powers of reason. Loneliness and lack of self-esteem led the individual to voluntarily destroy his own identity and enter into a symbiotic relationship with others. Such a person readily accepts leaders who liberate him from the burden of being free.

Similarly, Theodor Adorno and others pointed out in their seminal work, *The Authoritarian Personality,* that fascism relied on the "active cooperation" of a large majority, on "long-established patterns of hopes and aspirations, fears and anxieties that dispose them to certain beliefs and make them resistant to others." Thus, individuals were seen as willing victims of group norms, as captives of anxieties and beliefs.[5]

Neither Fromm nor Adorno considered the economic component in personality development. As we have seen, Germany moved with frightening speed from "Weltfremdheit" to "Weltgeltung"—from worldly innocence to a world reputation as an economic nation—in the nineteenth century.

Nothing in Germany's history prepared its citizens for this brutal change. Suddenly, personal identity was economized. Economic success became the national mission that thorough and obedient individuals were committed to serving. Orderliness became the national credo.

The masters of the average German—state officials, but also the new breed of entrepreneurs and managers—soon realized that they could consolidate their power by adopting militaristic postures. As we have seen, victories in the wars of unification stimulated public esteem of the army. Hardness became the military-economic ideal: the famous phrase "hart wie Kruppstahl" (hard like Krupp steel) adequately expresses this symbiosis. In social terms, the Wilhelmine businessmen were largely parvenus who avidly adopted existing norms. As we saw in the context of the Prussian ethos, the "Reserveoffizier" archetype became the ideal for the nonmilitary elite.

However, Germany was not an atomized society during the Wilhelmine period. Economic and technical progress was promoted and supervized by the state with the support of many communitarian institutions—guilds, associations and so on—that already existed. The individual was subjected to drill and discipline on the one hand, and protected by the state and these institutions on the other hand. Luther's religious corset, which created an inner community of faith, tightened the pressure on the individual. Personal compulsiveness was thus based on:

- Bekenntniszwang, a Lutheran compulsion of avowing one's faith.
- Gemeinschaftszwang, the compulsion of belonging to both a vocational and a national community.
- Erfolgszwang, a new compulsion to be successful.

The dynamism of economic progress was accentuated by the newness of united Germany, of a country founded in 1871 after the wars of unification. The cultural historian Norbert Elias makes the point that German national pride did not have the chance to slowly evolve as in England. This preempted a relaxed reflection on what it meant to be German.[6]

In retrospect, it seems important to emphasize the material success of Wilhelmine Germany. The average German witnessed an enormous increase in wealth during the latter part of the Kaiserreich. Since the social state and industrial expansion developed simultaneously, he profited from state welfare as well as from a rising income.

In the context of multiple compulsion, it was inevitable that the average German adopted norms of hardness rather than humanity. As a servant, he attempted to ape the manners of his masters. His personality was in fact characterized by compulsiveness rather than consciousness. He automatically accepted and internalized abstract norms of order and rules of orderliness without questioning their legitimacy.

Compulsiveness made most Germans susceptible to authoritarian influences. Lacking a supportive context for individualism, they blindly supported the monarchy until 1918 and later equally blindly National Socialism. It also however made them into excellent workers and officials.

The compulsive personality is the inner key to wealth creation in Germany. Each individual plays his role in optimizing the manufacturing process. The perfection of products "made in Germany" is not imposed by supervisors or management. It results from a compulsive commitment to perfection on the part of the individual. Similarly, the compulsive orderliness of the many Beckmessers in German business, the punctilious bookkeepers we encountered in connection with the Meistersinger of Nuremberg, ensures a high level of administrative efficiency.

Because of compulsiveness, individuals can internalize order so profoundly. Whether as managers or bureaucrats, manual or white-collar workers: the inner urge to create order ensures efficiency.

THE ECONOMIC LIMITS OF COMPULSIVE PERFECTIONISM

However, compulsiveness in management often reduces order to petty orderliness. Business psychologists Jürgen Hesse and Hans Christian Schrader point out that many of their patients are compulsive managers. These managers can best be described as narrow-minded hierarchs, who impose authority with a mixture of conscientiousness and self-righteousness.[7]

The credo of compulsive managers is order through control. At the beginning of the chapter on business mentality, we discovered that this "TÜV mentality" is an important German archetype. Compulsive managers justify their suspicious behavior by refering to "Sachzwänge," impersonal constraints.

The plea of Sachzwänge is a typical leadership ploy designed to divert attention away from personal compulsiveness. It also highlights the leadership cult of "Sachlichkeit" in Germany. Sachlichkeit means objectivity or impersonality. Sachlichkeit is a behavioral norm that Germans in all walks of life subscribe to. Those considered "unsachlich" are automatically disqualified.

In the business world, Sachlichkeit is imposed by organizational norms— and by compulsive leaders. In his perceptive study of German business, the French writer Gilles Untereiner comes to the general conclusion: "L'Allemand est sachlich," Germans are impersonal. Similarly, one leading German banker has been praised in the German press for his "cool impersonality."[8]

Sachlichkeit is the psychological credo of the business world. Relationships in German corporate cultures develop on the basis of mutual respect for specialized competence (Sachebene). Then, the contact slowly evolves from the Sachebene to the "Beziehungsebene," this being the more emotional level of contact. This contrasts both with the Anglo-Saxon emphasis on friendly informality and the Latin-countries' reliance on personal cordiality.

Compulsiveness coupled with impersonality is often responsible for counterproductive strategies and policies:

Over-engineering. As we saw in the chapter on business mentality, German products—particularly in sectors like machine building, automobiles, and machine-tools, are needlessly complicated. They are full of functions that the customers do not notice, full of safety precautions that the customer does not truly require. In the textile machines sector, alone the exaggerated craftsmanship of plug connections and sockets make the German machines 7 percent more expensive than those of producers from other countries.[9]

Over-regulation. Germany's bureaucracy has a great proclivity to over-regulate. Authorization procedures for industrial installations last longer in Germany than in other countries: an average of twelve months as against seven months in Great Britain and eight months in France.

Compulsive perfectionism can turn liberalization into a farce. The new financial market regulations designed to stimulate the German stock markets have for instance been widely criticized as being so perfectionistic that they dissuade rather than persuade foreign companies to get listed in Germany. Though the new regulations are modeled on those of the New York and London stock exchanges, they are far more complex and exacting. Attempts at liberalization in Germany are often self-defeating because of a compulsive tendency to perfectionize regulations.[10]

Compulsiveness and impersonality ensure a high degree of functional efficiency. Obviously, they also create enormous barriers for innovation and explain the German proclivity to constantly perfectionize existing products and processes rather than venturing into new forms of technology.

SECTION 2: THE PSYCHOLOGY OF CONSENSUS

The compulsive personality is the personification of the TÜV archetype: order through control. However, its traditionally strong influence on the economy is being progressively challenged by more relaxed and compromizing attitudes.

After the war, West Germany was soon reintegrated into the Western world. Occasional reports on neo-Nazi activities and the reassumption of important positions by Ex-Nazis made the headlines in the world press, but world opinion was mostly fascinated by the "Wirtschaftswunder," the economic miracle.

Perceptive visitors to postwar Germany like the journalist William L. Shirer and the philosopher Hannah Arendt had however commented on the peculiar lack of emotion of the Germans they encountered, on a proclivity to disown responsibility and assign the blame for the Nazi period to others. Such observations were generally ignored in a country that was understandably eager to forget the past and "make good" again.[11]

The first real debate in Germany on collective responsibility was provoked by a book called *The Inability to Mourn*, published by two German psychologists, Alexander and Margarete Mitscherlich, in 1967. The Mitscherlichs describe how a large cross-section of Germans refused to accept responsibility for the shame attributed to the Nazi period. In particular, an entire generation of Germans failed to mourn the death of Hitler, who had been emotionally cherished until 1945. This abrupt denial of allegiance and of the pain caused by the loss of the Führer were considered to be signs of regressive behavior.

The Mitscherlichs also contended that the economic miracle served to obliterate memories of Nazi inhumanity in and outside Germany, pointing out that "the world accepts German workmanship, whatever it might otherwise think of the Germans." Their accusations have been widely contested as being unjust or inquisitorial.[12]

In actual fact, the inability to mourn or to assume personal responsibility was inevitable. People with compulsive personalities have relinquished responsibility for their own conduct. In the same way as they projected their individual longings onto the person of the Führer during the Third Reich, so also could they make Hitler responsible after the war for everything that happened.

As seen earlier, personal identity was economized in nineteenth century Germany. The average German had learned to identify himself with his country's economic achievements. Thus, the inability to mourn and the readiness to identify with the Wirtschaftswunder were inevitable reactions.

One further aspect that both the Mitscherlichs and their critics ignore is the corporatization of identity in Germany. Individuals are members of guilds, professional and private associations. They thus lack a sense of personal responsibility. In the postwar period, both the corporatist institutions and the personality structures that they encouraged rapidly reestablished themselves.

By 1968, West Germany had achieved unprecedented prosperity. "A frigidaire for all Germans," the Wirtschaftswunder slogan, had become reality. The widespread distribution of wealth together with ambitious social welfare programs—in particular the pension reform of 1957—encouraged a more relaxed attitude to material wealth.

A series of events in the late 1960s and early 1970s promoted a change of consciousness:

- The students' movement attacked traditional German virtues: obedience, discipline, dutifulness, assiduity. It also stimulated a process of reflection on the Nazi period and on individual responsibility for the crimes committed.
- The Social Democrats gained power for the first time in postwar Germany in 1969. The new government under Willy Brandt embarked on ambitious programs to democratize and humanize society. Brandt's famous slogan was "Mehr Demokratie wagen," dare to be more democratic.
- The third influence on value change was the boom in "antiauthoritarian" methods of upbringing and "emancipatory" pedagogics. Designed to free the individual from social pressures, these highly controversial concepts soon lost their impetus. However, they modified the prevailing compulsiveness and promoted qualities like creativity and self-expression.
- In vocational education, there was a similar trend toward developing social competence in addition to the traditional craftsmanship skills.

However, without economic success, the process of change toward more balanced priorities would not have developed. Thus, the compulsive materialism of the postwar period ultimately promoted an evolution of attitudes toward work, consumption, and personal identity.

Work. Conservative circles in Germany have recently deplored an apparent decline in the country's work ethic. Relaxed attitudes to work and achievement in the 1980s and 1990s have been compared with the more ascetic values in the 1950s and 1960s.

However, as Helmut Klages, a leading value analyst points out, the initial postwar period was abnormal. The emergency situation after the war and the exigencies of rebuilding the economy displaced former values such as aesthetic sense and cultivated life-style. These values reasserted themselves after the need for sacrifice and self-effacement—and above all for an exaggerated work orientation—became less apparent.[13]

The results of opinion research—one survey indicated that only two-fifths of working Germans are willing to give work the highest priority in their lives as against two-thirds of working Americans—need to be seen in a proper context. German business is organized in such a way—through vocational education, trade unions, codetermination, and social insurance—that a communitarian orientation is structurally guaranteed. Thus, individualism is a healthy antidote for the enforced standardization of working life.

Seen in retrospect, the compulsive work ethic was a narrow, one-sided attitude to life that functioned well during the period when economic structures were clear-cut and mass production of conventional technology dictated working procedures. Things however have changed dramatically since then and the real question is whether the business world of today would be well-served by working attitudes that derive from the past. It seems more likely that Germany's corporations and enterprises profit from employees who are more individualistic than their predecessors, even if this entails a lower degree of uncompromising obedience.

Surveys show that the contemporary employee in Germany is committed both to Prussian virtues like precision and punctuality and to "communicative virtues" such as teamwork and openness. Signficantly, managers in Germany also subscribe to postmaterialist values to a greater extent than in the early 1980s. Thus, there is a consensus in attitudes to work, which forms an important part of the overall psychology of consensus in Germany.[14]

Consumption. The change in working attitudes and the reduction of working hours have led to a leisure boom. In his analysis of *Die Erlebnisgesellschaft, The Thrill-oriented Society*, the sociologist Gerhard Schulze describes how the aestheticization of leisure—through cultivated forms of eating and drinking, dancing, elegant clothes and so on—has given everyday life a new dimension.[15]

One prime form of consumerism is tourism. Tourism to Italy began in the 1950s and rapidly became a major business sector in the 1960s. Germans now spend more on their holidays each year than on all other leisure pursuits including sport. They also spend far more per capita than citizens in the United States and Japan. In spite of the recession of the early 1990s, the tourist industry has continued to grow. However, whereas group travel dominated in the early years of tourism, individual tours and "creative holidays," involving courses in languages, painting, and personal development, have progressively gained in popularity.

Are the Germans becoming hedonistic materialists? A number of opinion surveys indicate that the Germans are getting soft and enjoying life, in contrast to countries like Italy and France, which are more open to visionary ideas. One poll of "Euro-Trends" sees a larger proportion of hedonists—and traditionalists—in Germany than in the other European countries. It seems however that the real reason for these discrepancies is that the average German has a higher income and a correspondingly higher potential for hedonistic consumption. In the German context however, hedonism is a healthy antidote to the compulsive assiduity and asceticism of former years.[16]

By the 1980s, a broad spectrum of German society adopted the consumption habits of the former upper classes. Here again, a convergence of attitudes in the context of a Mittelstandsgesellschaft, the middle-estate society described exten-sively in this book, can be perceived. As we have seen, Germany's egalitarian Mittelstandsgesellschaft is the social basis for consensus.

Personal Identity. The average German is far from being part of a "lonely crowd." There is less loneliness today than in the early 1950s, as opinion polls indicate. However, though positive in human terms, this trend has also contributed to immobility. Many managers and employees are reluctant to leave their places of residence, even if they are assured better jobs and career possibilities elsewhere.

The 1950s were best characterized by the phrase "ohne mich," without me. Individuals avoided involvement in public affairs. This regressive attitude supported the compulsive work ethic and reflected an inward orientation. The average German citizen has now become more humane, more connected. He is more willing to personally participate in the rituals of consensus: debates on ecological and other issues, negotiations between vocational groups, and so on. *Innerlichkeit remains the core of personal identity, but it is complemented by communication.*

Patriotism is a more complex issue. The number of those proud of being German has increased somewhat since Almond & Verba's international survey of civic culture in 1959: in 1990 70 percent of all West Germans and 79 percent of the East Germans had positive attitudes, as against 59 percent of West Germans in 1959. Significantly, older people and those of lower educational levels were prouder of being German than the others, indicating that those of the younger generation in better positions are more critical of their national identity. The legacy of the Nazi period has made sensitive Germans suspicious of patriotic attitudes.

Germans are far less proud of their country than citizens in most other countries in the world. One survey of international youth showed that while Americans and Japanese expressed the greatest pride in their country's history and cultural heritage, German youth was by contrast most proud of its living standards. This again reflects the continuing economization of identity.

The collective psyche in Germany today is more mature than ever before. The social scientist Werner Weidenfeld describes today's Germans as "pragmatic," pointing out their closeness to Anglo-Saxon attitudes and values like tolerance and willingness to compromise.[17]

The psychology of consensus involves a new quality of commitment—more reflected and less compulsive. The new commitment is oriented toward both material and idealistic priorities. This is the inner core of balanced development.

SECTION 3: BETWEEN AMERICAN INDIVIDUALISM AND JAPANESE COLLECTIVISM—GERMAN IDENTITY

The many differences between Germany and the United States have been explored in the course of this book. Some examples:

- The German emphasis on manufacturing quality, economies of scope, and formalistic organization as against the U.S. emphasis on profitability, flexibility, and economies of scale (Chapters 1 and 2).

- The state role in defining and regulating economic order in Germany and the role of the trade unions in promoting an industrial partnership as against the atomistic, libertarian environment in the United States (Chapter 3).
- The egalitarian slant of the German educational system, which contrasts with America's elitist orientation (Chapter 4).
- The German tradition of Lutheran Protestantism and idealistic philosophy, as against Calvinism and pragmatism (Chapter 5).

Social cohesion in Germany is derived to a great extent from the vocational identity of the individual. The average German is committed, albeit unconsciously, to fulfilling a specific role in the Mittelstandsgesellschaft. In the United States on the contrary, early principles of commitment, as enunciated by Puritans like John Winthrop and protagonists of the American Revolution, in particular James Madison and Alexander Hamilton, were soon discarded. The religious and republican emphasis on community was later replaced by the rampant individualism of heroic settlers and "robber barons."

Influential Social Darwinists like Herbert Spencer justified and glorified the logic of individual achievement. Ever since, U.S. role models have favored "winners"—whether pioneers, entrepreneurs, football players, or film stars—and ignored losers.

A society consists however to a great extent of normally talented and qualified human beings. The U.S. emphasis on excellence blithely ignores what this book has defined as the middle level of achievement. *In contrast to the United States, Germany has promoted "losers," devoting major resources to developing the ambitions and activities of average members of the population. This is the basic logic of vocational and of life-long education.*

Thus, normal people have a different self-esteem in Germany. They have various means of participating and distinguishing themselves within the community.

The sociologist Robert N. Bellah and his colleagues have categorized individualism in their insightful study of American life, *Habits of the Heart*. They differentiate between biblical, civic, utilitarian and expressive individualism and also describe various ways in which Americans attempt to "transcend the limitations of a self-centered life."[18]

U.S. society has however greatly supported self-interest. The individual contributes to the community altruistically if at all. Opinion researcher Daniel Yankelovich has described changes in U.S. attitudes during periods of rising or falling wealth. In the "good" times, most citizens felt rich and secure enough to help poorer minorities. However in the context of recessions and unemployment, this altruistic attitude has changed into demands of reciprocity: those receiving welfare ought to be forced to earn what they get.[19]

Germany's citizens have lacked both altruism and Social Darwinism because the social state was imposed on them by Bismarck in well-meaning, authoritarian fashion. Ever since, it has belonged to the facts of life. Though Social Democrat and Christian Democrat governments in contemporary Germany have expanded or curtailed welfare programs, the basic commitment has never been questioned. In the consciousness of its citizens, Germany is a solidaric rather than Darwinistic polity and government has a social mission.

Because of their communitarian rather than individualistic status—as craftsmen and workers with specialized qualifications, as members of various associations—Germans have an implicit sense of Gestalt. They realize that the whole is more than the sum of the parts and are committed to contributing to a larger whole.

The progressive atomization of U.S. society contrasts with the continuous German search to level out the structure of society, to better integrate foreigners, the handicapped, and those with minimal education. Average Germans have not indulged in hero worship after Hitler: they realize that achievements often go back to privileged birth, socialization and exceptional circumstances. They believe that it is the many who count, not the few.

Germany's important protagonists are not robber baron entrepreneurs or whiz kids in management: they are social workers and transport coordinators, engineers in industry and educators at vocational schools and many others who contribute to the country's unique infrastructure. The self-esteem of Germany's quiet wealth-creators is supported by the context in which they live.

COLLECTIVIST HARMONY VERSUS AUTONOMOUS CONSENSUS

The differences between Germany and the United States are manifest. Those between Germany and Japan, which also possesses a culture of consensus, albeit within a radically different ethnic context, are less apparent. Both countries show a great degree of continuity in spite of change: the zaibatsu-keiretsu metamorphosis in Japan for instance is paralleled by the German knack of replacing old cartels by new power centers (see Figure 6.1).

Structural similarities mask fundamental differences in identity:

Economic Identity. Japan's business world is famous for its ritualized forms of achieving consensus. Its companies are justly admired for their ability to profit from the creativity of their employees and to establish corporate cultures based on mutual good will.

In Germany, corporate consensus derives from formalistic and functional considerations: "Sachkenntnis" and "Zuständigkeit," the specialized knowledge and specific responsibility of members of staff. Beyond this, it has been estimated that German managers spend 60–80 percent of their time dealing with obstacles in the decision-making process, while Japanese managers spend 20–30 percent. Germany's system of implementing suggestions from employees is also reported to be far less efficient than that of Japan.[20]

According to business management specialist Horst Albach, Japanese business has understood competition not in the Anglo-Saxon liberal sense, but in terms of social engineering, as a means of increasing the wealth of the population. The German economy on the other hand functions on the basis of segregated competition: product differentiation creates a series of specific market segments.[21]

Similar differences exist on commercial priorities. Japan's service orientation dates back to the feudal period, as the Japanese academic Tomoyasu Satow points out. The Mitsui family, which later founded one of the country's leading financial houses (zaibatsu), traded in the seventeenth century according to the motto "We should make our client happy, then the happiness will come back to us." The German commitment—from the Middle Ages onward—has been to the norms of craftsmanship. The Japanese have focused on human satisfaction, the Germans on abstract goals.[22]

The Japanese are more flexible than the Germans in emulating new technologies and using innovative marketing to develop and sell mass market products. The Germans evince, however, more inner flexibility in their socioeconomic evolution after the Second World War.

Thus, the Japanese excel in simultaneous engineering and in synchronized economic strategies coordinated by institutions like the MITI, while the Germans share simultaneous priorities on important issues like social justice and ecological change.

Germany's international orientation is genuine, while Japan's is purely instrumental. In his perceptive article, "Japan's Abiding Sakoku Mentality," Mayumi Itoh describes the way in which seclusion from the outside world (sekoku) remains a prevalent mindset in contemporary Japan. Thus, the country's economic internationalism faces major psychological barriers.[23]

Social Identity. Japanese socialization produces a collectivist harmony by repressing the individualistic potential for conflict, as many analyzes point out. The normal Japanese is taught to adhere to norms—in business, this involves following corporate goals—without questioning their basic legitimation. In Germany on the other hand, individualistic potential is generally integrated, not repressed.

Issues that disturb Japan's imposed consensus—whether war crimes, social injustice, or ecological deficiencies—are generally ignored or suppressed. Repressive welfarism characterizes industrial relations in Japan. Its trade unions have yet to recover from the draconian treatment they were subjected to in the years after World War II. Racialism has often manifested itself in public utterances of prominent Japanese and the apologies proffered tend to be formalistic. In Germany on the other hand, widely publicized discussions and investigations have tackled sensitive issues such as National Socialism.[24]

Through this process of painful self-reflection, Germany's social identity has changed organically. Japan's on the other hand seems to have changed only marginally, in stark contrast to its economic transformation.

Cultural Identity. Japanese religious attitudes are pragmatically prosaic, strongly oriented to success in this world. Zen Buddhism propagates the importance of profits and the "logic of capital." Confucian maxims, a second important influence, are equally down to earth. As a result, the Japanese have no interest in abstractions. They are interested in the "how" rather than the "why."

Of all Western countries, Germany is the most interested in the "why." The philosophical nature of German thought and the remarkable facility of the German language to convey abstraction have been discussed in the last chapter.

Figure 6.1
Patterns of Identity

U.S.A.

- Survival of the Fittest: Individualistic Ethic
- Large Gap between Top and Bottom
- Spirit of Antagonistic Atomism

Japan

- Linear Reasoning: Not Why but How
- Sociocultural Corset
- Spirit of Communitarian Collectivism

Germany

- Complex Reasoning: First Why, then How
- Economy without "Hard Edges" – Comparatively, not Superlatively Good
- Spirit of Conscious Consensus

Germany has constantly sought the absolute—whether in philosophical terms or in the perfectionism of industrial production. In Japan on the other hand, relativity is the key word. Ambition is less important than personal relations (amae), ethics less important than harmony. [25]

Japan's culture is one of undertones. Words are less important than nonverbal gestures. The Japanese language supports linguistic ambiguity. Germany on the other hand is a culture of overtones. In spite of occasional obscurantism, the German ethos is a search for clarity and truth.

National Identity. Japan constantly defines and redefines its national character. It very ostensively emphasizes its unique identity through Nihonjiron, the "theory" of Japaneseness. Nihonjiron has been called a form of "self-exoticization." Germany on the other hand stresses its normality as a European country, trying to be as self-effacing as possible in terms of national identity.

While the Japanese are often perceived as deferential in their behavior, but ultimately contemptuous of foreigners, Germans are genuinely self-critical and open to the outside world. One Japanese sociologist credits the Germans for having an "emancipated sense of responsibility," commenting simultaneously on the lack of an individual sense of responsibility in Japan.

The Japanese are thus not only incapable of mourning war crimes, as the Germans were in the first two decades of the postwar period (earlier in this chapter, the controversy on the inability to mourn the Nazi period was discussed). They are also incapable of grasping the need to mourn, the "why" as it were.

Their cultural mindset has allowed them to regret the shame brought on Japan's image through the war crimes, but not to grasp their collective responsibility for the crimes. As Ruth Benedict pointed out in her classic study, *The Chrysanthemum and the Sword*, the Japanese culture of shame led to a preoccupation with saving face, rather than self-questioning. In his recent comparison of German and Japanese attitudes toward World War II, the Dutch publicist Ian Buruma confirms Benedict's findings and highlights Germany's courageous openness, contrasting it with Japan's deviousness. [26]

The Japanese are thus more facile and flexible in their various identities than the Germans. They adapt quickly to changing needs because they have no real ideals. Japan adroitly bridges over the paradox of a supermodern economy and an archaic society, while lacking true orientation.

Behind   a flexible facade, the Japanese are more oriented toward collectiveness than consensus.   The German psyche is deeper and the interconnection between the socioeconomic and psychocultural spheres correspondingly intense. Progress is delayed by the need for connectivity. But when it occurs, socioeconomic progress is steady and organic.

In the final reckoning, U.S. socialization favors triumphant individuals and a context of antagonistic atomism. Japanese socialization fosters conformists in conditions of collectivist harmony. *German socialization supports autonomous individuals who are aligned toward reaching a consensus. Thus, individual identity tends to be more balanced than in the United States and Japan.*

BALANCED IDENTITY AND FUTURE WEALTH

Stable wealth is linked to balanced identity as well as to stable institutions. Countries that optimize the potentials of their own economic identity and that are aware of their own deficiencies are better equipped to create and distribute wealth.

As human beings, we possess various partial identities and can achieve balance through consciousness of these identities. Thus, opportunism is as much one of our "voices"—as the psychological approach voice dialogue describes our different selves—as enlightenment. Voice dialogue is an approach in humanistic psychology strongly influenced by Gestalt. It postulates that the individual's wholeness derives from a conscious dialog between subpersonalities.

In Germany, major voices like the achievement-oriented pusher and the compulsive perfectionist have traditionally dominated. However, in the context of the psychology of consensus, hitherto disowned selves like a search for dialogue and zest for pleasure have asserted themselves to a greater extent.

There is in fact no patent recipe for a country to achieve a balanced identity, just as there are no textbook strategies of consensus. Inner freedom involves standing between the personality extremes and bearing the tension, as the founders of voice dialogue, Hal Stone and Sidra Winkelman, point out.[27]

Consciousness rather than compulsiveness is the vital priority in Germany. In spite of postmodernist tendencies, Germany remains an old-fashioned country with a preponderance of traditional virtues like thoroughness and obedience. For the steady wealth of a nation, a judicious dose of these human qualities is invaluable.

Future wealth will depend on the extent to which Germany's identity becomes more balanced. It needs to move away from Lutheran compulsiveness toward a more relaxed sense of priorities. Balanced identity is constantly endangered by outside pressures. Many of the pressures of Germany's past have receded into oblivion, to be replaced by new challenges. Tocqueville's commentary that the Germans are possessed by abstract truths without considering their practical results is less alarming today than it was in the nineteenth century.

As we have seen, the Mittelstandsgesellschaft is comfortingly prosaic. Ecology for instance is an issue that stimulated an extremist ideology of purity in the 1980s. Public attitudes have since become more pragmatic, in keeping with the pervasiveness of consensus. The Greens and other pressure groups have been domesticized by the Mittelstandsgesellschaft.

However, *the German penchant for wholeness, the organic, Gestalt— valuable qualities that have contributed to Germany's ecological success—are potentially dangerous, because they host the roots of totalitarianism.* In recent years, fears have been voiced that the country's ecological consensus could lead to a dictatorship founded on purity.

Though the Green party is predominantly left-wing and subscribes to democratic values, right-wing fringe groups have expressed biologically founded ecological precepts uncomfortably close to those propagated during the Nazi period. A traditionally Teutonic zest for thoroughness coupled with a longing for the absolute makes ecology an issue that potentially threatens balanced identity.[28]

The reunification of Germany also challenged balanced identity. "Innere Einheit," inner unity, is an important issue that transcends the successful introduction of modern infrastructure and the social state into the East. In his analysis of the East German psyche, the psychologist Hans-Joachim Maaz discovered the same compulsive rejection of the past that took place in West Germany in the early years after the Nazi period, the same disownment of responsibility. East Germans are far from the psychology of consensus that has developed in the West.[29]

Prominent East Germans have complained stridently about the overbearing attitudes of the West Germans. The percentage of those who believe that "We are one people," declined between 1990 and 1994 from 45 to 28 percent in the East and 54 to 47 percent in the West. On the other hand, various surveys show that Germans in both parts of the country subscribe to the same basic values.[30]

It seems likely that current animosities will soon recede into the background, since the material foundations of inner unity exist. However, the East German process of adjusting to the Social Market Economy, the checks and balances of a Mittelstandsgesellschaft, and—above all—to the mechanisms and rituals of consensus, will last at least a generation.

Despite these challenges, Germany's identity is well attuned to balanced development. In the next chapter, we shall see that the dynamization of the consensus process is the key to future wealth in the German context.

NOTES

1. Erik H. Erikson, *Der junge Mann Luther* (Frankfurt: Suhrkamp, 1976), pp. 277ff.

2. Erikson, *Der junge Mann Luther*, particularly pp. 52–54, 72–73, 84–85, 110–111, 170–171, Ernst Troeltsch, *Aufsätze zur Geistesgeschichte und Religionssoziologie*, Aalen: Scientia, 1966, pp. 230–231; single testimonies of Luther's qualities are given by the theologian Gottfried Arnold (heartiness), the poet Heinrich Heine (heartiness), the state theorist Friedrich Julius Stahl (religious heroism), the writer Stefan Zweig (vehemence), the political academic Ludwig Uhland (Innerlichkeit), the philosopher Hegel (idealism), the theologian Karl Barth (peasant-like), the historian Gerhard Ritter (will power), the theologian Walther von Loewenich (excrement-orientation), see Hermann Glaser and Karl Heinz Stahl (eds.), *Luther gestern und heute* (Frankfurt: Fischer, 1983), pp. 59, 78–79, 85–99, 107–109, 111–114, 135–137, 157.

3. Friedrich List, *Das nationale System der politischen Ökonomie* (Stuttgart: Cotta, 1883), p. 81, see also pp. 153–154.

4. For a good overview, see Ute Gerhard and Jürgen Link, "Zum Anteil der Kollektivsymbolik an den Nationalstereotypen," in Jürgen Link and Wolf Wülfing (eds.), *Nationale Mythen und Symbole in der zweiten Hälfte des 19. Jahrhunderts* (Stuttgart: Klett-Cotta, 1991), pp. 16–52.

5. Erich Fromm, "Die autoritäre Persönlichkeit," in Hermann Röhrs (ed.), *Die Disziplin in ihrem Verhältnis zur Lohn und Strafe* (Frankfurt: Akademische Verlags-

gesellschaft, 1968), pp. 132–136; T.W. Adorno et al., *The Authoritarian Personality* (New York: Harper & Row, 1950), pp. 1–11, especially p. 10.

6. Norbert Elias, *Studien über die Deutschen* (Frankfurt: Suhrkamp, 1989), pp. 418–432; for a good commentary, see Stephen Kalberg, "The German Sonderweg Demystified: A Sociological Biography of a Nation," in *Theory, Culture & Society*, 1992, pp. 111–124.

7. Jürgen Hesse and Hans Christian Schrader, *Die Neurosen der Chefs* (Frankfurt: Eichborn, 1994), pp. 103–109; see also Barbara Bierach and Lothar Schnitzler, "Frage der Dosis," in *WirtschaftsWoche*, January 26, 1995.

8. Gilles Untereiner, *Le marché allemand* (Paris: Les éditions d'organisation, 1990); for references to the importance of Sachlichkeit, see "Deutscher Nachholbedarf bei Investor Relations," in *Börsenzeitung*, July 5, 1994 (importance of Sachlichkeit in investor relations), and "Aus der Deckung," in *WirtschaftsWoche*, September 16, 1994 (Commerzbank CEO Kohlhaussen is praised for his "kühle Sachlichkeit").

9. For a reference to textile machine manufacturing, see "Es gibt keine neuen Management-Konzepte," in *Süddeutsche Zeitung*, June 20, 1995.

10 For general over-regulation, see "Beschleunigung in Sicht," in *IWD*, February, 2, 1995, and Herbert A. Henzler, "Neuanfang in der Garage," in *Die Zeit*, November 25, 1994; for financial markets, see Reinhard Fröhlich, "Ausländer nicht vergraulen," in *Börsenzeitung*, December 10, 1994, and "Am Finanzplatz Deutschland muß weiter gebaut werden," in *Handelsblatt*, July 4, 1995.

11. William L. Shirer, *Berliner Tagebuch* (Leipzig: Kiepenheuer, 1994), particularly pp. 254–257, 270–273; Hannah Arendt, *Besuch in Deutschland* (Hamburg: Rotbuch, 1994).

12. Alexander Mitscherlich, *Gesammelte Schriften*, Book 4 (Frankfurt: Suhrkamp, 1983), pp. 17–30; for a more recent review, see Margarete Mitscherlich, *Erinnerungsarbeit* (Frankfurt: Fischer, 1993, pp. 13–35); for criticism of these ideas, see Tilmann Moser, "Die Unfähigkeit zu trauern: Hält die Diagnose einer Überprüfung stand?" in *Psyche*, 1992, pp. 389–405; Eckhard Henscheid, "Die Unfähigkeit zu trauern oder so ähnlich," in *Frankfurter Allgemeine Zeitung*, June 12, 1993.

13. Helmut Klages, *Wertedynamik: über die Wandelbarkeit des Selbstverständlichen* (Zurich: Interfromm, 1988), pp. 48–51.

14. For the results of various surveys, see Werner Weidenfeld, *Die Deutschen: Profil einer Nation* (Stuttgart: Klett-Cotta, 1991), pp. 39–47; Karl-Heinz Reuband, "Arbeit und Wertewandel—mehr Mythos als Realität?" in *Kölner Zeitschrift für Soziologie und Sozialpsychologie*, 1985, pp. 723–746; for manager attitudes, see Lilly Beerman and Martin Stengel, "Werte im interkulturellen Vergleich," in Niels Bergemann et al. (eds.), *Interkulturelles Management* (Heidelberg: Physica, 1992), pp. 15–16.

15. Gerhard Schulze, *Die Erlebnisgesellschaft* (Frankfurt: Campus, 1992), pp. 538–541.

16. Willi Herbert, "Wertewandel in den 80er Jahren: Entwicklung eines neuen Wertmusters?" in Heinz Otto Lthe and Heiner Meulemann (eds.), *Wertewandel—Faktum oder Fiktion?* (Frankfurt: Campus, 1988), pp. 140–158; see also Eleonore Grimm, "Der neue deutsche Typ: sorglos und materialistisch," in *Psychologie heute*, November 1990, pp. 34–36, 38–41.

17 Werner Weidenfeld, *Die Deutschen: Profil einer Nation*, p. 139; see also for patriotism pp. 130–131.

18. Robert N. Bellah et al., *Habits of the Heart* (New York: Harper & Row, 1986), pp. 20–47.

19. Daniel Yankelovich, "Das Ende der fetten Jahre," in *Psychologie heute*, March 1994, pp. 28–37.

20. Johannes Hirschmeier, "Grundlagen des japanischen Arbeitsethos: die Firma als Schicksalsgemeinschaft," in Constantin von Barloewen and Kai Werhahn-Mees (eds.), *Japan und der Westen*, Book 2 (Frankfurt: Fischer, 1986), pp. 270–277; see also K. John Fukuda, *Japanese Style Management Transferred: The Experience of East Asia* (London: Routledge, 1991), pp. 63–67.

21. Horst Albach, "Japanischer Geist und internationaler Wettbewerb," in *Zeitschrift für Betriebswirtschaft*, 1990.

22. Tomoyasu Satow, "A View of Service Attitudes in Japanese Business," in *Global Management* 1992 (Brussels: Management Centre Europe, 1992), pp. 117–122.

23. Mayumi Itoh, "Japan's Abiding Sakoku Mentality," in *Orbis*, 2/1996, pp. 235–245.

24. For industrial disputes, see Mikio Sumiya, *The Japanese Industrial Relations Reconsidered* (Tokyo: The Japan Institute of Labour, 1990), p. 33, and Hirosuke Kawanishi, *Enterprise Unionism in Japan* (London: Kegan Paul, 1992), pp. 3–4, 72–75.

25. Masahide Miyasaka, *Shinto und Christentum: Wirtschaftsethik als Quelle der Industriestaatlichkeit* (Paderborn: Bonifatius, 1994), pp. 213–222; for a general discussion of Japanese cultural and economy, see also Subhash Durlabhji, "The Influence of Confucianism and Zen on the Japanese Organization," in Subhash Durlabhji and Norton E. Markay (eds.), *Japanese Business: Cultural Perspectives* (Albany: State University of New York, 1993), pp. 65–74; see also Morishima Michio, "Confucianism as a Basis for Capitalism," in Daniel I. Okimoto and Thomas P. Rohlen (eds.), *Inside the Japanese System* (Stanford: Stanford University Press, 1988), pp. 36–38.

26. Ruth Benedict, *The Chrysanthemum and the Sword* (Boston: Houghton Mifflin, 1946), pp. 223ff; for an excellent recent comparison of Japanese and German attitudes to war crimes, see Ian Buruma, *Erbschaft der Schuld* (Munich: Hanser, 1994), especially pp. 14–20, 48–53.

27. Hal Stone and Sidra Winkelman, *Embracing Ourselves* (San Rafael, CA: New World Library, 1989); see also Hal Stone and Sidra Winkelman, *Wenn zwei sich zu sehr trennen* (Berlin: Simon und Leutner, 1992).

28. For right-wing activities, see Oliver Geden, *Rechte Ökologie* (Berlin: Elefanten Press, 1996).

29. Hans-Joachim Maaz, *Der Gefühlsstau* (Berlin: Argon, 1991), pp. 12–14.

30. For disaffection in both parts of Germany, see Elisabeth Noelle-Neumann, "Eine Nation zu werden ist schwer," in *Frankfurter Allgemeine Zeitung*, August 10, 1994; for similar East and West German attitudes, see Helmut Klages, *Traditonsbruch als Herausforderung* (Frankfurt: Campus, 1993), pp. 222–223.

CHAPTER 7

Past Miracles, Present Continuity, Future Consensus

Each of us knows that an act of historic importance, born out of the greatness of soul and of political wisdom, decisively contributed toward making the recovery a reality for us Germans: the decision of the former opponent in the Second World War, the United States of America, to include Germany in the U.S. foreign aid program.

—Bundesminister for the Marshall Plan
Foreword to a Report on the Marshall Plan, 1953

In 1953, the Federal Republic's minister for the Marshall Plan wrote a dedication to a progress report on the reconstruction of West Germany after the war. The report is full of charts and figures—and also includes lavish praise of the kind quoted above.

In 1945, Germany presented an apocalyptic picture of destruction—geographic, economic, psychological. In the years that followed, a series of dramatic events occurred: America's Marshall Plan promoted economic recovery and a dynamic statesman called Ludwig Erhard pushed through a currency reform in cavalier-like fashion. The Germans worked hard, successfully overcoming the Nazi past, and by the mid-1950s, a wondrous alchemy occurred: the country was prosperous again. This is the conventional view of Germany's postwar recovery.

In the United States, traditionalist and revisionist historians have debated on whether the plan was part of a defensive policy of containment or aligned to an aggressive strategy aimed at shutting the Soviet Union out of Western

Europe. Both lines of reasoning hold an obvious element of truth, though neither explains the entire story.

As John Gimbel points out, the reality of the plan was less glorified than its later interpretations. According to him, it "was actually a series of pragmatic bureaucratic decisions, maneuvers, compromises and actions." Beyond this, policymakers were apparently influenced by fears of a domestic recession and the need to promote international demand for U.S. products.[1]

In Germany, the Marshall Plan belongs to the shibboleths of postwar identity. For the generation that grew up in the 1950s, it was a symbol of U.S. benevolence, estimated as highly as the Wirtschaftswunder. Beyond this, a number of scholars have justified its importance for individual sectors like cotton and electricity and stressed its general economic benefits.

Revisionist historians like Werner Abelshauser have however contradicted these viewpoints. Abelshauser provides a wealth of evidence to prove that the public relations strategies of the Marshall Plan administration far outweighed the concrete benefits of product deliveries for the West German occupation zones. According to him, details revealed in confidential reports prepared by U.S. officials in Germany apparently varied from the official reports prepared for public consumption.

Abelshauser exaggerates when he characterizes the Marshall planners' self-advertising as a "modern multimedia information policy." However, his observations are confirmed by Germany's first Minister of the Economy, Ludwig Erhard, who complained vociferously in the early 1950s about manipulative statistics and misleading statements.

Understandably, Erhard and the other architects of the Social Market Economy (SME) wanted to take the credit themselves for having pulled Germany out of economic chaos. However, it seems likely that the plan's protagonists and administrators created a mythology of achievements. They exaggerated the significance of the plan and glossed over obstacles caused by red tape and by rivalries between the State Department and the Military Government in Germany. Beyond this, Britain and France received more aid than Germany: in the second year of the plan for instance, France received 21.7 dollars per capita, as against 12 dollars for Germany.[2]

The moral support provided by the Marshall Plan was more important than financial aid. One further advantage for Germany was that reconstruction became a European issue. The country was thus integrated within a European community of reconstruction.

The Marshall Plan was the catalyst of Germany's economic recovery, the match that fell through the rubble and ignited the immense oil field of potential that war destruction had covered. This oil field had grown vastly during the Wilhelmine era and even more so during the Nazi period.

SECTION 1: HOW MIRACULOUS WAS THE WIRTSCHAFTSWUNDER?

The Wirtschaftswunder is postwar Germany's most significant achievement. It is treated with a mixture of awe, envy, and respect across the world.

The narrative of the Wirtschaftswunder is suspenseful. It also illustrates the human need to believe in miracles.

"Das Wunder ist des Glaubens liebstes Kind," the miracle is religion's favorite child, according to Goethe. The world's major religions are full of supposed miracles that awe their adherents. Miracles are meant to be believed, not to be analyzed. We thus believe in miraculous achievements because we cannot imagine them happening in the real world. This indeed characterizes the mystique created around the Wirtschaftswunder.

In actual fact however, as this book has often demonstrated, German history reveals a vast continuity in economic, social, and cultural terms. As we shall see, the recovery after the Second World War was far less exceptional than the destruction during the war.

In 1926, a German author called Julius Hirsch published a book called *Das amerikanische Wirtschaftswunder, The U.S. Economic Miracle*. Hirsch was highly impressed by America's natural resources and its wide range of consumer goods. However, he also recognized the role of infrastructure, praising the excellent highways, marveling at the organization of work in U.S. factories and pondering on the strange gaps between private sector efficiency and public sector slackness, between wealth and deprivation.

Hirsch thus contradicts his book's title with the evidence he cites: the supposed miracle derives from America's resources mix. Hirsch's disenchantment with America's public administration was of course typically German, but it also indicated the country's weaknesses: lack of state commitment to balanced economic progress coupled with a corresponding lack of social organization.[3]

America's weaknesses are Germany's strengths. State commitment, allied with infrastructure, have always been the mainsprings of economic progress. Their significance has however been obscured and glossed over by the conventional explanations offered both by the Wirtschaftswunder's analysts and major protagonists.

The most balanced conventional view of the miracle was published by the Yale economist Henry C. Wallich in 1955. In his influential study, *Mainsprings of the German Revival*, Wallich stresses both transitory success factors like economic policies, the Korean war, and the immigration of refugees, and more permanent factors like demographic and economic structures.

Oddly for someone born in Berlin, though perhaps typically for a modern economist, Wallich is hesitant to explore the mentality oriented sources of success, though he does refer to the "born qualities" of the German people. For instance, he mentions the work ethic without pointing out vital differences between German and Anglo-Saxon attitudes. He wistfully wishes that the

Germans "might revert to being the people of poets and thinkers that they were in the past," ignoring the fact that since the mid-nineteenth century, the emphasis in Germany had constantly been on economic expansion and social security.[4]

Wallich thus describes the substance, but does not capture the spirit of the recovery. He writes about postwar public administration without considering the inherited bureaucratic skills of the Prussian tradition. He devotes a chapter to SME without considering the fact that a form of SME had been practiced in Germany since the Bismarck period. His description of trade unions and codetermination is equally unhistoric and superficial; Wallich denigrates codetermination by calling it a dream, ignoring its vital role in coopting the workforce into a constructive attitude toward change.

Wallich's treatment of cartel legislation and the reasons for its inefficacy in the German context is however insightful and illuminating. All in all, Wallich's treatise is well-researched, but it registers symptoms rather than diagnosing their causes.

The Wirtschaftswunder's protagonists offer equally conventional explanations. In his aphoristic book *Wohlstand für alle*, *Wealth for All*, Ludwig Erhard rejects the word "Wunder," while explaining postwar progress as the "consequence of the honest toil of an entire people, whom freedom gave the opportunity to use their energy and initiative." And Hermann Josef Abs, Chairman of the Deutsche Bank's Board of Directors after the Second World War and a confidant of Chancellor Adenauer, gave a similarly one-dimensional view, while praising American magnanimity.[5]

In contrast to these conventional modes of explanation, some observers in and outside Germany sensed that there was more to the miracle than first met the eye. In his impressive study, *Modern Capitalism*, Andrew Shonfield for instance very rightly points out: "The defeat, division, and chaos which Germany suffered in the 1940s did not wipe out the legacy of the past; it only lifted temporarily the pressure of history. When the Germans began to reconstruct their economy, they built upon the familiar structural foundation and plan, much of it invisible to the naked eye, as if guided by an archaeologist who could pick his way blindfold about some favourite ruin."[6]

The structural foundation that Shonfield refers to existed under the rubble—in terms of business mentality, environment, infrastructure, and culture. Most of the resources described in this book, which have contributed to Germany's wealth, in fact flourished during the Nazi period.

BUSINESS MENTALITY: SYMBIOSIS OF TECHNOLOGY AND ORGANIZATION

If there were one individual who symbolized the synthesis of technical and organizational skills that made German business so successful after the war, it was Albert Speer. Mostly known as Hitler's favorite architect and the creator of bombastic buildings like the Reichskanzelei in Berlin, Speer also became minister for armaments and munitions in 1942. For the last three years of the war, he supervized the manufacture and distribution of armaments with great efficiency.

Albert Speer and his "kindergarten"—a group of young talented technicians that he recruited—rationalized and optimized the organization of war production and supplies:

- Speer started by drafting a plan of organization that grouped rings of production units round individual weapons like tanks and submarines. All production and distribution processes were thus concentrated around the final product, somewhat like the Japanese just-in-time method of factory organization.
- Speer allotted full operational responsibility to the business leaders in the companies involved in the rings. Here, he was merely continuing in the tradition of the industrialist Walther Rathenau, who had similarly coopted industry into the military organistion during the First World War. Speer promoted standardization and the exchange of technical expertise between the participating companies within the framework of steering committees. This was a shrewd way of mobilizing the German business world's cooperative talents and of delegating responsibility.
- Speer not only allowed the private sector to participate in public sector activities, he also radically reduced bureaucratic procedures. One specific reform was that the minister communicated directly with industrial leaders and top administrators, instead of, as hitherto, through the state secretary. Speer kept asking his assistants to stop producing official notes and to communicate informally by telephone.[7]

Speer's ministry was actually criticized for being "dynamic" and he was accused of using "American methods!" However, his obvious success—weapon production rose by 60 percent within six months and tripled in the space of two years—temporarily silenced the critics. As one colleague pointed out: "His wealth of ideas, his dynamic activism, the impatient pressure for speed, his ability to throw customary practice into question and to find unconventional solutions for apparently insoluble problems were the source of his success."[8]

Speer remains an enigmatic personality. He was the only top Nazi to publicly apologize for his role in the regime and his memoirs were highly praised and avidly read in Germany. However, as the historian Karl Dietrich Bracher points out, Speer created his own legend as the "unpolitical specialist." He was not a fringe figure who was tragically compromized: on the contrary, he and many other specialists were a primary part of National Socialism and largely contributed to the Third Reich's efficiency. Speer and his fellow technocrats belong to the specialist character type that has—as the chapter on psychological roots shows—been principally responsible for wealth creation in Germany.[9]

Despite U.S.-style informality, Speer belonged to the German mold: an engineer with administrative talents. He and his brilliant fellow specialists— fanatical technologists who tended to be ideologically indifferent—were the epitome of Teutonic efficiency:

- William Werner for instance, born in the United States, had worked for Chrysler and studied at MIT. He rationalized motor construction and introduced new forms of processing techniques. Men like him contributed to quadrupling Germany's aircraft production in the course of the war.

- Willy Schlieker, one of Germany's best-known industrialists in the 1950s, became head of iron and steel production at the age of twenty-eight. He coordinated manufacturing units across occupied Europe from a bunker, equiped with telephones and telex machines. His organization was so perfect that it functioned until the last day of the war.
- A thirty-seven-year-old engineer called Albert Ganzenmüller became state secretary of traffic. An electrical train specialist with a talent for industrial organization, he reorganized transport logistics in France so efficiently that the train service functioned smoothly a mere three weeks after the country capitulated. Ganzenmüller, like Speer, loathed bureaucracy: he was known to refuse to sign any official document that was longer than four double-spaced pages.[10]

Rationalization experts and management consultants were employed to modernize working processes. Logistics were particularly sophisticated: raw materials and workers were encoded and registered on punched cards—an early computer application—and transmitted by telex all over Germany and the occupied areas, so that all factories and administrative units could localize materials and labor forces efficiently.

The Roles of Associations and Cartels

The German war economy's organizational achievements were as much due to the "Reichsvereinigungen," the industrial associations that coordinated production and distribution within the "rings," as to the activities of individuals. Many leading postwar entrepreneurs and managers held important positions in these associations: Thyssen CEO Hans-Günther Sohl and British-American Tobacco CEO Eduard Söring are two examples.

During the Nazi period, the formal extent of participation in associations was increased: in agriculture and crafts, membership was compulsory. Some associations were homogenous enough to resist the infiltration of Nazi ideology—in particular the supremacy of the Führer principle in contrast to traditional forms of committee decision-making. The craftsmen for instance were less "synchronized"—than the farmers. The Third Reich forced the business community to coordinate its activities and thus inadvertently strengthened the role played by associations.[11]

After World War II, business representation regained its former autonomy, while retaining its strong role in public life. The right of all Germans to form associations and societies is guaranteed in Article 9 of the Constitution. In the generally restorative climate of the Adenauer era between 1949 and 1963—postwar Germany's formative period—industrial associations in particular increased their influence on public sector decision-making.

Cartels were similarly important contributors to industrial efficiency. IG Farben, by far the most important cartel, was so powerful that an U.S. expert committee judged at the end of the Second World War that "without I.G.'s immense productive facilities, its far-reaching research, varied technical experience and overall concentration of economic power, Germany would not have been in a position to start its aggressive war in September 1939."[12]

IG Farben was an indelible part of the crimes of Nazi Germany: not only did the cartel supply synthetic gasoline and rubber for the war machine, it also raided the resources of the occupied countries and constructed a huge industrial installation in Auschwitz that used concentration camp inmates as slave labor.

These infamous deeds have generally distracted attention from the mindset that enabled IG Farben to reach its preeminent position. The major companies of the German dye industry had already started to settle prices and fix quotas for their products before the First World War, sometimes with the participation of manufacturers from other countries. In spite of the confiscation of their foreign subsidiaries and the reparations they were required to make, the "Interessengemeinschaft"—abbreviated IG, literally a community of interest—founded in 1920 steadily prospered.

The major reason for IG Farben's success, apart from the technical brilliance of its researchers and its excellent standards in production quality and service, was this construction of a community of interest. As Carl Duisberg, the architect of IG Farben put it: "The form of community of interest that we chose is particularly adequate for us Germans. It allows individual firms and the personalities involved to keep their individuality and is in economic terms so superior to a trust-like fusion that everything must be done to keep the community alive—while however removing impediments and damage resulting from undue individualism and decentralization."[13]

Individuality without undue individualism, autonomy without undue decentralization—this balance between individual and common interests, gently enforced by the IG Farben officials, explains much of the "community's" success. It is also an excellent example of the German capability to balance priorities, distribute responsibility, and thus achieve an efficient consensus.

Fritz ter Meer, the highest ranking scientist on the IG managing board at the end of World War II, also points out that the cartel's bosses were well aware of the drawbacks of a large centralized corporation and wanted to retain the traditional creativity and flexibility of individual companies like BASF, Bayer, Hoechst, and Agfa, all of whom belonged to IG Farben.[14]

To support this autonomy, IG Farben introduced various structures of cooperation between individual companies and factories:

– Regional networks were built in the form of "enterprise communities," where the managers of different companies in a given geographic area met regularly to discuss technical and entrepreneurial questions and to be informed of decisions made by the IG managerial board.
– A technical committee with experts from different managerial levels met one day before board meetings and passed resolutions that were presented for ratification by the board.
– A large number of specialized commissions manned by experts from the different companies dealt with specific technical issues.

This complex structure functioned because all companies shared the same emphasis on long-term prosperity and stability. Thus as one of IG Farben's most impressive leaders, Carl Bosch pointed out in 1926, the emphasis lay on reinvesting profits and the company felt itself more responsible to its 125,000 employees than to its shareholders.

This was not lip service: voluntary social benefits for employees far exceeded the officially prescribed contributions and reached up to 25 percent of the total amount paid for personnel. Opportunistic exploitation of the economic status quo during the Nazi period contrasted with exemplary management and personnel policies.

In postwar Germany, stakeholders also prevail over shareholders. Corporations invest in the skills of their employees. Associations organize communities of interest within sectors. *Thus, IG Farben remains a German archetype, not in diabolic but in structural terms.*

Major factors that led to postwar Germany's business success—manufacturing proficiency, organizational efficiency, cooperative zeal—had continued to develop during the 1930s and early 1940s. There was no dramatic gain in expertise after the war.

BUSINESS ENVIRONMENT: TRUE ORIGINS OF THE SOCIAL MARKET ECONOMY

Like the business mentality, the business environment during the Third Reich provided major impulses for the postwar revival. The most spectacular example of this hidden continuity is undoubtedly SME. Often portrayed as a brave new beginning in policy orientation after the coercion of Nazi totalitarianism, the principles of SME were in reality enunciated during the 1930s under the patronage of the regime.

Ludwig Erhard's ideas of a socially oriented market economy were by no means subversive: on the contrary, they were reflected in the deliberations of members of the Nazi establishment. Erhard himself was supported by highly placed bureaucrats at the Ministry for Economic Affairs (Reichswirtschafts-ministerium) and by German industrialists who belonged to the influential association Reichsgruppe Industrie.

Recently published documents reveal that Erhard was by no means the freedom-loving anti-Nazi he was later portrayed as being. In the 1930s, he praised the new regime for favoring cartels and regulating prices. After war broke out, he used his high-level contacts to gain lucrative market-research contracts in the occupied territories. Erhard in fact played an advisory role in the economic exploitation of these territories.[15]

Similarly, leading ordoliberals and neoliberals were well established and given ample opportunities to publicize their views during the Nazi period:

– Alfred Müller-Armack, who coined the term Social Market Economy, developed his concept of the state's dynamic role in determining economic order as early as 1933 and welcomed the new regime for providing a strong "Nationalstaat," capable of dominating the economy. He was a great admirer of Italian fascism, judging that the Mussolini regime had managed to integrate society into state-imposed order.

- Walter Eucken, later the most prominent ordoliberal, propagated the need to grasp economic order as part of a larger order of things and emphasized the importance of "Leistungswettbewerb," in company with other ordoliberals during the 1930s and early 1940s. This was later to become a key SME concept. Both Müller-Armack and Eucken were strongly influenced by the right-wing philosopher Carl Schmitt, in particular by his concept of the "totaler Staat," strong enough to resist social pressure.[16]

Eucken was a firm believer in the efficacy of a strong state, which granted a measure of liberty after having established economic order. The ordoliberals flourished both under a fascist regime and later under democratic conditions because they were masters of ambiguity. During the Third Reich, they emphasized state-imposed order, while after the war, they propagated liberal principles.[17]

As the historian Werner Abelshauser cogently points out, SME did not fall like "manna from heaven" after 1945. It belonged to the viable alternatives of economic policy during the Third Reich.

Even in terms of vocabulary, premonitions of the Wirtschaftswunder ethos could be found during the Nazi period. Erhard's famous phrase, "Wohlstand für alle," Wealth for All, was used by a Nazi publicist called Fritz Nonnenbruch as far back as 1936. The Nazis certainly did not evenly distribute wealth, but they did succeed in ensuring social security for those who belonged to the Volksgemeinschaft.[18]

Bureaucratic Continuity and Estate Organization

A key link in the chain between the Nazi period and the Wirtschaftswunder was the public-private sector coexistence. Economic bureaucracy during the Nazi period mostly continued to carry out policies that had been drafted in the last years of the Weimar Republic. The National Socialists had no clear-cut economic strategy apart from vague ideas about autarky and protective tariffs. They were neither the agents of big business, nor did they dominate the private sector.

Bureaucracy in Germany has remained innately conservative, whatever the regime. As one analysis of administrative structure in Germany points out, the Republic of Weimar was forced to rely on a bureaucracy for whom republican values were anathema, whereas the National Socialists could be assured of general support on the part of civil servants, who appreciated the return to supposedly conservative norms. At the same time, the public administration sought to retain its own autonomy and assert itself against the party functionaries with a fair amount of success.

National Socialism's myth of a homogenized state with radical priorities was belied by the reality of administrative continuity. Hitler made no secret of his dislike and distrust of the "stupidity" and "egoism" of the bureaucrats, including them in his general hatred for jurists. Yet, though the National

Socialist party and a number of newly created administrative units put pressure on the administration, the result of these efforts was confusion rather than change.

Hitler made the mistake of ignoring the organic character of the administration, though he pretended to have a vision of the state as a "living organism." As one expert puts it, the Führer state produced an "organized chaos" of competing administrative units and represented an "atavistic personal association," rather than a collective entity.[19]

After the fall of the Nazi regime, a large percentage of the bureaucrats were able to continue their careers in West Germany. They ensured a valuable amount of administrative continuity—but also a restoration of procedures and modes of thought prevalent in the past.

The nearness of industry and government—in particular that of the industrial associations to official bureaucracy—was supplemented during the Nazi period by the ideological framework of the "ständischer Aufbau," the estate-oriented structure. Each business sector—for instance the Mittelstand—belonged to a separate estate and formed a part of a larger whole. This organic model, which saw the state as the peak of a hierarchic pyramid of autonomous associations, was propagated by the Austrian theorist Othmar Spann and fervently supported by influential industrialists like Fritz Thyssen.

Though the organizations founded to propagate these ideas—the "Amt für ständischen Aufbau" and the "Institut für Ständewesen"—soon lost influence, the spirit of estate-orientation persisted during the Nazi period and proved a unifying influence during the postwar period.

One example of this harmonious approach to development is the revitalization of the industrial heart of Germany, the Ruhr region, after World War II. Far from proving how talent and free enterprise can move mountains, the resurgence of the Ruhr is a superb example of how a basic consensus between the state, business and labor stimulated Germany's resurgence.

The need to stimulate investment in the Ruhr region and rebuild the industries that had contributed to Germany's wealth in the past was apparent. Chancellor Adenauer invited entrepreneurs and trade union officials to an economic summit in 1951, where committees were formed and the role-play defined: the associations organized private investment in Ruhr industries, the government supported these activities by passing an "investment promotion law," and the trade unions participated without however influencing decision-making. All this would not have been possible in an atomistic, Anglo-Saxon setup: the advantages of Germany's estate-orientation are apparent.[20]

Social Modernization

The deepest contribution of the Nazi period toward postwar stability and prosperity was the modernization of society. In his social history of the Third Reich, David Schoenbaum considers the creation of a new social consciousness to be National Socialism's great triumph. Though the conditions under which social modernization occurred were brutally totalitarian, cohesion increased markedly.[21]

The formal mechanisms of industrial partnership were destroyed by the Third Reich. Trade unions and works councils were abolished, many of the trade union functionaries were assassinated, arrested, or forced to emigrate. A law regulating "the order of working conditions" in 1934 established the Führerprinzip: a principle assigning all responsiblity to the "factory leader." The working class was compulsorily organized in the German Working Front, a kind of corporatist representation.

The pseudo-egalitarian rituals of the Volksgemeinschaft (literally: people's community) proclaimed by the Nazis and the pseudo-socialist Nazi ideology were accepted by the vast majority of the workforce, because they seemed closer to the interests of the common man than the class-bound Kaiserreich and the intellectually oriented Republic of Weimar. Perversely enough, the Nazis reaped the harvest of what the Social Democrats had sown during the Kaiserreich and the Weimar Republic—a proletarian sense of self-worth, coupled with a sense of belonging to the community.

Though the German Working Front under its drunken leader Robert Ley was a parody of true representation, workers gained rather than lost identity during the Third Reich. The mechanisms of industrial partnership changed momentarily—but not the spirit of participation.

Both before and after the Nazi period, the German approach to capitalism stressed the value of work at least as much as the importance of profits. Workers were not exploited and discarded at the whims of their masters as in more ruthlessly capitalist countries: they were integrated into economic order. They and their employers played assigned roles through their representatives. The working class was thus successfully coopted into its supporting role, long before SME came into being after World War II.

The National Socialists not only ensured social security: they also emphasized the need to improve efficiency. Nazi ideology stressed women's domestic role. Despite this, the percentage of women involved in the working process during the 1930s was high in comparison to other countries. The workforce also become more mobile in the 1930s, with large numbers of craftsmen and farmers entering the factories.

Qualified workers were at a premium and could demand high wages. Here, the outlines of the postwar "Mittelstandsgesellschaft," the middle-estate oriented society described extensively in this book, can be perceived. The Nazis also made ambitious plans in terms of housing, motorization, and social aid. These plans were shelved during the war, but the expertise that enabled them to be made could be summoned up in the "Stunde Null," the often dramatized Zero Hour after the war.

The Nazis propagated an ideology of achievement that was remarkably close to the ethos of the Wirtschaftswunder. As late as 1944, the magazine *Die deutsche Volkswirtschaft, The German Economy*, reported that the motto for the Deutsche Arbeitsfront, the unified trade union and welfare organization of the Nazi period, was "Leistung und Aufstieg," achievement and (social) climbing. This reflected the ideology of social modernization that had been propagated in the 1930s. *Thus, the very metaphors of the postwar ethos—reconstruction through achievement and social leveling—were gleaned from a vocabulary used during the Nazi period.*[22]

Similarly, *Die deutsche Volkswirtschaft* reported in 1944 on the progress made in alloting tax-free benefits to pension funds. The context of course is grotesque: while the country was being bombed into virtual extinction, economists were calmly discussing the modalities of the social state. Here again, the roots of the social security that supported the "inner readiness" of the Germans to rebuild in the face of chaos after the war can be clearly perceived.[23]

The social cohesion achieved by the Nazis enabled postwar Germany to survive the currency reform without social divisiveness. All commentators of the reform agree that it was highly unsocial: it favored a minority of entrepreneurs and owners of property at the expense of the vast majority of the population, whose savings were wiped out by the drastic devaluation. Erhard's economic policies were highly business-oriented, with low tax rates and strong investment benefits.

Basic elements of the welfare state survived the war and ensured the underprivileged a minimum of subsistence. However diametrically opposed both the Weimar Republic and the Third Reich had been to the Bismarck period, they had continued and enlarged both the spirit and substance of Bismarck's reforms. Thus, postwar policies, which would have been ruinously divisive elsewhere, could succeed in Germany. The cohesion and consensus of postwar Germany derive from a continuity of enlightened social policies.

SOCIOECONOMIC FOUNDATIONS: CONTINUITY IN THE FACE OF CATASTROPHES

Just as in the Sherlock Holmes story, the fact that the dog *didn't* bark was of decisive importance, so also is the continuity of Germany's infrastructure during the twentieth century an amazing achievement. Despite two world wars and two ruinous spells of inflation, the country retained its basic orientation of investing heavily in and constantly improving its infrastructure.

The most visible infrastructure achievement of the pre-Wirtschaftswunder period was undoubtedly the Autobahn. Construction of the German highways was a key project for the Nazis because Hitler could thus kill several birds with one stone: create employment, improve transport logistics in the context of planned military activity—and, last but not least, impress the world with a symbol of German engineering brilliance.

In actual fact, the Autobahn was far less important and successful than it seemed to be. The myth of the hundreds of thousands who worked to build the highways is untrue: 700 started in 1933 and the average number of workers involved till the outbreak of war was 80,000. Considering the fact that two million Germans found employment in the 1933–36 period, the contribution of the Autobahn was minimal compared to that of the private sector, which absorbed the vast majority of those unemployed.[24]

The second myth attached to the Autobahn concerns its significance for the mobility of Germany. Mobility did improve: however, of the originally planned 12,000 kilometers of highways, only 3,700 kilometers were constructed until 1940, when work stopped. Though the railways were neglected during the Third Reich, rail traffic increased and the Reichsbahn remained a symbol of efficiency until the end of World War II. It was by far the most important means of military and civil transport, accounting for 70–80 percent of all traffic. It did not however escape wartime destruction.

As the historian Eugen Kreidler points out in his analysis of the Reichsbahn during the Second World War: "Nearly six difficult war years reduced the Reichsbahn, which had hitherto enjoyed worldwide respect and which was greatly admired for its achievements by Germany's war enemies, to a shambles. Immediately after the capitulation, many industrious people started the infinitely difficult task of reconstructing the railways."[25]

Railway reconstruction was not in fact infinitely difficult in organizational terms: the Reichsbahn was renowned for a remarkably high standard of operational efficiency. The railway officials shared a high ethos of achievement both before and after the war. As one overview of German history in the twentieth century points out, there were no spectacular changes in transportation between 1914 and 1945. The Nazis inherited a high standard of performance—and maintained this standard. After the war, the same standard prevailed.[26]

Similarly, there were practically no new impulses for education in the 1914–45 period. On the one hand, the Nazis dismissed and liquidated an entire generation of Jewish and leftist scientists and scholars and broke with the classical Humboldtian ideals. On the other hand, there were few basic changes in Germany's vocational and primary education apart from the founding of some ideological schools (the "Nationalpolitische Erziehungsanstalten" and the "Adolf-Hitler-Schulen"). Germany's vocational education remained untouched, in spite of the attempt to draft a new law.

Further education expanded massively during the Nazi period. In spite of its ideological orientation, the Third Reich promoted a learning environment. Participation in the various courses, lectures and journeys organized by the Deutsche Volksbildungswerk increased from 2.2 million in 1937 to 5 million in 1942. Educational propaganda was subtler than the spectacular outdoor events organized by Goebbels' propaganda ministry. It enabled a large percentage of Germans to participate in cultural activities of various kinds.[27]

Hitler's Social Darwinism could only triumph in those spheres where total power led to total control, as in the political and racialist policies of the Third Reich. In the socioeconomic sphere, he was unable to achieve the same results. The autonomy of the business associations, vocational education, and other aspects of Germany's traditional estate order successfully resisted Nazi influence. The country's transport and education infrastructure continued to thrive during the Nazi period.

CULTURE: THE GAP BETWEEN IDEOLOGY AND REALITY

The Americanization of popular culture in Germany after the Second World War has often been commented on as a fundamental change in cultural orientation. This assertion is only partially true.

In spite of cultural propaganda that opposed "liberalistic American egotism," the concrete amount of contact between the two countries in the 1930s was remarkably large:

- Göring's magazine *Der Vierjahresplan* promoted study trips to the United States, allowing German technicians and industrialists firsthand contact with U.S. productivity. German civil engineers analyzed the consistency of U.S. cement in the context of the Autobahn construction and Ferdinand Porsche visited the Ford and General Motors factories while planning the Volkswagen beetle, which was mass-produced after the war.
- Similar study trips were offered for lawyers, advertising experts, craftsmen, farmers and so on by other organizations.
- The unified trade union, Deutsche Arbeitsfront, offered a series of study trips to America and the Carl Schurz association supported youth exchange.[28]

Beyond this, the overt and covert U.S. presence in Nazi Germany was enormous. Hollywood films were shown all over Germany until 1941. Swing and other forms of jazz enjoyed a large and clandestine clientele throughout the Nazi period, though official propaganda derided "nigger music." Ironically, Goebbels himself was a great admirer of jazz and organized special private concerts for an inner coterie during the war years.

In Berlin's Sportpalast, where Goebbels held his infamous speech in 1944, calling on the people to participate in the "total war," the walls were plastered with advertisements for "ice-cold Coca Cola." Ford advertised widely in radio jingles. Reports on America increased rather than decreased during the Nazi period, as one quantitative analysis of the *Berliner Illustrierte* between 1927 and 1938 shows.

Even during the final war years, most Germans had positive attitudes toward the United States. American pilots, who were forced to parachute into German territory, apparently encountered German officials who attempted to talk with them in the English they had learned at school and would offer them a cup of ersatz coffee.[29]

WONDER AFTER WONDER...

Germany's postwar miracle was not the first, but the third "Wirtschaftswunder" in this century. Writing in 1930, at a time when the German economy was beginning to collapse in the context of the New York stock exchange crash, Columbia University economist James W. Angell commented on the wondrous boom during the 1923–29 period and called this upsurge the "drama of a reconstruction, that has not seen its equal in world economic history."[30]

Strong words: Angell was understandably impressed by the phoenix-like rise of a country after hyper-inflation, the burden of enormous reparations, and the wartime loss of traditional markets. Like Wallich, who commented on the "Wirtschaftswunder" some twenty-five years later, Angell's economics-oriented worldview led him to believe that only a miracle could have restored Germany's economy so quickly.

Miracle number two: in 1936, a German emigrant called Hans E. Priester published a book called *Das deutsche Wirtschaftswunder*. This opponent of the Nazi regime pointed out in the foreword to his book that "an economic miracle without parallel has occurred." Priester was at pains to point out the vital role of the National Socialist state in the upsurge after 1933, but like Angell and Wallich, he ignored the elements of continuity in Nazi Germany's economic progress.[31]

Wonder after wonder. In reality, Germany never did anything miraculous. Its success—in 1923, 1933 and 1948—vindicated the efficacy of the traditional German approach to economic progress. The real wonder since 1948 is that stable world politics have enabled West Germany—and since 1990, unified Germany—to consolidate its wealth.

In retrospect, the debt that the postwar recovery owes to the Nazi period seems inevitable. How else could a destroyed country have developed economic policies, business strategies, and the sociocultural grounding that enabled these policies and strategies to succeed? The three years between 1945 and 1948—the year of the currency reform and the supposed beginning of the Wirtschaftswunder—were simply too brief a period for any other ethos to have developed.

Both the Nazi period and the postwar era are situated within a larger continuity. Both demonstrate the resilience of structures and attitudes derived from the past and the incapability of ideology to transform the organic. The Gestalt of the German economy has slowly mutated, but its phenomena, foundations, and roots recognisably adhere to patterns derived from the past.

SECTION 2: CONTINUITY RATHER THAN CHANGE

We live in an Age of the Superlative. Never has economic change been so immense, has technology advanced so fast, have social norms evolved so dramatically. *The rhetoric of change is omnipresent. Reality however tends to be less dramatic.*

Germany's postwar development is a case in point. At first sight, the change between 1945 and 1995 could hardly be greater: a country in ruins as against the leading economic power in Europe, a country released from fascism as compared with a democratic state. All this is true—and yet, far less has changed than has remained the same. The rhetoric of change contrasts with the reality of continuity.

This is most apparent in the economic sphere. As the institutional economist Egon Matzner points out, Germany is far from being a free-market economy: "In a nutshell, West Germany was, and Germany will be, a political economy rich in rigid non-market institutions such as strong trade unions, industry-wide collective bargaining, compulsory trade associations, a heavily and centrally regulated vocational training system, strong employment protection, statutory participation of workers and so on.[32]

Matzner's list can be extended further: supervisory authorities for banks and insurance companies, the "Handwerksordnung" (order of craftsmanship) and the "Gewerbeaufsicht" (trade supervision) effectively govern major sectors of the economy. Most of the institutions involved are old and their ways of functioning have changed only marginally in the last fifty years.

It is not only institutions that have survived and consolidated their roles in the course of time. In his book, *The End of the Economic Miracles*, the Hungarian economist Franz Jánossy saw an implicit continuity in Germany's economic progress since the late nineteenth century, emphasizing its "human capital" approach to progress. Other authors have emphasized the general importance of "social capabilities" and "immaterial capital."[33]

ECONOMIC IDENTITY: BALANCE

As we have seen, the German economy incorporates balance rather than dynamism. With a sureness that verges on the uncanny, like a somnambulist wandering down paths known from the past, postwar Germany has pursued an amorphous strategy of sharing out funds and responsibility, distributing benefits, and linking them to market conditions.

Employment stimulation schemes, "social plans" for those affected by retrenchment, bankruptcy compensation for employees, paid holidays and financial incentives for pregnant women and mothers, tax benefits for employees with savings accounts—the list of schemes directly involving state welfare in Germany is enormous. Equally enormous are the infrastructure investments in education, ecology, transport, and utilities.

The dead weight of these policies and projects makes it virtually impossible for any government to make dramatic changes or indeed follow fundamentally new policies. Thus, *the German commitment to continuity is profound—and implicit.*

The policies mentioned above have ensured an invaluable basic stability in Germany's economy and society. At the same time, they reduce the flexibility of both the public and private sectors in periods of crisis. In particular, high levels of wages, fringe benefits, and the overall complexity of labor laws have discouraged entrepreneurs from creating employment.

Unemployment has become a virtually insoluble problem, a bleak impasse for a polity dedicated to providing social welfare and personal well-being to its citizens. Germany has a greater degree of unemployment than its major rivals: over 10 percent as against around 3 percent in Japan and 6 percent in the United States No convincing strategy for eliminating unemployment and for dealing with the effects of rationalization and outsourcing has developed so far. Vocational specialization and social insurance regulations continue to restrict job creation.

A further example of structurally imposed inflexibility is the constitutional provision for tax sharing between the various states ("Länderfinanzausgleich"), designed to ensure even living conditions throughout Germany. The word "Ausgleich"—compensation—is in fact a key to understanding the peculiar complexity of the German economy. The German state has traditionally guaranteed that its citizens are compensated for the many mishaps that life can pose: after the war, there was a "Lastenausgleich" for the refugees. The local authorities in structurally weak regions receive "Ausgleichszahlungen," compensatory payments.

Rather like a universal insurance company, the postwar German state guarantees social security and egalitarian living conditions. Dynamic change is thus blocked by the search for parity.

Germany's parity orientation reflects its emphasis on balanced development. Social legislation and administrative regulations have expanded correspondingly. In 1950, West Germany published around 800 pages of laws and regulations each year. Thirty years later, it published four times as many pages. These restrictions curb industrial investment, restrict the expansion of the service sector, and thus make it difficult to tackle unemployment.

However, the German emphasis on integrating workers into a mesh of social security and vocational participation is a sound long-term strategy, which contrasts with the laissez-faire approach to industrial policy. The political scientist James Kurth divides the U.S. economy into high and low service sectors. The high sector consists of financial services and globally active corporations, while the low sector incorporates low-skill jobs for the local market.

Kurth then points out: "In a sense, postindustrial workers in the low-service economy are like preindustrial workers in a subsistence economy who contribute nothing to the wider economy beyond their own immediate locality. In contrast, in an efficient and competitive industrial economy, most workers produce for the global market, or they provide services directly supporting that production."[34]

This in a nutshell is the fundamental difference between the United States and Germany. The U.S. performance is more impressive at first sight but is bought at the cost of a profound disparity between privileged "knowledge workers" in financial services, software, and other high-touch/high-tech areas on the one hand and a "service proletariat" on the other hand. In Germany by contrast, a large percentage of employees both in large corporations and Mittelstand enterprises contribute to exports. Service jobs are closely linked to the industrial sector.

Downward vocational mobility is massive in America and marginal in Germany, as one comparative study has shown. Since the cost of downward mobility cannot be quantified, it tends to be overlooked in purely economic estimates of success. However, it contributes to the gradual disintegration of society and demolition of wealth's foundations.[35]

Industrial partnership, in particular codetermination, enables German companies to achieve a specific kind of flexibility. Corporations like BMW and Trumpf, for instance, have developed innovative flexitime models oriented around equally flexible manufacturing installations. Since these models are codetermined by the works councils and approved of by the trade unions, they tend to be highly stable. Models to create employment can build on jobs created by flexitime.

The German process of structural change will be gradualist because of its consensus orientation. Gradual change has already occurred in one vital area: the environment. As we have seen, *the ecological transformation in Germany transcends technocratic policies and business strategies. It marks a new attitude toward growth, a more balanced attitude that stresses quality of life as much as quantity of growth without however ignoring the country's need to achieve competitive advantage in international markets.*

This is an organic metamorphosis, one that has not upset the delicate balance between the state, business, the trade unions, other interest groups and society at large. It has also bettered rather than worsened Germany's long-term competitiveness, acting as an impetus for innovations aligned toward reducing costs of raw materials, creating new machines, refashioning manufacturing processes and increasing the efficiency of industrial organization.

SOCIAL IDENTITY: MITTELSTANDSGESELLSCHAFT

The first twenty years after the Second World War have generally been called restorative, best construed as a return to bourgeois values, as personified by the Biedermeier period in the nineteenth century. One caustic description of 1949–68 calls it "post-totalitarian Biedermeier." The word "bieder," which originally signified uprightness but now denotes simple-mindedness, adequately describes society during the Adenauer and Erhard administrations.

Traditional values like perseverance and orderliness were stressed—values that the Nazi period had partially modified, but never really changed. The Germans of 1945 were basically as hard-working, as well-organized and as homogenous in their attitudes as they had been in 1933. Thus, the social continuity of the postwar years built on a solid foundation. Erhard himself openly longed for a "formed society," a term that awakens associations with the estate orientation of the Nazi Volksgemeinschaft, where everyone had his allotted place.

The year 1968 was different. Self-questioning was the leitmotif of student protest. The order of things—at the universities, in business, in bureaucracy—was questioned and the hypocricy of a society that continued to ignore the implications of the Nazi period was exposed.

Both the compulsive materialism and the blind pro-Americanism of the postwar period were attacked, both lost some of their orientational importance in the decades that followed. The social consensus of historic forgetfulness was broken: after 1968, "Vergangenheitsbewältigung" (literally, mastering the past) became the catchword for a process of earnest reflection on the horrors of Nazi Germany.

In true German fashion, this process of coming to terms with fascism has been formalized and functionalized. But the admittedly ritualistic process of questioning the past matured German society and made it susceptible to the development of groups of citizen activists, later to be called "Bürgerinitiativen." By 1980, around a thousand registered "Citizens' Initiatives" united some 300,000 members. The peace movement, the anti-atomic energy protests, women's lib—and, most significantly, the ecological party—derived from the spirit of 1968. The students had demonstrated the potential of organized protest and other social groups were quick to follow. The protests of specialized groups tended to be more focused—and thus more effective—than the ideologically motivated student revolt.[36]

Ecology and other issues cater to an incipient need, in the context of a Mittelstandsgesellschaft, to subscribe to a cause and to contribute to the common good. In Germany, it satsfies the deep need to moralize that dominates political controversies and media commentaries and that—as we have seen—makes German rhetoric so boring. It also serves as an escape valve for the frustrated energy of a society that has been constrained to moderation after the excesses of the Nazi period.

The sense of proportion and of balance that characterises the Mittelstandsgesellschaft also curbs the longing for the absolute that is rooted in a variety of phenomena examined in this book: product perfection, organizational thoroughness, romanticism. Thus, many Germans have been on the implicit lookout for something symbolizing goodness, purity, rarification—and ecology is an ideal issue.

"Eco Pax," a change in values emphasizing the ecological fundament to life, has transformed German society. Ever since, progress—whether it means new Autobahns or industrial settlement—has to legitimize itself. Eco Pax is a built-in corrective to heedless growth. It has reinforced rather than reduced Germany's enormous social consensus—and predestined Germany to excel in the practice of sustainable development.

CULTURAL IDENTITY: INNERLICHKEIT

At first sight, cultural change after 1945 was spectacular. Until 1933, Germany was one of the world's leading cultural powers, full of world-famous romanciers, philosophers, social and natural scientists.

The Third Reich changed all this. A large percentage of Germany's cultural establishment was either forced to emigrate or discredited because of complicity with the regime. Many cultural personalities declined to return to West Germany, among others Thomas Mann and Max Beckmann. Thus, a cultural vacuum developed.

The high priests of "Kulturkritik"—the traditionally influential cultural criticism—condemned the Americanization of society and the banality of popular culture after the war. With scant success, as the publicist Christian Graf von Krockow points out: "America above all incorporated freedom and space. The Germans kept dreaming the American Dream." Similarly, the philosopher Jürgen Habermas has drawn attention to the contemporary Westernization of the German mind, while the educationist Hartmut von

Hentig discerns an uncommon amount of Anglo-Saxon common sense in postwar Germany.[37]

However, we have seen that close contacts with the United States and the "American way of life" existed during the 1930s and 1940s. The occupation of Germany after the war merely reinforced a tendency that already existed.

While mainstream intellectuals in the 1950s and 1960s played the roles of "Aufklärer," trying to enlighten their countrymen on a variety of issues, the trend since the 1970s has been toward Innerlichkeit, a more romantic concentration on inner values, coupled with a search for idyllic modes of life. The German predilection with ecological issues, above all the fear of Waldsterben, of forest death, can be traced back to the Innerlichkeit of romanticism.

As we have seen, Innerlichkeit is the key to Germany's cultural identity. Ever since Luther, "Tiefe des Gemüts," depth of the soul, is a norm that German literature and the fine arts have aspired to. *From this depth comes the longing for wholeness and for the organic that makes German society so cohesive and the ecological consensus so profound.*

Styles of writing and of oral expression have become crisper in the German media in the 1990s, reflecting the boom in private TV programs and trend-setting magazines. Germany's jeunesse dorée speaks excellent English and is very much into international trends.

At first sight, the German "Sonderweg," the legendary non-Western "special direction" involving a different approach to both politics and culture, seems well and truly over. At second sight, the opposite is the case: as we have seen, German idealism and romanticism coexist with urbanity and continue to foster an often excessive degree of moralism and sensitivity. Values like "Befindlichkeit" (sensitivity) and "Betroffenheit" (dismay) continue to dominate German culture. As the sociologist Erwin Scheuch points out, Kulturkritik remains a uniquely German predilection.[38]

Displaying dismay at the state of the world and the badness of mankind still belongs to the rituals of public discussion. The ethos of pessimism, described in various contexts in this book, remains vitally important. This is the cultural reason why ecology is such an important issue in Germany: it offers an enormous number of opportunities for pontification on the terrible condition of the air, the soil, the forests. Major shibboleths of German culture have thus remained the same, despite the urbane facade.

Balance, Mittelstandsgesellschaft, Innerlichkeit: the invisible quintessence of German identity is the "inner middle." As seen earlier, Germany's contemporary identity is strongly oriented toward the middle rather than toward extremes. The Mittelstand, the impeccable mediocrity of German managers, the egalitarianism of a working community, are external evidence of the middle. *The inner middle however also draws on the German emphasis on depth rather than superficial brilliance, on wholeness rather than quick results. Without an inner middle, the German approach to balanced development would lack consistency and depth.*

SECTION 3: THE DEEPENING OF CONSENSUS

In his search for West Germany's "efficient secret," the English political scientist Gordon Smith discovered the complex nature of its consensus process: "The strength of the synthesis has to be admitted; its hallmark is the value placed on securing wide agreement, and its style is best suited to the slow accretion of policies in well-defined directions that are generally understood. It amounts to a version of politics posited on consolidation rather than change. A successful leader appreciates how the elements of consensus are composed and the limits within which changes can be made."[39]

As we have seen, German leaders play the role of moderators, relying on consensus in the policymaking process. This puts obvious brakes on change and explains why Germany often appears to be irritatingly static. As we have also seen, change in the German context is an organic process that evolves slowly, but when change occurs, it is profound and rarely retracted.

The word consensus has acquired different connotations, depending on cultural context. In Roman law, contracts were sealed by an act of will, a sign of consensus between the parties to a contract. In the Anglo-Saxon tradition, articulated by philosophers like John Locke, consensus is the foundation of civil government. Democratic states postulate a fundamental consensus (Grundkonsens) that all citizens participate in, even if governments depend on majority support.

German philosophy, in particular Hegel, emphasized Volksgeist, the spirit of the people, rather than the Grundkonsens. This dangerous romanticism weakened the Republic of Weimar and contributed to the perversion of law and of basic human values during the Nazi period.

However, after Germany became a democracy in 1949, aspects of Volksgeist—in particular what the sociologist Ralf Dahrendorf has called the German "longing for synthesis"—ensured a valuable continuity in a country torn apart by war and division. The Germans used the Anglo-Saxon democratic framework and augmented it by a constant process of dialogue: between capital and labor, the public and private sectors, and representatives of interest groups and bureaucrats. The balance of power, priorities, and responsbility analyzed in the context of the business environment have encouraged complex forms of consensus.

Basically, two types of consensus have been investigated in this book:

- An ostensive search for consensus on controversial issues such as energy and transport. The ostensiveness of consensus is mirrored by the use of language: the "Energiekonsens" for instance belongs to Germany's contemporary vocabulary and designates a negotiation ritual that has continued for several years.
- An implicit alignment toward consensus visible in ecology and in the functioning of industrial fairs. These deeper forms of consensus are based on shared values and priorities.

Contemporary Germany has become a sophisticated democracy with well-functioning institutions, but has retained a wordless understanding of community (Gemeinschaft) that transcends the rudimentary bonds provided by a modern society (Gesellschaft). German society today is far removed from the enforced communitarianism of the Nazi Volksgemeinschaft: it is a community of shared values and priorities rather than a community founded on racial roots.

Shared values and priorities are characteristic of a deeper and more dynamic consensus, one that goes beyond the Grundkonsens of majority rule and common law to mold society and modify the economy, as is the case in ecology. *This Gestaltungskonsens—literally, formative consensus—is Germany's key to future wealth.*

Arriving at and implementing the Gestaltungskonsens involves an enormous amount of negotiations and administrative activity. The danger here is an exaggeration of the importance of petty issues: the French term "querelles allemandes" adequately expresses the German propensity toward petty squabbles. Sometimes indeed, a "Konsens über Nonsens" is achieved, a consensus on nonsensical matters. But the optimization of consensus could well become the German bridge to the twenty-first century. *Because of the way Germany's economic, social, and cultural identity supports the consensus process, the German bridge to the future seems stabler than the more technocratic bridges that the United States and Japan are busy building.*

CONSENSUS AND INTERNATIONAL PREEMINENCE

Despite appalling conflicts in formerly united, ethnically disparate entities like the Soviet Union and Yugoslavia, the world is slowly moving toward structures of consensus, as visible in the development of various alliances between countries, such as NAFTA, ASEAN, MERCOSUR, and APEC. The North and South Americans, the Southeast Asians and the Australians are cooperating in loose federations that adopt certain features of the European Union (EU), which can look back to the largest amount of expertise and experience in molding member-states out of nation-states.

The EU is not only the most established international federation but also the most coherent. Its fifteen members are culturally linked and subscribe to similar norms of democracy and social welfare. Beyond this, the union has grown organically: from six members in the middle of Europe in 1958 to fifteen stretching from the extreme north to the extreme south of the continent. Geographic proximity has promoted trade, just as normative proximity has enabled a free trade zone to evolve into a customs union, a common market, and to gradually mutate into an economic and monetary union.

This contrasts vividly with other international federations of nation-states:

APEC. The Asian Pacific Economic Cooperation is for a number of reasons a nonstarter. Despite a series of "vision statements" since 1989, APEC is far from constituting a coherent group of countries with common norms, let alone an economic community. To start with, the eighteen-member group is highly disparate in economic and cultural terms: United States, Canada, Mexico, and Chile coupled with Australia, China, Indonesia, and Japan.

Beyond this, the geographic gulf between the Asian and "Pacific" nations is enormous. Intra-Asian trade has expanded to now account for almost 50 percent of East Asia's total trade, This regional focus, which also characterizes trade in the EU, excludes the Pacific countries. Conversely, the United States's prime trading partner—both for imports and exports—is Canada, not Japan.

Regional focus would seem to favor the purely East Asian affiliations ASEAN, ARF, and EAEC. However, glib protestations of common interests and of "Asian values" are belied by the nationalistic postures and economic egotism both of China and other major Asian countries. As we have seen, Nihonjinron, the "science of Japaneseness," makes Japan an unlikely candidate for leadership in Asia.[40]

NAFTA. The North American Free Trade Association is an equally ineffective federation, though it only consists of three geographically adjacent states. Economic and cultural divergence between Canada and the United States on the one hand and Mexico on the other hand is too significant to be overcome by a loose association of states.

Canada and the United States also differ on fundamental policy priorities. Canada maintains an European-style social state with correspondingly high taxes and state quota. it relies more on demand-oriented than supply-side policies. Trade with the United States has considerably increased because of NAFTA, while trade with Mexico remains minimal. However, U.S. allegations of Canadian protectionism have led to a number of acrimonious trade disputes. Canadians have also attempted to protect their cultural identity by restricting film distribution and book-retailing from the United States. Thus, the three countries are far from constituting a coherent association.[41]

MERCOSUR. Mercato sur, Latin America's common market, has a greater chance of success. Geographic and cultural proximity between its members— Brazil and Argentina, Uruguay and Parguay—has boosted trade ever since MERCOSUR was founded in 1991.

This federation of states has yet to evolve into a full free-trade area and is far from becoming the common market that it aspires to be. Nor is it likely to feature a supranational institution like the European Commission. However, the MERCOSUR countries have already achieved more intra-Latin trade, and are poised to increase trade with other federations of states, in particular the EU.[42]

Free trade alone is an insufficient foundation for a community of states. EFTA, the European Free Trade Association, founded in 1959 with seven members, is the best proof of this argument. From the beginning onwards, commitment to EFTA was tenuous. Its founder Great Britain tried, albeit unsuccessfully, in 1961 and 1967 to join the European Community (EC) and ultimately succeeded in 1974. Other countries like Denmark and Portugal later followed the same tactics.

EFTA lacked a cohesive ethos and signally failed to promote wealth creation. The EU on the contrary has progressively developed an ethos of partnership for mutual benefit, despite perpetual frictions on specific issues such as agricultural subsidies, industrial policies, and ecological restrictions.

Growth rates, inflation levels, and general standards of living have converged in the EU to an increasing extent:

- In 1984, average inflation in the EC was 9 percent, in 1996 it was 2.4 percent, reflecting the high degree of financial stability of the fifteen member states. Simultaneously, the difference between the highest and lowest inflation in member states declined from 26.9 to 8.9 percent during the same time frame.
- A similar convergence in standards of living has occurred. In 1983, average income in Ireland for instance was 63 percent of the EU average, in 1996, it reached 90 percent.

The next decades will see the EU expanding eastward. The CEFTA countries—Poland, Hungary, the Czech and Slovak republics, and Slovenia—are likely to be the next candidates, followed by the Baltic Council states (Lithuania, Estonia, and Lettland).

Through its various institutions—European Parliament, European Council, European Court—the EU has promoted democratic values as well as economic progress. Decision-making by consensus rather than imposition characterizes EU policies. This has supported the transition to democracy of member-states like Spain, Portugal, and Greece, which experienced dictatorial regimes until the 1970s. It will also help the CEFTA countries and other formerly socialist states to achieve the same transition.

Germany profits greatly from the fifteen-nation EU: it is now in the middle of a large, stable community. Its trade volume with the central and east European countries that are likely to become new EU members is already higher than that with the United States.

Germany's ability to contribute to consensus within the EU presages its world role, just as France's obstructionism, centralism and narrow-minded nationalism have prevented it from becoming truly influential. As one French commentator judged in 1994: "Here is a country paralyzed by unemployment and by self-doubts on its role in the world, its European policies, its institutions and its identity. There is a country whose reunification is a success, which has modernized its social relations and restructured its economy and is now starting to assert itself in foreign affairs."[43]

ORDNUNGSPOLITIK AND COHESION IN THE EUROPEAN UNION

Legislation and policies in the EU are increasingly being influenced by German "Ordnungspolitik," by policies that establish a common economic order, while allowing for a reasonable amount of private-sector autonomy. Beyond this, Germany's specialists play quietly influential roles in the many technical committees that set the union's industrial standards and guidelines. This is particularly the case with ecological laws and regulations.

Ordnungspolitik in the German context is linked with subsidiarity—with social policies aligned toward autonomy rather than centralism. Germany's former chief justice, Ernst Benda, compared U.S. federalism with German subsidiarity and came to the following conclusion: federalism in the United States is an unstructured process often described as a "state of mind."[44]

The precepts of subsidiarity in Germany by contrast are clearly enunciated and anchored in the constitution. The practice of subsidiarity is ensured by widespread competences exercized by the federal states and by the formalized role of private-sector organizations in administering welfare.

The Treaty of Maastricht, valid since 1993, emulates the German constitution by adopting the same principles of subsidiarity: the European Commission's purview is restricted to issues that member states cannot resolve individually.

To ensure cohesion despite regional diversity, the German constitution prescribes "Bündnistreue," the loyalty of both the states and the central government to common aims. Central policies enforce cohesion: the "Länderfinanzausgleich" described earlier evens out the economic diversities between the different German states by redistributing revenues.

Similarly, the EU promotes social cohesion by providing subsidies and technical assistance to underdeveloped regions. The union's "cohesion funds" are allotted to ensure reasonably equal standards of living in all member states and have largely contributed to Ireland's dramatic upsurge.

Cohesion in the German context is however more than a policy of distributing subsidies. As we have seen in the course of this book, organizational cohesion characterizes corporations, formalized interest representation ensures cohesion in the entire economy, and social cohesion is at the core of the Mittelstandsgesellschaft. The efficacy of Germany's consensus mechanisms is founded on cohesion. Similarly, the EU consensus process will improve to the extent that a greater degree of cohesion is achieved.

The depth of Germany's influence in the EU transcends its more visible preeminence as the union's leading economic state. *The normative Germanicization of Europe is a gradual, largely invisible process, just as the continent's Americanization—in terms of financial markets, media, and consumer goods—is more ostensive and superficial.*

No country in the world is now strong enough to impose its own norms and concepts of order, as Great Britain and the United States did in the past. Neither a Pax Nipponica nor a Pax Teutonica is likely to succeed the Pax Britannica and Pax Americana of former times. Thus, future strength will be measured by the closeness of a country to the global consensus process, by its capability to integrate within the international mainstream of socioeconomic development. It is a process in which the moderator, not the pace-maker, gains influence.

Germany is both geographically and culturally better equipped than the United States and Japan to play a worldwide moderator role, just as in the EU, it is better equipped than France and Britain.

BALANCED DEVELOPMENT: BALANCING WEALTH, WELFARE AND WELL-BEING

Germany's great competitive advantage in the future will be the way it has invested in social welfare and psychic well-being rather than exclusively in wealth. While subscribing to the same wealth norms as its major competitors, growth and productivity, it has balanced these aims with other values and priorities. *Cohesion and consensus have consolidated balanced development. Germany's Gestaltungskonsens will optimize the constant search for a policy balance.*

Productivity and growth are seemingly abstract words, when used in economic theory. They are linked however to the competence and potential of human beings. Adam Smith's revolutionary statement—that the wealth of a nation is not measured in gold or silver but in the quality and quantity of a nation's labor force—needs to be reformulated. National wealth in the long term is linked with the access of those involved in productive activity not only to wealth but also to welfare and well-being.

In postwar Germany, economic growth has simultaneously humanized society. As we have seen, Germans today are more open-minded and less compulsive than they have ever been before. The fifty years after the Second World War have not only been the most prosperous in Germany's history, they have also been the stablest and the most humane.

There is a delicate, a nonquantifiable link between the wealth of a nation and the welfare of its people. Welfare encompasses schooling, housing, medical care, cultural facilities. If welfare is widespread, it provides stable foundations for future wealth.

Great Britain ignored this insight with tragic results. It lived off the fat of the land—or rather, from its pioneer industrial and mercantile skills, from its colonies and from its remarkably stable democracy—without creating the foundations of long-term wealth. When it tried to introduce the social state, it was too little and too late. Above all, welfare was not organic—it was patronisingly humanitarian.

Conversely, welfare cannot survive without the constant creation of wealth. The production and distribution of goods and services, the give-and-take of international trade are vital elements of the health of an economy. Sweden is an excellent example of a country that disregarded this hometruth at its peril, attempting in splendid isolation to maintain its own welfare model. It lost competitive standing in world markets and has been forced to seriously curtail its social state and restructure its economy.[45]

Equally delicate is the link between welfare and well-being. Germany has exaggerated somewhat in its provision of welfare—six weeks of paid holidays for most employees and exaggerated health care schemes are two examples—but it has generally grasped the need for the balance between the three Ws. Germans today live in a sophisticated world of relatively high wealth, welfare, and well-being.

The specific balance of the three Ws depends on norms derived from the "inner middle," as seen earlier. On a more concrete level, it relies on the

Mittelstandsgellschaft, which favors the active many rather than the happy few, in contrast to American elitism. And the active many voice their welfare and well-being needs more confidently than their counterparts in Japan. A large cross-section of German society thus contributes more consciously to national wealth, to social welfare, and to their own personal well-being than in America or Japan.

The practice of balance involves the mastery of a subtle mixture of incentives and restrictions, of state control and private-sector autonomy. It is the policy mix best attuned to long-term wealth. No amount of ideology, whether capitalist or socialist, or of superficial success can permanently obliterate the need for balance in the distribution of wealth, provision of welfare, and pervasiveness of well-being.

The demise of bureaucratic socialism in Eastern Europe and elsewhere in the 1980s and 1990s has rendered the ideological arguments of free-market economies unnecessary. Even more irrelevant are former prognoses of the demise of capitalism, made, for a variety of reasons, by Karl Marx, Joseph Schumpeter, and Werner Sombart, among others. The basic question—to what extent are governments and societies satisfying the material and nonmaterial needs of their citizens—can no longer be answered by mere declarations of faith in the all-healing powers of the market—or in the inevitability of socialism.

Many countries still cultivate their own illusions, but they are doomed to reawaken to reality. The pageantry of the Kennedy and Reagan eras has vanished. Epigonal attempts at neo-Reaganomics and neo-Thatcherism cannot mask a basic evolution toward realism and social justice. *In this context, the country with the fewest illusions and the most realistically enlightened values and priorities is destined to lead the world—not by imposing its own norms but by integrating into the world economy and setting the norms by which other countries voluntarily abide.*

TOWARD AN AGE OF SUSTAINABLE DEVELOPMENT?

In an essay on futurology, aptly entitled "On the Limits of Economic Prediction," the economist Robert L. Heilbroner draws attention to contemporary attitudes: "Ours is not the first age to believe it could foretell the future. The Greeks consulted the oracles; the Middle Ages the clergy; the Enlightenment the philosophers and historians. The difference is that we ask the scientists."[46]

We live in a scientific age and many of us trust the quantitative, facts-and-figures approach that the natural sciences in particular embody. The use of systems analysis, scenarios, and global models gives forecasts an aura of scientific respectability.

Heilbroner comments on the inadequacies of short-term forecasts in particular. They imply that the predictors can functionalize behavioral response, ignoring the "potential perversity of behavior." Long-term forecasts have, according to him, slightly better chances: for cultural reasons, collective economic behavior remains roughly the same. However, their accuracy is seriously diminished by difficulties in predicting the effects of new commodities on consumer behavior and of technology on society.

These problems are virtually insoluble. As John Kenneth Galbraith succinctly puts it: "Forecasts are, in fact, inherently unreliable." However, the cultural background referred to by Heilbroner is, as we have seen in this book, a prime determinant of economic activity. Thus, future strengths and weaknesses can be partially deduced by reference to the culture of a country. The links between economics, society, culture, and psychology provide a frame of reference for reflections on how countries can respond to future change.

The real question to be asked about forecasts, models, scenarios and visions is: How close are they to the identity of the countries they cover? The inherent problem with global predictions is that the entity they attempt to encompass is too complex. Beyond this, the methods used by the vast majority of scientific predictions are too linear. They ignore the organic nature of human activity.

Projections of the future thus tend to say more about the personalities and cultural backgrounds of their creators than about epochs to come. Their success also seems to depend more on the Zeitgeist than on the premises or methodology they use. Thus, in the optimistic 1960s, the Hudson Institute forecasts of Hermann Kahn were en vogue, just as in the post-oil crisis 1970s, the pessimistic Club of Rome forecasts touched a nerve.

Similarly, optimistic prognoses are generally favored in the United States, because they satisfy the collective desire to think positively. In Germany on the other hand, most visions of the future are pessimistic, because they confirm the habitual gloominess that many thoughtful Germans cultivate. In a country in which the "lust for downfall"—as one German political scientist points out—is a basic intellectual attitude, forebodings of doom find receptive audiences.[47]

The future manifestly cannot be predicted. However, the ability of countries to cope with unforeseen future developments can certainly be estimated.

SUSTAINABLE DEVELOPMENT: THE MASTERY OF COMPLEXITY

It seems likely that the world of the future will fulfill neither Francis Fukuyama's optimistic "end of history" nor Samuel Huntington's pessimistic "clash of civilizations" prophecy. Reality will be less dramatic and more complex, involving clashes within cultures and cooperation between different cultures.

This complexity also applies to attitudes and approaches to economic progress. Increasingly, market mechanisms will be seen as functioning within a larger context. Sublimation of the free market as the arbiter of progress will diminish accordingly.

Sustainable development (SD) has become the catchword for a more ecological orientation toward progress. A country's wealth derives from its capability to simultaneously grow and to save resources, in other words to balance the needs of the economy and those of ecology (see Figure 7.1).

Figure 7.1
Rivaling Models of Development

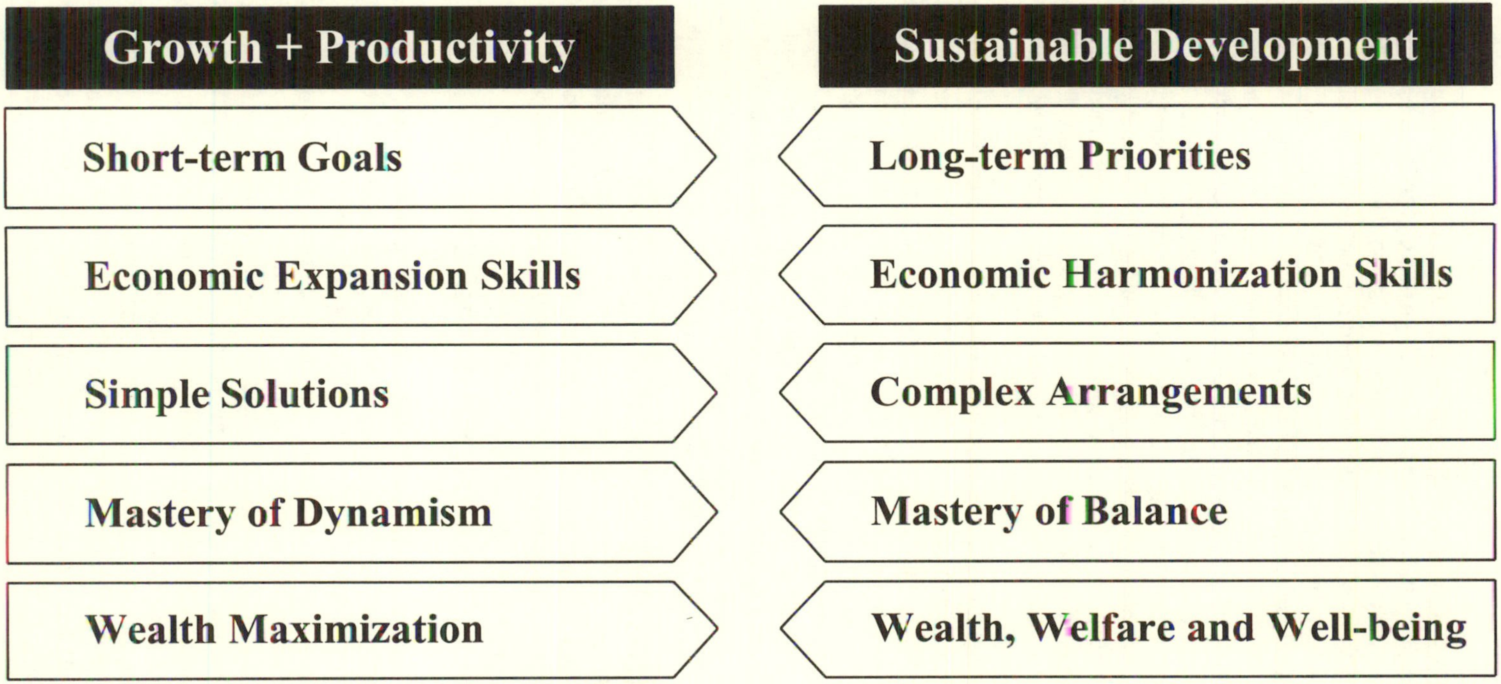

Growth + Productivity

Short-term Goals

Economic Expansion Skills

Simple Solutions

Mastery of Dynamism

Wealth Maximization

Sustainable Development

Long-term Priorities

Economic Harmonization Skills

Complex Arrangements

Mastery of Balance

Wealth, Welfare and Well-being

A global consensus in favor of SD is slowly evolving. The UN conference on ecology in Stockholm in 1972 signaled a growing interest in ecology on the part of industrialized countries, just as the Rio conference held twenty years later focused worldwide attention to the ecological issue. However, perceptions of sustainability are too narrowly linked to ecology: the financial, social, and cultural dimensions have yet to be adequately explored.

Financial stability—both monetary and fiscal—is a prerequisite for the sustainability of all economic policies. Alexander Lamfalussy, former president of the European Currency Institute (which will become the European Central Bank as soon as the common EU currency, the Euro, is launched) has for instance observed that member states of the EU will qualify for monetary union if they show a sustainable commitment to the prescribed criteria. SD requires both a stable currency and long-term fiscal policies that support resource-saving, eco-integrated production techniques, and other aspects of ecological progress.

Equally, SD can only be a success if it enjoys social support. Consumer attitudes and habits, in particular with regard to energy, transport and packaging, need to evolve accordingly. In cultural terms, sustainability is closer to the asceticism of the Enlightenment than to hedonistic postmodernism.

Because of these variables, the international implementation of SD varies widely. As we saw in the chapter on business mentality, Germany's ecological consensus has enabled it to implement policies, restructure industries, and adopt new norms and values more effectively than the United States and Japan. The German commitment to ecological purity is culturally grounded and enjoys strong social support. The antithesis between economic goals and ecological imperatives is rapidly evolving into a synthesis.

Ecological experts are cooperating with economic planners, industrialists, and interest groups to imbue Germany's Social Market Economy with an ecological dimension. *Germany's ability to balance wealth, welfare and well-being enables it to master the complexity of sustainability.*

WELTGÜLTIGKEIT, NOT WELTGELTUNG

The spirit of mercantile capitalism characterized Great Britain in the nineteenth century, just as ecological sociocapitalism constitutes the quintessence of Germany at the end of the twentieth century. The British success recipe was simple and visible, a manifestation of pragmatic philosophy. The German recipe is complex and deeply structured, characteristic for this country's deeper philosophical traditions. The world of the nineteenth century was one of simple values and power relations, just as the present world shows a growing degree of complexity. The former optimism of development at any price constasts with today's skepticism about the durability of economic development in the context of depleted resources.

In the complexity of an age of sustainable development, the Germans will excel, because of their mastery of balance and complexity. Their ecological sociocapitalism is likely to move from European preeminence to

Weltgültigkeit, world validity. World validity does not mean a model to be copied but an orientation on basic issues. Germany's values and priorities will permeate the world more imperceptibly and effectively than any amount of material colonization could ever achieve.

As the philosopher Arthur Schopenhauer pointed out, the supreme personality in world history is the Weltüberwinder, the world-overcomer and not the Welteroberer, the world-conqueror. *The most influential contributor to the future world economy will be the country that overcomes the extremes of individualism and collectivism to achieve the normative middle.*

The normative middle is diametrically opposed to geographical fixations like "Mitteleuropa." The national-liberal publicist Friedrich Naumann's vision of a middle European federation of states under German tutelage was well-meaningly imperialistic. Published during the First World War, it foresaw German preeminence in a world of races constantly battling for supremacy. More recently, a number of Austro-Hungarian publicists have attempted to revive the spirit of Mitteleuropa—without however touching a chord in Germany.[48]

Germany's role in an age of sustainable development would be the exact opposite of Naumann's geopolitical Darwinism. Its power would derive from its nearness to the normative middle, not from economic clout or political machinations. Weltgültigkeit is based on norms, just as Weltgeltung, the chauvinistic zest for world renown of the Wilhelmine and Nazi periods, was oriented toward power at any cost.

The future will reveal the need for a new kind of modesty—one that recognizes the limits of true change and the importance of continuity. Perceptions will sharpen to the insight that countries like human beings have identities, that are subject to the formative influence of their history, living conditions, and cultural norms. Their wealth potentials depend on their ability to first recognize and then develop their identities.

The United States for instance has always been and will always be good at specific kinds of activity: spectacular pioneering achievements in technology and marketing, manufacturing productivity, and service sector innovations. The Americans are enormously talented and dynamic—and if they grasp the issues at stake in SD, they are capable of implementing unconventional solutions. To a certain extent, the Americans can adjust toward the German form of consensus and its balance of priorities, but they will never master these issues in Teutonic style. Their way toward a balance of wealth, welfare and well-being needs to be specifically American, featuring heroic individuals, improvization, and the pioneer spirit. Otherwise, it cannot succeed.

The Japanese face similarly serious deficiencies in welfare and well-being. Japan has done remarkably well in material terms with a culturally imposed Spartan ethos, but at the cost of social and psychological backwardness. This disparity between economic and technological superdevelopment and psychosocial underdevelopment is the Japanese barrier to future wealth in the context of SD. But the Japanese are superb assimilators and if their policy elite can adapt to the balance of the three Ws as skillfully as their predecessors imported Western economic activity, Japan can continue to be an economic superpower and develop a deeper foundation for future wealth.

Thus, Germany's future superiority is by no means inevitable. But to surpass Germany, the United States and Japan would need to organically develop a new Weltanschauung, rather than to mechanistically implement linear strategies. Short-cut solutions will not suffice.

Fifty years after the catastrophic end of the Second World War, Germany is poised toward a normative world role. "Am deutschen Wesen soll die Welt genesen"—literally, the world should be cured of its ills by the German character—was an arrogant postulate of German nationalism till 1945. It paraphrased and misconstrued a verse written by the nineteenth century romantic poet, Emmanuel Geibel: "Und es mag am deutschen Wesen, Einmal noch die Welt genesen," the world could perhaps once be cured by the German character.

Significantly, Geibel perceived German strength as deriving from its "inner middle," not from the outer strength that the nationalists gloried in. He discerned Weltgültigkeit—a normative influence based on Innerlichkeit, the inward orientation that is central to Germany's identity—while the nationalists were in a self-defeating pursuit of Weltgeltung.

The norms of the inner middle will be the foundation of Germany's profound and humane preeminence in a world of sustainable development.

NOTES

1. John Gimbel, *The Origins of the Marshall Plan* (Stanford: Stanford University Press, 1976), see especially Introduction and Conclusion; see also Charles L. Mee, Jr., *The Marshall Plan* (New York: Simon and Schuster, 1984), pp. 20–25, 34–43, 89–95, and Charles Kindleberger, *Marshall Plan Days* (Winchester, MA: Allen & Unwin, 1987), pp. 25–30.

2. Werner Abelshauser, "Hilfe und Selbsthilfe," in *Vierteljahreshefte für Zeitgeschichte*, 1989, pp. 85–89; for opposing viewpoints see Knut Borchardt and Christoph Buchheim, "Die Wirkung der Mashallplan-Hilfe in Schlüsselbranchen der deutschen Wirtschaft," in *Vierteljahrshefte für Zeitgeschichte*, 1987, pp. 317–348; for statements from the Erhard circle, see various articles in the magazine *Währung und Wirtschaft*, among others, Ludwig Erhard, "Stabiler Preisstand," 1949–50, pp. 3ff, the editorial "Lügen," 1950, pp. 109–110, "Geschichte und Geschichten vom Marshall-Plan," 1950–51, pp. 93ff, "Das große Einmaleins des Marshall-Plans," 1949, pp. 143ff.

3. Julius Hirsch, *Das amerikanische Wirtschaftswunder* (Berlin: Fischer, 1926), pp. 7–15.

4. Henry C. Wallich, *Mainsprings of the German Revival* (New Haven: Yale University Press, 1955), pp. 20–21, 106–112, 328–334.

5. Ludwig Erhard, *Wohlstand für alle* (Düsseldorf: Econ Taschenbuch), p. 157; Hermann Josef Abs, *Germany and the Marshall Aid* (speech at the 1st Luxembourg-Harvard conference in Luxembourg, 1987).

6. Andrew Shonfield, *Modern Capitalism* (London: Oxford University Press, 1965); see also Alfred Müller-Armack, *Wirtschaftsordnung und Wirtschaftspolitik* (Freiburg: Rombach, 1966), p. 89, and Peter Lawrence, *Managers and Management in West Germany* (New York: St. Martin's Press, 1980), pp. 12–15.

7. Jost Dülffer, "Albert Speer," in Ronald Smelser and Rainer Zitelmann (eds.), *The Nazi Elite* (London: Macmillan, 1993), pp. 212–254; for first-hand information, see Albert Speer, *Erinnerungen* (Berlin: Propyläen, 1969), pp. 219–239; for the Reichsvereinigungen see Hans Kehrl, *Krisenmanager im Dritten Reich* (Düsseldorf: Droste, 1973), pp. 260–268.

8. Quoted in Jost Dülffer, Albert Speer, p. 220; see also Albert Speer, *Erinnerungen*, pp. 219–239.

9. Karl Dietrich Bracher, *Die deutsche Diktatur* (Cologne: Kiepenheuer & Witsch, 1993), pp. 545–547; see also Ralph Giordano, *Wenn Hitler den Krieg gewonnen hätte* (Hamburg: Rasch und Röhring, 1989), pp. 119–123.

10. Anton Zischka, *War es ein Wunder?* (Hamburg: Mosaik, 1966), pp. 42–45; Kurt Prizkoleit, *Die neuen Herren* (Vienna: Desch, 1955), pp. 444–464; for titles and responsibilities, see the handbook *Wer leitet? Die Männer der Wirtschaft und der öffentlichen Verwaltung* (Berlin: Hoppenstedt, 1941/42).

11. Ingeborg Esenwein-Rothe, *Die Wirtschaftsverbände von 1933 bis 1945* (Berlin: Duncker & Humblot 1965), pp. 136–144.

12. Quoted in Joseph Borkin, *The Crime and Punishment of I.G. Farben* (New York: The Free Press, 1978), p. 1.

13. Fritz ter Meer, *Die IG Farben* (Düsseldorf: Econ, 1953), p. 23.

14. Ibid., p. 24.

15. For a commentary on Erhard's role and for original documents, see Karl Heinz Roth, "Das Ende eines Mythos," in *1999*, 4/1995, pp. 53–80.

16. Alfred Müller-Armack, *Staatsidee und Wirtschaftsordnung im neuen Reich* (Berlin: Junker und Dünnhaupt, 1933), pp. 20–21, 40–41; Walter Eucken, *Die Grundlagen der Nationalökonomie* (Jena: Gustav Fischer, 1943), pp. 61–71; similar ideas were expressed in a juristic context by the Freiburg ordoliberal Franz Böhm in *Die Ordnung der Wirtschaft als geschichtliche Aufgabe und rechtsschöpferische Leistung* (Stuttgart: Kohlhammer, 1937), pp. 7–11, 48–53. For a critical review of the roles of ordoliberals in National Socialism, see Dieter Haselbach, *Autoritärer Liberalismus und soziale Marktwirtschaft* (Baden-Baden: Nomos, 1991), pp. 37–61, 123–127.

17. See in this connection Keith Tribe, *Strategies of Economic Order* (Cambridge: Cambridge University Press, 1993), pp. 203–214.

18. Martin H. Geyer, "Soziale Sicherheit und wirtschaftlicher Fortschritt," in *Geschichte und Gesellschaft*, 1989, p. 390.

19. Dieter Rebentisch, *Führerstaat und Verwaltung im zweiten Weltkrieg* (Stuttgart: Steiner, 1989), 31–35, 533–553.

20. Heiner R. Adamsen, *Investitionshilfe für die Ruhr* (Wuppertal: Hammer, 1981), pp. 13–17, 156–167.

21. David Schoenbaum, *Die braune Revolution* (Cologne: Kiepenheuer & Witsch, 1980), pp. 90–93, 106–113.

22. See *Die Deutsche Volkswirtschaft* 20/1944, p. 572 and 11/1944, p. 310; see also"Der Leistungskampf der deutschen Betriebe," in *Soziale Praxis*, 1938, pp. 599–603, and "Verwirklichung des Sozialismus," in the same magazine, 1938, pp. 915–918.

23. *Die Deutsche Volkswirtschaft* 18/1944, p. 509.

24. Fritz Prizkoleit, *Die neuen Herren*, pp. 12–15.

25. Eugen Kreidler, *Die Eisenbahn im Machtbereich der Achsenmächte während des Zweiten Weltkrieges* (Göttingen: Musterschmidt, 1978), p. 289; for the Autobahn, see Kurt Prizkoleit, *Gott erhält die Mächtigen* (Düsseldorf: Rauch, 1963), pp. 12–15.

26. Wolfram Fischer (ed.), *Handbuch der europäischen Wirtschafts- und Sozialgeschichte*, Book 6 (Stuttgart: Klett-Cotta, 1987), pp. 434–435.

27. H.-Elmar Tenorth, "Bildung und Wissenschaft im Dritten Reich," in Karl-Dietrich Bracher et al (eds.), *Deutschland 1933–1945—Neue Studien zur nationalsozialistischen Herrschaft* (Bonn: Bundeszentrale für politische Bildung, 1992), pp. 240–255; see also Wolfram Fischer, *Handbuch der europäischen Wirtschafts- und Sozialgeschichte*, pp. 425–426.

28. For an in-depth description of these phenomena, see Hans Dieter Schäfer, "Amerikanismus im Dritten Reich," in Michael Prinz and Rainer Zitelmann (eds.), *Nationalsozialismus und Modernisierung* (Darmstadt: Wissenschaftliche Buchgesellschaft, 1991), pp. 199–215.

29. Schäfer, "Amerikanismus im Dritten Reich," pp. 199–215.

30. James W. Angell, *Der Wiederaufbau Deutschlands* (Munich: Duncker & Humblot, 1930), p. 3.

31. Hans E. Priester, *Das deutsche Wirtschaftswunder* (Amsterdam: Querido, 1936), pp. 9–11.

32. Egon Matzner and Wolfgang Straeck (eds.), *Beyond Keynesianism* (Aldershot, Hants: Edward Elgar, 1991), p. 10.

33. Franz Jánossy, *Das Ende der Wirtschaftswunder* (Frankfurt: Verlag Neue Kritik, 1966), pp. 207ff; for a review of human capital arguments, see Rolf H. Dumke, *Reassessing the Wirtschaftswunder: Reconstruction and Postwar Growth in West Germany in an International Context* (Munich: Universität der Bundeswehr, 1992), pp. 20–22.

34. James Kurth, "Toward the Postmodern World," in *Dialogue*, 2/1993, p. 12.

35. For a comparison of German and U.S. conditions, see Hans-Peter Blossfeld et al., "Is There a New Service Proletariat?" in Gosta Esping-Andersen (ed.), *Changing Classes* (London: Sage Publications, 1993), pp. 114–115.

36. For a general overview of Citizens' Initiatives, see Ilona Kroll, *Vereine und Bürgerinitiativen heute* (Pfaffenweiler: Centaurus, 1989), pp. 32–63, and Rob Burns and Wilfried van der Will, *Protest and Democracy in West Germany: Extra-Parliamentary Opposition and the Democratic Agenda* (London: Macmillan, 1988), pp. 164–185.

37. Christian Graf von Krockow, *Die Deutschen in ihrem Jahrhunder* (Reinbek: Rowohlt, 1990), p. 277; for the Habermas and Hentig quotes, see Hermann Glaser, *Kulturgeschichte der Bundesrepublik Deutschland* (Munich: Hanser, 1989), pp. 10–11.

38. Erwin K. Scheuch, *Wie Deutsch sind die Deutschen?* (Bergisch-Gladbach: Lübbe, 1991), pp. 52–53.

39. Gordon Smith, "Does West German Democracy Have an 'Efficient Secret'?," in William F. Patterson and Gordon Smith (eds.), *The West German Model* (London: Cass, 1981), p. 174; Dahrendorf is quoted in Heinrich Oberreuter, "Defizite der Streitkultur in der Parteiendemokratie," in Ulrich Sarcinelli (ed.), *Demokratische Streitkultur* (Bonn: Bundeszentrale für politische Bildung, 1990), p. 79; see also other essays in the same book, including Siegfried Weischenberg, "Gladiatoren oder Propagandisten?" pp. 101–143.

40. Jonathan Clark, "APEC as a Semi-solution," in *Orbis*, Winter 1995, pp. 81–95; see also Daniel Bell, "Will the Twenty-First Century Be the Pacific Century?" in *Dissent*, Spring 1995, pp. 195–201, and various articles on "Pacific myths" in *Foreign Affairs*, November-December 1994.

41. Bernard Simon, "Canada's Strength, Canada's Pain," in *Financial Times*, September 5, 1996, and "Singing the NAFTA Blues," in *Business Week*, December 9, 1996, pp. 26–27.

42. For a balanced overview of Mercosur, see the special survey "Remapping South America," in *The Economist*, October 12, 1996, pp. 1–26.

43. Eric Le Boucher, "L'Allemagne et l'identité française," in *Le Monde*, October 19, 1994.

44. Ernst Benda, "Die USA, Deutschland und Maastricht: Erfahrungen mit und Prognosen über Föderalismus und Subsidiarität," in Werner Weidenfeld (ed.), *Reform der Europäischen Union* (Gütersloh: Bertelsmann Stiftung, 1995), pp. 135–155.

45. For basic ideas of the Swedish model, see Gunnar Myrdal, *Jenseits des Wohlfahrtstaates* (Stuttgart: Gustav Fischer, 1961); for a recent technocratic view of the Swedish crisis, see Assar Lindbeck et al., *Turning Sweden Around* (Cambridge, MA: MIT, 1994); see also Siegfried Thielbeer, "Das Ende des Wohlfahrtsstaates," in *Frankfurter Allgemeine Zeitung*, November 28, 1992.

46. Robert L. Heilbroner, *Between Capitalism and Socialism* (New York: Vintage, 1970), p. 259.

47. See in this connection Kurt Sontheimer, "Die Lust am Untergang," in *Universitas*, 10/1989, pp. 971–979; see also Reinhard Rode, "Deutschland: Weltwirtschaftsmacht oder überforderter Euro-Hegemon?" in *Leviathan*, 1991, pp. 229–246.

48. For Naumann's ideas on Mitteleuropa, see Friedrich Naumann, *Werke—Politische Schriften*, Book 4 (Cologne: Westdeutscher Verlag, 1964), particularly the introduction, pp. 375–388; for a typical recent endorsement, Milo Dor, *Mitteleuropa: Mythos oder Wirklichkeit* (Salzburg: Otto Müller, 1996).

Selected Bibliography

This bibliography provides an overview of substantial sources—both primary texts and commentaries. The notes attached to the different chapters contain a more substantial cross-section of the books, journals, periodicals and newspapers refered to by the author.

INTRODUCTION

Eucken, Walter. *Die Grundlagen der Nationalökonomie*. Berlin: Springer, 1965.
Giersch, Herbert et al. *The Fading Miracle*. Cambridge: Cambridge University Press, 1992.
List, Friedrich. *Das nationale System der politischen Ökonomie*. Stuttgart: Cotta, 1883.
Porter, Michael. *The Competitive Advantage of Nations*. New York: Free Press, 1990.
Smith, Adam. *An Inquiry into the Nature and Causes of the Wealth of Nations*. Oxford: Clarendon Press, 1976.
Sombart, Werner. *Das Wirtschaftsleben im Zeitalter des Hochkapitalismus*. Book 1. Munich: Duncker & Humblot, 1927.

1. THE MITTELSTAND: MICROCOSM OF THE GERMAN ECONOMY

Albach, Horst, and Held, Thomas (eds.). *Betriebwirtschaftslehre mittelständischer Unternehmen*. Stuttgart: Poeschel, 1984.
Chandler Jr., Alfred D. *Scale and Scope*. Cambridge, MA: Harvard University Press, 1990.
Miegel, Meinhard. *Wirtschafts- und arbeitskulturelle Unterschiede in Deutschland*. Gütersloh: Bertelsmann Stiftung, 1991.

Piore, Michael T., and Sabel, Charles F. *Das Ende der Massenproduktion*. Berlin: Wagenbach, 1985.
Winkler, Heinrich August. *Mittelstand, Demokratie und Nationalsozialismus*. Cologne: Kiepenheuer & Witsch, 1972.

2. ORDER AND THE BUSINESS MENTALITY

Aleman, Ulrich von (ed.). *Neokorporatismus*. Frankfurt: Campus Verlag, 1981.
Bleicher, Knut. *Organisation— Formen und Modelle*. Wiesbaden: Gabler, 1981.
Eberwein, Wilhelm, and Tholen, Jochen. *Euro-Manager or Splendid Isolation?* Berlin: de Gruyter, 1993.
Ghaussy, A. Ghanie, and Schäfer, Wolf (eds.). *The Economics of German Unification*. London: Routledge, 1993.
Halstrick-Schwenk, Marianne. *Die umwelttechnische Industrie in der Bundesrepublik Deutschland*. Essen: RWI, 1994.
Jaeger, Hans. *Geschichte der Wirtschaftsordnung in Deutschland*. Frankfurt: Suhrkamp, 1988.
Moore, Curtis, and Miller, Alan. *Green Gold: Japan, Germany, the United States and the Race for Environmental Technology*. Boston: Beacon Press, 1994.
Pfeiffer, Hermannus. *Die Macht der Banken*. Frankfurt: Campus, 1993.
Schein, Edgar H. *Organizational Culture and Leadership*. San Francisco: Jossey-Bass, 1986.

3. COMMITMENT AND THE BUSINESS ENVIRONMENT

Bergmann, Joachim, and Shigeyoshi, Tokunaga (eds.). *Economic and Social Aspects of Industrial Relations*. Frankfurt: Campus. 1987.
Dlugos, Günter et al. (eds.). *Management under Differing Labour Market and Employment Systems*. Berlin: de Gruyter, 1988.
Erhard, Ludwig. *Wohlstand für alle*. Düsseldorf: Econ, 1991.
Eucken, Walter. *Grundsätze der Wirtschaftspolitik*. Hamburg: Rowohlt, 1965.
Jeserich, Kurt G.A. et al. (ed.). *Deutsche Verwaltungsgeschichte*, Book 2. Frankfurt: Deutsche Verlagsanstalt, 1983.
Mill, John Stuart. *Principles of Political Economy*, Volume 1. New York: The Colonial Press, 1900.
Müller-Armack, Alfred. *Wirtschaftsordnung und Wirtschaftspolitik*. Freiburg: Rombach, 1966.
Tönnies, Ferdinand. *Gemeinschaft und Gesellschaft*. Berlin: Curtius, 1926.

4. THE SOCIOECONOMIC FOUNDATIONS OF WEALTH

Bauersfeld, Heinrich, and Bromme, Rainer (eds.). *Bildung und Aufklärung*. Münster: Waxmann, 1993.
Baumert, Jürgen et al. *Das Bildungswesen in der Bundesrepublik Deutschland*. Hamburg: Rowohlt, 1990.
Goedegebuure, Leo. *Hochschulpolitik im internationalen Vergleich*. Gütersloh: Bertelsmann Stiftung, 1993.
Marsh, David. *Die Bundesbank*. Gütersloh: Bertelsmann, 1993.
Reidenbach, Michael. *Verfällt die öffentliche Infrastruktur?* Berlin: Deutsches Institut für Urbanistik, 1986.

Ringer, Fritz. *The Decline of the German Mandarins*. Cambridge, MA: Harvard
     University Press, 1969.
Seitz, Konrad. *Die japanisch-amerikanische Herausforderung*. München: Bonn Aktuell,
     1994.
Sombart, Werner. *Die deutsche Volkswirtschaft im 19. Jahrhundert and im Anfang des
     20. Jahrhunderts*. Darmstadt: Wissenschaftliche Buchgesellschaft, 1954.

5. THE CULTURAL ROOTS OF ORDER AND COMMITMENT

Bucholz, Arden. *Moltke, Schlieffen, and Prussian War Planning*. New York: Berg,
     1991.
Ciafardone, Raffaele (ed.). *Die Philosophie der deutschen Aufklärung*. Stuttgart:
     Reclam. 1990.
Eglau, Hans Otto. *Erste Garnitur*. Düsseldorf: Econ, 1980.
Elias, Norbert. *Über den Prozess der Zivilisation*. Book 1. Bern: Francke, 1969.
Gadamer, Hans-Georg. *Vernunft im Zeitalter der Wissenschaften*. Frankfurt: Suhrkamp,
     1976.
Gay, Peter. *The Enlightenment: An Interpretation*. New York: Knopf, 1967.
Hampden-Turner, Charles, and Trompenaars, Alfons. *The Seven Cultures of Capital-
     ism*. New York: Currency Doubleday, 1993.
Kaufmann, Franz-Xaver (ed.). *Zur Soziologie des Katholizismus*. Mainz: Grünwald,
     1980.
Knittermeyer, Hinrich. *Schelling und die romantische Schule*. Munich: Reinhardt, 1929.
Müller, Adam. *Die Elemente der Staatskunst*. Meersburg a. Bodensee: F.W. Hendel
     Verlag, 1936.
Müller-Armack, Alfred. *Religion und Wirtschaft*. Stuttgart: Kohlhammer, 1968.
Novak, Michael. *The Catholic Ethic and the Spirit of Capitalism*. New York: Free
     Press, 1993.
Smith, Adam. *The Theory of Moral Sentiments*. Oxford: Clarendon Press, 1976.
Weber, Max. *Die protestantische Ethik und der Geist des Kapitalismus*. München:
     Siebenstern, 1993.

6. THE PSYCHOLOGICAL ROOTS OF ORDER AND COMMITMENT

Adorno, Theodor W. et al. *The Authoritarian Personality*. New York: Harper & Row,
     1950.
Brezinka, Wolfgang. *Erziehung in einer wertunsicheren Gesellschaft*. Munich:
     Reinhardt, 1986.
Elias, Norbert. *Studien über die Deutschen*. Frankfurt: Suhrkamp, 1989.
Erikson, Erik. *Der junge Mann Luther*. Frankfurt: Suhrkamp, 1976.
Glaser, Hermann, and Stahl, Karl Heinz (ed.). *Luther gestern und heute*. Frankfurt:
     Fischer, 1983.
Klages, Helmut *Wertedynamik: Über die Wandelbarkeit des Selbstverständlichen*.
     Zurich: Interfromm, 1988.
Link, Jürgen, and Wülfing, Wolf (eds.). *Nationale Mythen und Symbole in der zweiten
     Hälfte des 19. Jahrhunderts*. Stuttgart: Klett-Cotta, 1991.
Mitscherlich, Alexander. *Gesammelte Schriften*, Book 4. Frankfurt: Suhrkamp, 1983.
Röhrs, Hermann (ed.). *Die Disziplin in ihrem Verhältnis zur Lohn und Strafe*.
     Frankfurt: Akademische Verlagsgesellschaft, 1968.
Schulze, Gerhard. *Die Erlebnisgesellschaft*. Frankfurt: Campus, 1992.

7. PAST MIRACLES, PRESENT CONTINUITY, FUTURE CONSENSUS

Gimbel, John. *The Origins of the Marshall Plan*. Stanford: Stanford University Press, 1976.

Glaser, Hermann. *Kulturgeschichte der Bundesrepublik Deutschland*. Munich: Hanser, 1989.

Matzner, Egon, and Straeck, Wolfgang (eds.). *Beyond Keynesianism*. Aldershot, Hants: Edward Elgar, 1991.

Patterson, William F., and Smith, Gordon (eds.). *The West German Model.* London: Cass, 1981.

Rebentisch, Dieter, and Teppe, Karl (eds.). *Verwaltung contra Menschenführung im Staat Hitlers*. Göttingen: Vandenhoeck & Ruprecht, 1986.

Schmölders, Günter (ed). *Der Wettbewerb als Mittel volkswirtschaftlicher Leistungs-steigerung und Leistungsauslese*. Berlin: Duncker & Humblot, 1942.

Schoenbaum, David. *Die braune Revolution*. Cologne: Kiepenheuer & Witsch, 1980.

Siegel, Tilla, and Freyberg, Thomas. *Industrielle Rationaliserung unter dem National-sozialismus*. Frankfurt: Campus, 1991.

Tribe, Keith. *Strategies of Economic Order*. Cambridge: Cambridge University Press, 1993.

Wallich, Henry C. *Mainsprings of the German Revival*. New Haven: Yale University Press, 1955.

Weidenfeld, Werner (ed.). *Reform der Europäischen Union*. Gütersloh: Bertelsmann Stiftung, 1995.

Zischka, Anton. *War es ein Wunder?* Hamburg: Mosaik, 1966.

Index

About the Author

KAEVAN GAZDAR has worked as a journalist and lecturer, and also as Project Manager at one of Germany's leading management consultancies. He is the author of three books in German on economic and technological issues.